at once.

I also enclose under this cover, an official acknowledgement of Dr. Reeves's official letter.

"The Census of Canada" compiled under directions of my department — but far from perfect, I am sorry to say, will go out by this mail, to the Academy

With other thanks for the paper, on the Morlihan monumental stones, (recd by last mail.)

Believe me,
My Dear Ferguson
Your very obbijedt
Thos. Darcy McGee

Saml. Ferguson Esq. Q. C.
Dublin.

THE ARDENT EXILE

THOMAS D'ARCY McGEE, AT THE TIME OF CONFEDERATION

*From Morgan: "Types of Canadian Women
Past and Present", Wm. Briggs, 1903.*

MARY THERESA McGEE

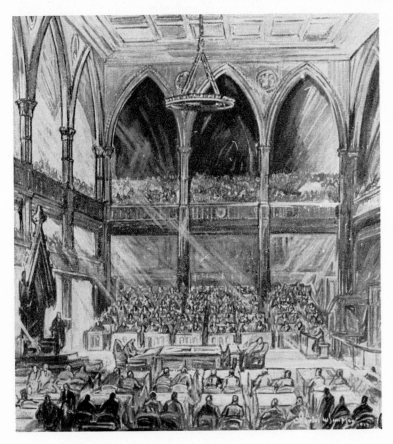

FUNERAL PROCESSION OF D'ARCY McGEE, MONTREAL, 1868.

THE ARDENT EXILE

By JOSEPHINE PHELAN

THE LIFE AND TIMES OF

Thos. Darcy McGee

Josephine Phelan

apr 18/78

TORONTO
THE MACMILLAN COMPANY OF CANADA LIMITED
1951

To

THE MEMORY OF

MY AUNT

JOSEPHINE AGNES DELORME

CONTENTS

CONTENTS

PROLOGUE

A<small>N OLD MAN</small> sat in the sun and thought of the friends of his youth. It had been good to be young in the 1840's. All over Europe eager students and journalists had formed societies, printed papers and schemed to overcome old wrongs by the force of enlightened public opinion.

Sir Charles Gavan Duffy, warming his old bones in the Mediterranean sunshine, could recall them all; though his thoughts naturally lingered on his own group, Young Ireland, and his own paper the *Nation*, which he had published in the days before he had titles and honours when he was just plain Mr. Duffy of Dublin.

In each country of Europe youth had sought a different goal. The Hungarians strove for freedom, the Italians for unity, the French socialists wanted to guarantee all workers jobs, the Germans craved a constitution. Gavan Duffy and his friends had undertaken to make the Irish a harmonious people.

Great things were afoot.

In 1848 an epidemic of revolution, beginning in France, swept Europe and was put down by outraged authority. Then all the young men, their fine plans riddled by gunfire, were scattered into exile. The Hungarians fled to Paris and the French to England. The Irish—those who were not caught by the English government and sent to the penal settlements of Australia—fled to America.

Gavan Duffy's thoughts reached back into the past—to 1848 and the men of 1848. Serenely, as one whose leisure would be broken by no interruption but the final one, Duffy worked over his diaries and letters and the files of his old paper the *Nation* and from this material wrote the story of his friends.

He had outlived most of them. To look back over their careers was like reading in the book of fate. They had all been swept away in the great migration that had poured towards the New World in the mid-nineteenth century. Only the bold affection of friendship would have attempted to trace their several destinies. Some had won distinction, some had died in their prime. The most brilliant of them all, the leader, Thomas Davis, had died before the crisis of 1848. One, years after, had taken his life in Washington, one had died in an accident on the Missouri River, another had been assassinated in a Canadian city.

As he wrote during the long summer days in the south of France, each character took on life and individuality. From the growing pages of Duffy's reminiscences the blunt features and intelligent eyes of D'Arcy McGee seemed to look back at him. D'Arcy had been the youngest of their band, more poorly endowed than the others with formal education and social background, remarkably homely, remarkably talented and silver-tongued. Wrenched like the rest of them from the land they all longed to serve he had been more fortunate than the others in finding a country to replace the one he had lost. He had come closer than any of the others to fulfilling the intention of the leader of Young Ireland—the ideal of the scholar in politics.

"McGee in wide sweep of imagination, in the persistency and variety of his labours," wrote Duffy, "in everything but in qualities where Davis was unapproachable, closely resembled the master who was lost."

He could give no higher praise.

Part One

YOUNG IRELAND

Chapter One
THE MAKING OF A JOURNALIST

In the year 1842 a seventeen-year-old Irish boy immigrated to the New World. At that time it was possible to cross the Atlantic in two weeks on a fast steam packet. But this was for the luxury trade. Thomas D'Arcy McGee travelled economically on a sailing ship engaged in the lumber trade between Wexford and Boston. The voyage took two months. The captain, who was a friend of D'Arcy's father, gave favourable rates for the passage and kept a friendly eye on D'Arcy and his sister who travelled with him. After the most acute phase of home-sickness and sea-sickness had passed the travellers began to look about them and by the time they were in sight of America, like thousands of young immigrants before and since, they were eager to start their new life. The land of liberty lay before them. The future was theirs.

D'Arcy had literary ambitions inherited from his mother and from his grandfather who had been a book-seller in Dublin. In his scanty baggage were a number of poems written by himself and a book won as a prize for a speech he had made before a juvenile temperance society. The book he sold to a Boston pawnshop shortly after he landed; the poems, which did not prove saleable, he kept. In due time they were published. D'Arcy McGee had not been long in America before it became known that here was a young man of talent.

Boston in the 1840's was a pleasant city of prim steepled meeting-houses and red brick or white frame homes with green shutters. To travellers coming from the age-darkened cities of Europe it looked as bright and pretty as a toy town.

3

Its clean tree-shaded streets spread over three hills, Beacon, Copp's and Fort, the last since levelled. In the commercial district oyster cellars provided diners with the famous delicacy of the New England seaboard, not the mean coppery little oysters of the British Isles, but succulent specimens served in every way the cook could devise. At the foot of Boston's hills lay the harbour from which vessels set out for all the ports of the world. The commerce of this harbour made possible the staid culture of New England. The descendants of the Puritans were a wealthy people who, although they frowned on the garish display of noisy newly-rich New York, willingly spent money on worthy causes— foundations, universities and intellectual luxuries such as imported author-lecturers like Mr. Dickens and Mr. Thackeray.

On the Boston Common and at suitable places throughout the city open-air meetings celebrated the fourth of July. Speeches were made; bands played. D'Arcy McGee, weaving in and out the edges of the crowd before Fanteuil Hall, thrilled to this demonstration of patriotism. During a lull in the programme he hoisted himself onto a wagon and began, *ex tempore*, to address the crowd. The bystanders hearing a strong clear voice turned and drifted around him. They saw an undersized, shabby boy with untidy black curly hair and a grotesquely Irish face. They heard some high-flown sentiments given with a notable command of language and in a voice that, to ears accustomed to nasal Yankee accents and blurred peasant brogue, sounded dulcet.

He addressed them on the glory of liberty and the American Republic.

"Who is that?"

"Some young Paddy fresh from the old land."

"Would to God the old land would send us more of the same."

At this point one begins to suspect that the story may be as much legend as fact, but certainly by some such means, prompted more by enthusiasm than calculation, D'Arcy McGee made his immediate world aware of him. Within a week he had joined the staff of a respectable Irish American journal, the Boston *Pilot*.

The newspapers or journals of the early nineteenth century were intended not so much to publish news as to support a cause. The modern daily bringing last-minute news to a multitude of readers belongs to the age of telegraphs and rotary presses. In the 1840's dailies, telegraphs and rotary presses existed, but only in a small way. Their great day lay ahead.

The typical newspaper of the 1840's was a weekly with a circulation of a few thousand. News was acquired by clipping items from other papers to which the editor subscribed on an exchange basis so as to have a constant supply of material. Clipping was so universally accepted by journalists that a paste pot and a pair of shears were as necessary as a printing press for issuing a weekly paper.

But if the editor clipped nearly everything else, he or his associate editor always wrote the paper's editorials. It was not for the stale news, bits of poems or serial stories that the subscriber paid his yearly fee, but to enjoy the editor of his chosen weekly fulminating and pontificating on a subject of interest to him. The more successful the editor was in turning the subject into a cause, the more highly he was regarded by his readers.

The nineteenth century was optimistically dedicated to reform. Any theory for the improvement of mankind that was worth considering had a journal to advance it. There were weeklies to support temperance, socialism and the abolition of slavery. There were journals advocating obscure cults such as phrenology, homeopathy and the fashionable health cult, hydropathy. There were journals for semi-religious subjects such as spiritualism and freemasonry, as well as journals to oppose them. There were also journals to advance the cause of Irish nationalism. The Boston *Pilot* with which McGee took his first job was one of these last.

The only indispensable people on a weekly's staff were the editor and the printer. If the staff were to be brought to an irreducible minimum, the printer remained the key man. The editor produced the ideas but the printer produced the paper in tangible, saleable form. At a pinch the printer also could produce editorials and might even yearn to write them. In the history of American journalism from Benjamin Franklin to Horace Greeley so commonly was the editor a former printer that this development from printer to editor seemed to have been the rule. To this rule McGee proved an exception. He began his career in journalism not as a printer's devil but among the paste pots and news files of the *Pilot's* office.

These files contained the exchange copies of all the Irish newspapers both American and Old Country, as well as pamphlets, printed speeches and books on Irish history. McGee, fascinated, greedily read them all. This was not his introduction to the woes of Ireland, but never before had he come upon so much printed matter to fortify his patriotism.

It would hardly be exaggeration to say that D'Arcy McGee had absorbed Irish politics with his mother's milk. Certainly he had learned Thomas Moore's poems with his prayers at his mother's knee.

> "Land of song," said the warrior bard,
> "Tho' all the world betrays thee,
> One sword at least thy rights shall guard,
> One faithful harp shall praise thee."

Verses like these young Tommie, prompted by his mother and approved by the company, would recite when the McGees had guests.

D'Arcy's mother, Catherine Dorcas McGee, despite the care of a growing family, had time for poetry and music. She delighted especially in teaching Tommie D'Arcy, one of the youngest, her songs and stories. Perhaps she found in him more than in her other four children her own joy in whatever was romantic and imaginative in her country's literature. Socially she was somewhat her husband's superior. James McGee, a coastguard who had advanced to the

6

modest security of a collector of excise, made a decent living for his family and left politics alone. But his wife's family, the Morgans, consistently opposed the government and some of them had been out in the rebellion of 1789. Furthermore, her father had been a book-seller with some claim to being a literary man and one of her cousins was a bishop. This record of patriotism and piety conferred prestige on the Morgan family beyond anything the McGees could show.

Catherine McGee died when D'Arcy was eight, but he never forgot the proud ideas of country and family she had taught him. The Irish are democratic only in a limited sense. Any Irishman likes to claim connection with a fine old family; and the peasants are descended from kings.

When he joined the *Pilot* staff McGee not only avoided the usual apprenticeship as a printer but he rose rapidly from a junior to a senior position in the editorial office. Before many months had passed he was performing the highest journalistic functions, writing editorials and acting from time to time as special correspondent in the towns around Boston.

His duties as a correspondent were complex. He did not so much seek out and report news as make news by giving a lecture and reporting it to his paper. This procedure served a number of ends. McGee's speech made money, advertised the *Pilot*, secured new subscribers and kept the paper in touch with the state of affairs in New England. Finally the lecture, revised and printed, became an editorial. The whole cycle gave the lad an early taste of fame.

Lectures were popular in New England since they offered to the earnest Puritan-bred population a form of entertainment disguised as self-improvement. The lecturer's fee varied. Charles Dickens, the most popular lecturer of the period, made as much as $1,500 in an evening with his readings. D'Arcy McGee, at the height of his fame in Canada, mentioned two hundred and fifty dollars as his share of the proceeds from one of his lectures. But the usual

fee was fifty dollars plus expenses for an hour's lecture.
McGee was launched on a promising career.

His audiences were Irish and he lectured on Irish topics
because like most immigrants his listeners had left their
hearts in the Old Country. Many of them were day
labourers working at the docks or with the railway construction gangs or as domestic help in hotels and taverns. They
had peasant virtues of honesty and decency. They saved
money and sent for their families to join them. But they
were prompted more by generosity than thrift. They lacked
the true peasant instinct to take up land and seemed content
to live a hand-to-mouth life in the cities. The sociability
and excitement of city life attracted them, the fiercely
political fraternal societies and the volunteer fire brigades
which they joined with enthusiasm, all the while yielding
more and more to their particular weakness for drinking
and fighting.

The factory owners and the shipping and construction
firms of New England were glad to have cheap Irish labour.
But the classes with whom the immigrants competed for
work feared them because they were numerous and resented
them because they were Catholics. D'Arcy McGee's business was with the political rather than the economic or social
life of his countrymen. From the platform and through the
editorial columns he spoke to them of repeal and Daniel
O'Connell.

In 1801, after a cruelly unsuccessful rebellion, William
Pitt, then Prime Minister of England, manoeuvred to have
the Irish Parliament abolished and Ireland united to England under one Parliament in London. From that day the
supreme goal of the Irish was to get back their own Parliament. "Repeal" was a fighting word in the nineteenth
century, meaning different things in different places. In
England, for instance, "repeal" meant removing taxes on
imported grain to lower the price of food for city workers.
But to an Irishman anywhere from America to Afghanistan
"repeal" meant only one thing, dissolving the hated Union,

the forced marriage between Ireland and England.

When D'Arcy McGee addressed his audience he spoke in this tradition. "A Union! Oh, it was a strange nuptial scene. Ireland was wooed in words of terror; there was merrymaking on the slippery scaffolds; she was all laden with chains at the altar. The aisles of the church were strewn with bones, and the skulls of the dead grated beneath the feet of the betrothed as they led her to the sanctuary. Her step was feeble and she tottered as she went, but it was all a groundless timidity. The marriage was consummated, and in the dungeon of those jealous protestors, Tone and Fitzgerald, the echo of her epithalamium was heard."

The audience may not have understood all the words, but the spirit was as familiar to them as their own names.

During the time of trouble and discouragement following the Union the Irish found a leader who fought their battles in the English Parliament with the combined force of a remarkable personality and powerful oratory. Daniel O'Connell was a Kerry lawyer who taught his impetuous countrymen a new technique in political warfare. Instead of armed rebellion he taught them the use of constitutional and parliamentary methods and the non-violent expression of public opinion. This was a novel doctrine for the Irish. By these methods O'Connell obtained concessions which no Irish Catholic nor English Catholic had enjoyed since the Reformation. His countrymen had complete confidence in his ability ultimately to repeal the Union and obeyed him implicitly.

A nation-wide temperance crusade preached at this time by Father Mathew seemed providentially designed to support O'Connell's doctrine of restraint. Men and boys took the pledge by tens of thousands. Breweries went out of business. When Daniel O'Connell called for peaceful mass demonstrations the wild Irish turned out in their thousands and conducted themselves with the dignity and sobriety of a New England Sabbath meeting. It looked as though the Irish with their correct deportment and constitutional tactics might beat the English at their own game.

All during the summer of 1843 huge peaceful meetings were held. This year, O'Connell had promised grandiloquently, would see the repeal of the Union.

The pressure of Irish public opinion at last forced the British government to act—but not in the direction of repeal. Troop ships were sent into Dublin Bay and the day before the final repeal meeting of the season at Clontarf a public proclamation forbade its taking place. This was an old trick when trouble was brewing in Ireland to force it into the open at a time and place most favourable to the authorities. But O'Connell avoided the issue by cancelling the huge meeting in the matter of a few hours. When the soldiers gathered at Clontarf in the chill October morning only bare fields and empty, ancient ruins awaited them.

This occasion was declared a great moral victory for the cause of repeal. It is true the prompt and decisive action had demonstrated the superb organization of the Repeal Association throughout the country. But the wisest knew that O'Connell this time had gained no victory. At best he had made a strategic retreat. It was hard to beat the English at their own game.

These mass meetings, staged on historic sites like Tara and Mullaghmast, had made splendid copy for the *Pilot* and McGee's speeches during the summer of 1843. For an address he was to give at Watertown, Massachusetts, on November 10, he planned a vivid outline of Irish history with the latest meeting at Clontarf as the climax. But by that time the real news of Clontarf had made the ending of his speech, as he had prepared it, an anti-climax. Baffled and distressed he summoned all the power of his not inconsiderable oratory to meet the situation.

"Never were a people more worthy of sympathy than the Irish," he told his audience at Watertown. "We see them stand upon the precipice of civil war and with a steady eye and firm voice preach patience to their own sufferings ... How majestic is the calmness without and the courage within that has paralysed the hands of soldiery and frozen in their hour of preparation the awful machinery of war!

The fortress walls of Ireland gleam with the crimson livery of a foreign force, but when the setting sun flings out its purple banner over ocean wave and mountain top the people go up in thousands to the sound of music to worship freedom in the high places."

With fine phrases McGee covered up the defeat of the Repeal Association. Fifteen years later he would know better how to gauge the event and even when speaking publicly he would have learned to speak plainly. But at this time he was only eighteen; his oratorical powers were much in advance of his political experience and his emotions were inclined to get the better of both.

Even though the cause of repeal was suffering reverses McGee's personal fortunes continued to rise. His writings in the *Pilot* had come to the attention of repeal leaders in Ireland. O'Connell himself was reported to have referred kindly to "the inspired writings of an Irish boy in America". In 1845 McGee accepted the offer of Wilson Gray, editor of the Dublin *Freeman*, to go to London at a good salary as the paper's correspondent. In July, after having spent three years in the New World, he returned home.

Whether McGee had any idea that his stay in the Old Country would be temporary it is impossible to say. Certainly he would have been greatly surprised if anyone had suggested that he would not only return to America but end by going to Canada. No one but a clairvoyant could have told him that the most brilliant portion of his career would be set in Canada and that some of those who would be his colleagues in this great episode were already taking part in public life there. Ireland was to teach him hard lessons from which another country would benefit. In 1845 many changes of fortune lay ahead of him. Canada remained hidden in the future.

Chapter Two
EDITORS IN DUBLIN

In August Dublin was deserted by people of
any importance. They went to the country to enjoy the
indifferent hunting and good fishing or to carry on political
agitation among the rural communities. Even when the
Dublin world was complete with ordinary people going
about ordinary affairs while their betters practised the social
graces, there was still something forlorn about the town.
Too many symbols reminded the people that all was not
well with the country. The long quays stretched along the
Liffey where it flowed into Dublin Bay almost deserted by
shipping because trade laws favoured England. The empty
silent Parliament House affirmed more plainly than the Act
of Union that Ireland was no longer a nation.

D'Arcy McGee, arriving in town during this off month
of August, attracted more attention than if he had come
when the city's activities were in full swing. The few
journalists remaining in town were disposed to take note
of the young editor from America, and McGee quickly discovered that he had landed into the middle of a literary
revival very congenial to his temperament.

The Dublin *Freeman,* the paper that employed McGee,
was a sober-toned weekly possessing the solid backing of the
Irish merchants who supported O'Connell and repeal for
the practical reason that under the Union Ireland had not
been prosperous. Repeal of the Union they hoped would
improve trade. They heartily approved of O'Connell's non-
violent agitation, since disorder also was bad for trade.

The *Nation,* the other outstanding journal, was a much
livelier sheet. It had been started by three young men con-

12

cerned about the good of Ireland. Three years before, Gavan Duffy and John Dillon had sat under a tree in Phoenix Park listening to the political philosophy of Thomas Davis.

There were only two parties in Ireland—that is how the Welsh-Irish Protestant Davis explained his ideas to his two Irish Catholic companions. They were not Whigs and Tories, not Protestant and Catholic, not Anglo-Irish and Celtic-Irish, not north and south. There were only two parties in Ireland, those who suffered from her degradation and those who profited by it. And this degradation was more spiritual than material. For a century and a half Irish letters had almost ceased to exist. For a people like the Irish who were imaginative, literary and keenly conscious of history, this was death. To revive among Irishmen the writing and reading of their own history and literature was as necessary as the revival of trade. Nationalism was the key to Ireland's freedom.

All over Europe this heady doctrine of nationalism in slightly varying forms was being taught. The younger generation was discontented. It had been different just after the Napoleonic Wars. Then the peoples of Europe had been weary. They had let the astute Austrian Metternich and his fellow-statesmen impose on them the peace of the Congress of Vienna. But it was not natural for the restless and diversified Europeans to remain satisfied for long with a policy that said things should not change, that there was a place for everyone and everyone should stay in it. The bright slogan of the French Revolution, "Liberty, Equality and Fraternity", which had led the French into high adventure and much trouble had not lost its glitter. It was still part of the doctrines of liberalism and nationalism to which the young people of Europe were responding hungrily and joyously just as Duffy and Dillon responded to the ideas of Davis.

They must establish a paper immediately, declared Duffy, to teach the Irish that they were a nation.

Alas, replied Davis and Dillon, they had no money for such an undertaking.

But Duffy had a small inheritance and this he was ready to devote to the purpose. This was the beginning of the Dublin *Nation*.

Within three years the paper's circulation reached 9,000 a week, the largest circulation of any Irish paper. The three hundred Repeal Association Reading Rooms, the only thing remotely approaching a public library, subscribed. Even the most isolated hamlet had at least one or two private subscribers who passed on their copies to others. The paper was a financial success, a gratifying but merely incidental circumstance. More important to Duffy and his friends, the *Nation* was being read by all classes in Ireland, especially the young farmers and mechanics. As for the young gentlemen, they not only read the paper, many of them wrote for it too. Nor would it do to mention only the young gentlemen as contributors. From humble and un-expected quarters verse and comments came to Duffy's desk to prove that the cause of Irish letters, like Sleeping Beauty, was not dead but needed only the right voice to awaken it.

The staff and the Dublin contributors met once a week at the home of one of them. The forthcoming issue was planned and the assignments given out. The articles and poems in the preceding number were discussed with much personal bantering and witticism. Replies were composed to the letters to the editor. According to Duffy many of the more felicitous turns of thought that found their way into the replies were crumbs from the conversation at the supper table.

When Duffy tried in his memoirs to recapture these evenings, the quick play of wit, the easy companionship, the unquenchable confidence eluded his pen. These weekly gatherings glowed with Thomas Davis's peculiar genius. Unlike most of his oratorically-inclined countrymen he had no liking for addressing crowds at political meetings, though when the occasion demanded he could do so effectively. But in these intimate meetings with a few of his followers, the passionate scholar could communicate to them something of himself.

Under his influence they were beginning to read history, not only Irish history, but recent history of other countries, especially small countries. Only fifteen years before Belgium had become independent of Holland. Norway had claimed her national rights and peaceably separated from Sweden. Even the obscure politics of the Canadas fascinated them. Already less than ten years after the Rebellion of 1837 men who had been called rebels took their seats honourably in a Canadian Parliament. All the British North American communities with only a few thousand people in each had their own Parliaments, while ancient Ireland with a population of 7,000,000 was deprived of hers. Why? The *Nation* wanted to know. And from the columns of the *Nation* the question passed into the Irish mind.

"Young Ireland" their critics derisively termed the writers for the *Nation*. The name at first disconcerted them. It bracketed them with Mazzini and his Young Italy, foreign fellows given to secret societies, irreligious theories and—who knows—even home-made bombs. But after a while they accepted the name and bore it proudly.

Within a week of his arrival in Dublin, D'Arcy McGee had met both leaders of the Young Ireland party.

Wilson Gray, on friendly terms with Duffy, occasionally attending a weekly supper meeting, introduced his new London correspondent. Duffy, who was always interested in a journalist, casually invited him to join him some time for breakfast. As he was at a loose end in Dublin, McGee acted on the invitation more promptly than Duffy had expected. He came the next morning when Duffy had arranged to visit Davis. There was nothing to do but take him along.

This was one of the most agreeable things that had happened to D'Arcy since his return to Ireland. These men of his own generation, cultured, witty and patriotic were the most congenial companions he had ever met. In his effort to make a good impression he became over eager and talked too much. The editors of the *Nation* did not quite know what to make of him. There was not only his forward manner, but also his appearance—such an odd-looking boy, shabby and unkempt.

A true Irish heart, Davis said, but spoiled by the Yankees.

Duffy had to admit that the newcomer to the *Freeman's* staff was slovenly and unformed, but his discerning mind noted that McGee's homely appearance was offset by a voice "singularly sweet and flexible" and he recognized in him an alert and original mind. Duffy did some quick planning. A holiday at any distance from Dublin was out of the question for him. But a few days in the Wicklow Hills could be arranged. He invited McGee to go with him on a walking tour.

Dublin was almost an English city. No statue nor monument, not even a street name commemorated any famous or heroic Gael. Only English governors, better forgotten, had given their names to its streets and squares. But the County of Wicklow, beloved by Dubliners, was unspoiled Ireland, a country of lush green hills and valleys, of streams celebrated in Moore's poems, ancient Celtic crosses and vaguely melancholy ruins. The very place names sang to the ear, Clara and Dunran, Glendalough, Glenmalure and the Vale of Avoca.

Drifts of mist veiled and unveiled the masses of hills, scudding rain alternated with sudden sunshine. Not the pleasantest summer weather one could have asked, but good enough for vigorous walking, especially if one were well clad and shod, with the prospect of a good inn and hot supper at the end of the day. A bad year for crops. The potatoes were ruined, the farmers said. But of course the farmers always complained about the weather.

They tramped through the quiet countryside, McGee listening while Duffy told him how the *Nation* had been started and of the brilliant leadership of Thomas Davis. To think he had wasted his youth in America knowing nothing of Young Ireland!

In conversation with this new friend, wise and experienced in the ways of Irish politics, McGee could now ask the questions that had lingered in his mind since the failure of the Clontarf meeting. Duffy could only underline more blackly his misgivings. Since Clontarf the virtue seemed to have gone out of O'Connell. He hesitated and refused to take a definite course. The young men of the *Nation* were his political and spiritual heirs. But as sometimes happens in the natural order the father could not understand his sons. Daniel O'Connell had once been a young man passionately determined to right Ireland's wrongs. But even under the passion and exuberance of the young man had lain the hard core of a practical nature. It was an inspired, but calculating lawyer who had scored the victories over the English authorities. What had this battered veteran of many, sometimes sordid, political battles in common with these studious idealists who read history, wrote ballads and attempted by means of a newspaper to educate everyone? Beneath the scrupulous loyalty and unfailing courtesy of Davis and the young men the old tribune suspected a secret contempt for his own massive but slightly tarnished achievements.

"Young Ireland!" he would roar when they dared to cross him. "Young Ireland! Well, I stand for Old Ireland and I have some idea Old Ireland will stand by me!" And the older Repealers would applaud uproariously while the earnest young men tried despairingly to make their point. He had the most scurrilous tongue in the three kingdoms when he let himself go, but he never laid the full weight of his wrath on the Young Irelanders. They were so high minded, so ignorant of the world, he had not the heart. Sometimes if he thought he had gone too far he would be among them, an arm over Davis's shoulder, saying something like "Sure you're good boys. I know it and I love you all"—thereby confusing the earnest young men more than ever.

There was one simple answer to this riddle of O'Connell's last years. After Clontarf he was a dying man, suffering from an insidious, progressive brain disease. But this was only known after his death. Duffy could give McGee no

17

satisfactory answer to his questions. Young Ireland was in the hard position of having pledged its loyalty to a leader in whom it no longer had complete confidence.

The charm of Duffy's companionship and the misty, tender beauty of Wicklow County proved irresistible to the impressionable boy from America. D'Arcy left for London with his head full of poetry and the philosophy of Young Ireland. Duffy reported to Davis that he thought they would find in McGee a serviceable recruit.

Young Ireland was soon to have need of serviceable recruits. It was to be a year of calamities. In September, just as some of the *Nation's* contributors were returning to Dublin, fresh from holidays and eager for work, Davis fell ill of a mild attack of scarlet fever. He was ill only a few days, but the first day he ventured out he suffered a relapse and died very suddenly the same night.

The staff of the *Nation* not only lost its leader in Davis, but through sheer mischance began to fall to pieces. Dillon was ill with tuberculosis and was ordered by his doctor to a southern climate. One of the most brilliant contributors went insane. Two of the most active younger members were obliged to leave for England to continue their law studies.

The miserly summer yielded a poor harvest. As the pessimists had warned, the potato crop was ruined.

That winter there was famine in Ireland.

Chapter Three
McGEE ATTENDS PARLIAMENT
AND DISCOVERS THE BRITISH MUSEUM

Sir Robert Peel, the Prime Minister, had decided that the British working-people should have cheap bread. His conscience told him this was right and his political sense that if he did not see to it his opponents would. In the industrial cities of England the agitation for the repeal of the Corn Laws, which prevented the importation of cheap foreign grain, had reached a point of tension comparable to the agitation for the repeal of the Union in Ireland. But the British government was directly responsible to the English people in a way it was not to the Irish. It could not evade popular demands in England as it did in the case of Ireland.

The Prime Minister's policy embarrassed many in the House of Commons. Some of the Tory party felt that as their party had been elected by landowners and farmers to protect English agriculture, they had no right to change their policy and pass an act against the interests of their electors. The Tories were split between those who were willing to follow Peel and those who felt they must stick to their principles.

The Whig party realized that the repeal of the Corn Laws was inevitable. Some Whigs would have liked their party to be the government that would have the honour of this reform, but shrewder and more experienced members reflected that the government that removed the tariffs would be bitterly unpopular with the farming and landowning classes. It might be as well to let Peel and his Tories have the dangerous honour. Once the act was passed the

19

Whigs could ride to power on the wave of agricultural resentment that would follow.

Thanks to this situation the House of Commons, when McGee began his duties as correspondent in the autumn of 1845, did not lack parliamentary drama. But like chess the game of politics was more exciting to the players than to the spectator. Peel deliberately kept the debate as unsensational as possible, making long speeches stiff with statistics wherein he snipped off first one and then another import tax, step by step leading his reluctant Tories to the final act.

D'Arcy McGee, an obscure reporter in the Commons' press gallery, looked upon the Mother of Parliaments and found that presumably august assembly far from impressive. Members of the Whig and Tory parties faced each other on either side of the Speaker's dais, lounging in their seats with the informality of a gentleman's club. Most of them wore their hats, fashionable tall beavers or conventional black stove pipes. During a seemingly endless speech a member would tip his hat over his eyes and remain in an attitude of deep repose. One might almost have said that the honourable gentleman slept. Even the surroundings were unimpressive. The old Parliament had been burnt down in 1834 and until the handsome new Houses of Parliament were completed the Commons met in various makeshift quarters in the neighbourhood of Westminster.

McGee had the privilege not only of listening to the deliberately dull speeches of Sir Robert, but of seeing and hearing the two great statesmen of the future, William Ewart Gladstone and Benjamin Disraeli. Neither of them did much to enliven the debates. Even as a young man Gladstone's eloquence was weighty and earnest, and although it was impossible for Disraeli to speak without brilliance, at this period he was consciously trying to conform to the sober atmosphere of the House. He was playing the game intensely and subtly, using others whenever possible to express his views.

McGee may have seen Daniel O'Connell who occupied

his seat briefly during the session. But the sight of that broken hulk of a giant could only have distressed the boy brought up to regard O'Connell as the Liberator, a being apart and above the ordinary run of humanity.

This Parliament of Englishmen had nothing for Ireland. Peel used the threat of famine in Ireland as another argument for free trade, but Irishmen knew that the poor of Ireland depended on potatoes, not on grain, for their food. There was plenty of grain in Ireland, but it was harvested for sale in England. Daniel O'Connell with an upsurge of his old force told the government that an emergency measure should be passed to hold the wheat and oats in Ireland against the famine. But Irish landowners, many of whom were English and lived in England, would not hear of forgoing their privilege of selling their grain at a good price in the protected English market; a privilege, that in view of the impending legislation, they would soon no longer enjoy. The Irish members in the House of Commons were little better than petitioners to the dominant English parties and like importunate suitors they could be fobbed off.

In contempt McGee turned from what he considered elaborate dilly-dallying with vital problems.

In spite of the sense of tedium and unreality that Parliament gave the impatient onlooker, the game of politics as played at Westminster was a fine one of its kind, one that attracted some of the most talented men in England. Many of them by reason of wealth and family were placed above the cruder temptations of personal ambition. Their predecessors in the Commons had left great records of public service. The standards were set high. Only the best in statesmanship could win them place and honour there. The institution of Parliament was beginning to feel the pressure of nineteenth-century democracy. Slowly by complicated, halting processes characteristic of the stubborn British mind, this venerable, aristocratic assembly was being moulded into a form that the British people would be willing to accept as representing themselves.

In later life D'Arcy McGee too would play the game of

politics and play it with distinction. He would recall the
hours spent in the House of Commons and the notable
people he had watched. But at the time he was reporting
them, the proceedings bored him. London, an immense
drab city smothered in fog, did not attract him. And he
does not seem to have made friends.

But if neither Parliament nor London interested him, it
was not because of doltish inability to profit by the opportunities that one of the great cities of the world had to offer.
On the contrary, if he was indifferent to the variety of London life it was because soon after he came he found the
unique gift London had for him. He discovered the Library
of the British Museum.

Like Parliament this noble institution had a life independent of the building in which it happened to be housed.
The present magnificent circular Reading Room was only
a paper plan at the time McGee used the Library. It was
contained in a Georgian house facing Great Russell Street
with two wings forming a courtyard. Here in an anonymous
freemasonry of the intellect D'Arcy McGee kept company
with the great figures of the Victorian age, people whom he
was never to meet personally. The members from the House
of Commons—both Disraeli and Gladstone used the Library
—he would know by sight, but he may not have recognized
others who came and went during the winter he was in
London: Richard Cobden, champion of free trade, Matthew
Arnold the scholar, Thomas Carlyle, Gabriel Rossetti the
artist, Mazzini the exiled leader of Young Italy.

A few years earlier he would have seen Charles Dickens,
a parliamentary reporter like himself, avidly reading to
supplement a scanty education. A few years later he would
have shared the reading tables with Thomas Huxley the
scientist, Louis Blanc the French socialist and Karl Marx
the German communist. The Library of the British Museum
had a strong attraction for these stormy petrels of radical
thought.

The Library's collection included a section on Ireland
containing the recently published works on archaeology by

Eugene O'Curry and John O'Donovan as well as their trans-
lations of ancient Celtic manuscripts. McGee delved into
them with the wide-eyed joy of Keats first looking into
Chapman's translation of Homer. The poem in which
McGee later commemorated John O'Donovan rings with
the excitement of his own discovery. In these books he
found a scholarly reconstruction of Irish life before the conquest, a reaffirmation of the Christian Celtic culture that had
survived in Ireland when the rest of Europe was swept by
the barbarian invasions of the dark ages.

In other fields of knowledge science and research were
breaking to pieces traditional beliefs and leaving a trail of
rational doubts and bleak materialism. "The sea of faith
was once, too, at the full", wrote Matthew Arnold, who had
suffered the disillusion of the new science, "and round
earth's shore

> Lay like the folds of a bright girdle furl'd.
> But now I only hear
> Its melancholy, long, withdrawing roar,
> Retreating to the breath
> Of the night wind, down the vast edges drear
> And naked shingles of the world.

But D'Arcy's studies, without destroying his childhood
beliefs, helped him to cast them into a more mature form.
In these weighty, carefully annotated volumes he found the
bedrock of Celtic history. The old legends were based on
facts, the mythical saints and heroes had actually taught
and fought. The stories his mother had told him were
essentially true.

More and more these Irish studies became the centre of
his life, while the world of the 1840's and the convolutions
of Parliament faded into the London fog. Over the thresh-
old of the British Museum opened a world more to his
liking. Each time he checked his hat, signed for his books
and settled himself at one of the tables he entered upon
the most delightful and dangerous experience a Celt can
know. He was living in the past.

Or rather he would have been living in the past if his driving energy had not impelled him to give expression to everything he learned. Even as he pored over the tomes his imagination strained ahead, eager to create from the solid mass of scholarship new poems and histories for Young Ireland. Knowing that the *Freeman* would have no use for this material he tentatively sent some poems and articles to Gavan Duffy. They were promptly accepted.

This kind of writing was excellent for the *Nation* which frankly favoured literature and history. Duffy, however, noted that McGee's political articles for the *Freeman* were "a little wild and speculative". Wilson Gray, the *Freeman's* editor, was with good reason even more concerned about his London correspondent, who was writing as one bemused by the ancient glories of Ireland to the exclusion of the economics of free trade.

In April Wilson Gray came to London to find out what was wrong. He made it clear that he had expected reports based on the proceedings of Parliament and not on the archives of the British Museum.

Did Mr. McGee know who wrote the "Letters from London" for the *Nation*?

Yes, D'Arcy admitted. He wrote them.

Dr. Gray considered this conduct astonishing since Mr. McGee had been specifically engaged as correspondent for the *Freeman*.

D'Arcy was deeply offended. What he had written for the *Nation* had been done in his own time. If Dr. Gray found anything amiss with that he, D'Arcy, had no choice but to resign.

Since Gray had come to London with the intention of dismissing McGee this high behaviour took him aback. The interview ended with dissatisfaction on both sides. A little later Gray wrote McGee that the *Freeman* would no longer require his services.

Perhaps Wilson Gray judged his correspondent's neglect of duty too harshly because, although D'Arcy was giving much of his energy to his studies he had an enormous capacity for work. All his life he did several things at once, if not with equal skill, certainly very vigorously. It does not seem to have occurred to either of them that he was poorly equipped by experience and temperament to serve as a reporter. How could a young man of twenty who had been allowed to wield the editorial pen since he was seventeen be expected to conform to the exacting work of a parliamentary reporter? Having more than once experienced the excitement of an audience's response to his own words, could he be constrained calmly to listen to others in debates in which he was not allowed a part?

Dr. Gray left in London a young man badly worried not because he had lost a good position but because his conduct had been questioned. D'Arcy wrote Duffy a full account of what had happened, ending: "Since you are our literary mentor I wish to know whether I acted as became an Irish writer and a man of honour?"

The point he had raised was a delicate one. Duffy, as an editor of a paper, could understand Gray's annoyance. But if he could not counsel D'Arcy in a matter of conscience he could at least offer a practical suggestion. Would McGee care to remain in London as correspondent for the *Nation*?

In June 1846, two months after McGee had broken with the *Freeman*, Parliament passed the act repealing the Corn Laws.

The ponderous game had been played to its final move. Three times, according to custom, the bill had come before the House. The first reading and debate was the critical stage. It had gone on for weeks with Parliament often sitting far into the night. Disraeli, who was leading the dissenting Tories, several times stepped out of his demure role to attack the Prime Minister, his old chief, with cruel wit and eloquence. Even to a supercilious young reporter some of it must have been exciting. And the future parliamentarian was given the opportunity to observe an exceptionally complete example of the slow process of legislation at every stage. Beneath his surface boredom McGee's acute mind, half unconsciously, noted and recorded it all.

The vote ending the first debate assured the passage of the bill. The second debate was on points of detail. With the final reading and vote in June the machinery of parliamentary procedure ground to a close. The bill had been accepted by the House of Commons.

It now came before the House of Lords where it had already been thoroughly discussed. The Lords had learned from stormy experience that it was usually useless to veto a measure that had received the approval of the Commons. The House of Lords passed the bill after one reading and little debate.

The Queen's signature was the last step that made the bill officially an Act of Parliament and the law of the land. For better or worse England was now committed to free trade. Henceforth Britons would import their food and concentrate on becoming the foremost industrial and commercial nation of the world.

Then, by one of those manoeuvres that the more astute of the Whigs had foreseen, the parliamentary chess-board was swept clean. The Whigs, who had dropped their uneasy alliance with the government as soon as the bill was passed, joined with those Tories who had refused to follow Peel and with the Irish members who were against any government that held Ireland to the Union.

This combination of parties proved too strong for Peel's government which was defeated on one of its measures and obliged to resign. The Queen called upon Lord John Russell, the leader of the Whigs, to act as her Prime Minister and form a new government. The Whigs now sat on the government benches to the right of the Speaker's chair, while the defeated Peelites took their seats to the left on the opposition benches. The pieces had been set up anew and another game began.

Towards the end of the debates on the Corn Laws McGee returned to Dublin. He had accepted Duffy's invitation to work on the *Nation* for a repeal closer to his sympathies, the repeal of the Union between England and Ireland.

Verses from the Poem

Commemorating John O'Donovan

His fortress was a nation wreck'd,
His foes were falsehood, hate, neglect,
    His comrades few;
His arsenal was weapon-bare,
His flag-staff splinter'd in the air,
    Where nothing flew!

He toiled to make our story stand
As from Time's reverent, runic hand
    It came, undeck'd
By fancies false, erect, alone,
The monumental arctic stone
    Of ages wreck'd.

With gentle hand he rectified
The errors of old bardic pride,
    And set aright
The story of our devious past,
And left it, as it now must last,
    Full in the light!

Happy the life our scholar led
Among the living and the dead—
    Loving—beloved—
Mid precious tomes, and gentle looks,
The best of men, and best of books,
    He daily moved.

Kings that were dead two thousand years,
Cross-bearing chiefs and pagan seers,
    He knew them all;
And bards, whose very harps were dust,
And saints, whose souls are with the just,
    Came at his call.

THE ARDENT EXILE

O'er all low limits still his mind
Soar'd catholic and unconfined,
 From malice free;
On Irish soil he only saw
One state, one people, and one law,
 One destiny!

Chapter Four
IN THE OFFICE OF THE *NATION*

Dublin was gay in the spring. The social season was at its height. Those who had gone to the continent for the winter or to London for the sitting of Parliament were in town before starting on the summer exodus to the country. Socially eligible Young Irelanders could count on a round of invitations to breakfasts, dinner parties, receptions, art displays and the theatre.

Dublin was not a wealthy city; entertainment was on a modest scale, but nowhere in Europe would you find wittier conversation or better company. Dubliners felt that their dinner parties, alone, gave their society claim to Athenian brilliancy.

D'Arcy McGee, removed from the spell of the British Museum, no longer lived in seclusion. Even if the stately Georgian doors of the houses in Merrion Square did not open to him he was included in the weekly supper parties of Young Ireland. These, although now lacking Davis's inspiration, were as hilarious as ever.

Famine had pinched the farmers and fishermen of the western counties that winter. This proved, said politically-minded Dubliners, that Ireland should have her own Parliament to look after the country's welfare. Food had been scarce all over Europe following the poor harvests of 1845, but other small countries like Switzerland, Holland and Belgium had spared their people by forbidding food exports.

Peel's government had not considered this necessary for Ireland. The only effort made to ease the food shortage had been to import corn meal from America to be used for poor relief. The Irish did not know what to do with this strange food. "Peel's brimstone" they called the horrible bright yellow porridge they made with it. Their pride and their stomachs rejected it.

Truly, trouble and Ireland belonged together. It was nothing new for the people to go hungry. In Dublin wit was sharper and spirits more reckless because of what was happening in the west. As yet no one realized that this famine would grow to a calamity as black as any ever suffered by that calamitous country.

Duffy continued to publish the *Nation* from Davis's old office. In this dingy room lit at night by hot glaring gaslight and constantly cluttered with newspapers Duffy and his friends spent some of the tensest and happiest hours of their lives.

Here D'Arcy McGee met his new colleagues, some of them about his own age, fresh from school: Thomas Francis Meagher, foppish and languid, unaware that the English accent and mannerisms acquired during his school years with the English Jesuits at Stoneyhurst contrasted oddly with his high-pitched patriotism; Thomas Wallis, a decidedly intelligent young man gifted or cursed with a critical mind and a blistering tongue; Devin Reilly, a moody, overgrown lad given to hero-worship of Gavan Duffy and resentful of D'Arcy from the first.

Following Davis's death and Dillon's departure for Madeira, Duffy had taken as his associate editor John Mitchel. This Protestant Ulsterman had been won over to Young Ireland by Duffy in the course of a walking tour similar to the jaunt during which he had won the mind of D'Arcy McGee. Mitchel was interested in the Irish land problem. He was able to take over the column in the *Nation* that Dillon had always written on this subject. For the moment Duffy, who did not wish the *Nation* to become an exclusively Catholic paper, was well pleased with his latest recruit.

There were contributors who were seldom seen around the *Nation* office. One poet who wrote regularly for the paper was never seen except by Duffy. A strange, afflicted personality, drug-ridden, almost ignored by his contemporaries, James Clarence Mangan wrote poetry touched with the fire of genius that survived the writings of all the rest. Dark Rosaleen, the sad, unearthly Ireland of his songs, lived on to inspire the poets who came after.

Other mysterious and invisible beings wrote for the paper. These were the ladies. Love of Ireland inspired them, but some also were lured from afar by the romantic personalities of Thomas Davis, Gavan Duffy and the handsome John Dillon. From preference or convention the ladies kept away from the *Nation* office, except on the occasions when, owing to the exigencies of Irish politics, all the male members of the staff were either in jail or in hiding. Then, emerging from maidenly seclusion, the ladies would take over the office and bring out the paper.

If the cause to which Thomas Davis had devoted his short life outlasted him it was because he left in his friend Gavan Duffy an ardent and well-informed disciple. These two had planned for the future. Duffy used these plans as his guide when he found himself alone.

"Educate that you may be free" was the motto of the *Nation*. The scars of the penal laws from which O'Connell had rescued his countrymen still showed rawly. Irishmen had developed some of the characteristics of an oppressed people, over-amiable servility alternating with rash violence. The Irish, Davis and Duffy had believed, could do with a great deal of educating. They had worked out a number of projects to advance national culture. To satisfy the unquenchable Irish delight in poems, songs and stories, the *Nation* successfully encouraged the revival of Irish ballad literature. But the dearest project of all was the Library of Ireland, a series of volumes to be written by different members covering Irish history and biography. Davis's biography of Wolfe Tone was left unfinished at his death, but other volumes were published at the rate of one a month for nearly two years.

Among the new recruits Duffy had attracted to Young

Ireland, D'Arcy McGee best understood its purpose. The bent of his mind was scholarly and literary. Remembering the fruitful hours with the works of the archaeologists, he could think of no career he would prefer to continuing their work of discovering Ireland to herself. He joyfully accepted a contract from Duffy, with an advance of £100, to write a biography for the Library of Ireland series. At the same time he set to work on a ballad history of Ireland for the *Nation*, spinning it out in issue after issue of the paper with tireless invention. Its popularity proved that the subscribers were as ready to read verses as he was to write them.

His activities did not stop here. He became honorary secretary of the semi-political Dublin Trades Union. He loyally supported national culture by attending art exhibits. At one of these he met Mary Caffrey, the first and only girl to play an important part in his life. He had never liked London and he no longer missed the British Museum. Who would want to live anywhere but in Dublin?

Although bringing new members into the ranks of Young Ireland was not difficult, controlling them was another matter. Duffy lacked the rare gift that Davis shared with Father Mathew and Daniel O'Connell of making prudent counsels as inspiring as a call to battle. Although the principles of Young Ireland remained the same as when Davis was alive, individual members recklessly compromised them.

John Mitchel wrote an editorial urging that in case of troop movements against them, the people be instructed in the best way to wreck a train. Duffy, as editor of the paper, was brought to trial for this article; even though, as he explained privately, he had money invested in railways and no wish to see trains wrecked.

Thanks to his lawyer, Duffy and the *Nation* were cleared of the charge of sedition. But the trial alarmed O'Connell whose lifelong objection to physical force had become in old age an obsession. Duffy wanted the incident dropped and forgotten. But the discussion of physical force and if it were ever justified was too great a temptation for the nimble tongues of Young Ireland.

The climax came at a meeting of the Repeal Association in Conciliation Hall. O'Connell was not present. He came infrequently now to meetings. His son John O'Connell was presiding, a middle-aged man of ordinary abilities who fancied himself his father's successor. He had no fondness for Young Ireland. Nevertheless Thomas Meagher chose this time to rise and deliver an oration on "The Sword". It was a remarkable effort composed with elaborate care, adorned with erudite allusions, pitched in an exalted strain and producing a dramatic effect. Many considered it the finest speech ever given in Conciliation Hall. Tom Meagher was afterwards known as "Meagher of the Sword".

The chairman shattered the spell. The speech, he declared, was seditious and must not go on. Meagher protested. John O'Connell refused to hear him. Meagher, thereupon, said his rights of free speech had been violated and left the Hall. Those who were in sympathy with Young Ireland followed him. Some, like Duffy, left regretfully. Perhaps the break between Young Ireland and the Old Repealers was inevitable, but Meagher's Sword Speech made it a fact.

McGee felt deeply concerned in the withdrawal from Conciliation Hall. His own application to join the Repeal Association had been turned down. The fact that he wrote for the *Nation* was enough at the moment to make him undesirable. He joined with the others in defending Young Ireland against the intolerant attitude of the Old Repealers; in this cause he made his first speeches in Ireland. He did not have the advantages of Meagher's fine clothes and gentlemanly appearance. Everything about his appearance suggested the wild-eyed, wild-haired revolutionist. People therefore were surprised to hear him speak forcefully but reasonably. Indeed some who favoured the firebrand type of oratory criticized him as being "too universally conciliatory".

It was Meagher who made barbed remarks about the Church in politics and talked of "levelling the altar rather than see it defiled by clerical bigotry". It was the unguarded remarks of Mitchel and Meagher that left an opening for the campaign of malice and lies indiscriminately aimed at all the members of Young Ireland after the Sword Speech episode. Irish eloquence had many aspects. It could grace a Dublin dinner party or, turning venomous, become a weapon to undo an enemy. Before the malice now turned upon Young Ireland had spent its force, the *Nation* had been banned from every Repeal Reading Room in the country and the Bishop of Armagh had said that he thanked God there were no schoolboy philosophers or Voltairean newspapers in his diocese.

McGee, older in experience than in years, was more attracted to Duffy, Mitchel and the senior members of Young Ireland than to those of his own age with their adolescent enthusiasms and friendships. Meagher of the Sword, his natural rival, he did not see very often. Meagher, who did not have to earn a living, wrote only when in the mood and preferred to devote his talents to patriotic speechifying up and down the country. Devin Reilly was often about the *Nation* office but his work was so far inferior to McGee's that he hardly qualified as either rival or colleague. To McGee his moods and jealousy seemed childish. Each was soon giving the other the sharp edge of his tongue.

By summer Duffy was eager to get away from town. The social distractions were preventing him from working on his book for the Library of Ireland. Besides, Dublin was not without its vexations. He had stood trial for Mitchel's editorial about wrecking railways; he had seen Young Ireland forced out of the Repeal Association. Even the office was no longer peaceful with McGee sarcastic and Reilly sulking.

Duffy took a house at Dundrum in the Wicklow Hills. There he retired for the summer, trustfully leaving Mitchel in charge of the paper. Dillon had returned, his health greatly improved by his winter in the south. In September

Thomas Carlyle visited Duffy at Dundrum where his host invited all the Young Ireland writers to meet him. As McGee was writing regularly for the *Nation* it may be assumed in absence of other evidence that he was among those who paid their respects to the noted philosopher and historian.

A curious lifelong friendship existed between Gavan Duffy and Carlyle in spite of the difference in age and temperament. Each was a missionary for his own ideas, but neither ever succeeded in converting the other. Duffy maintained that from Carlyle he learned not Carlyle's ideas but how to think for himself.

As for Carlyle he remained unsympathetic toward repeal and on the whole toward the Irish who, in his stern opinion, brought their troubles on themselves. But he warmed his dour nature with the youth and high spirits of Duffy and his friends, commending them as "honest and manly fellows". He would not have dreamed of admitting that what he really liked was not their honest manliness, but their gaiety, their happy faculty, of which he had not an iota, of stepping easily from shabby realities into a world of imagination and laughter.

Chapter Five
BLACK '47

A WOMAN, carrying a child wrapped in her shawl, walked slowly along the road leading from Skull in the county of Cork. A passerby noticing her halting step and dazed look spoke to her.

The child, she said, had died of hunger. She herself had the fever upon her, but she would make a hole in the graveyard to bury the poor innocent before the rats gnawed the body. This incident occurred in the second year of the famine, the winter of 1847, remembered in Ireland as Black '47.

Hunger is an insidious thing, draining away the strength and numbing the mind like a drug. Those who went into the worst famine areas wondered at the apathy of the people. Since they did not know the fine points of the science of nutrition they did not recognize the symptoms of malnutrition. They imagined that a man who was starving to death would be a savage, desperate fellow. Instead, entire families died helplessly of starvation and fever almost within sight of the cereal, meat and butter waiting at the docks for shipment to England. In the streets of the southern ports gaunt wanderers were everywhere: the women in lines before the Poor House clamouring for soup tickets; the men at the Public Works Commission waiting sullenly for a job on the road. When given work they were, more often than not, too weak to perform it.

In remote villages even this feeble life was gone. Some were completely deserted. The dead in the shanties lay unburied, half eaten by dogs and rats. Those who had set out for the town weakened on the way and crept into quarries and ditches to die.

There is a kind of wild exaggeration about the stories of the famine that might cause the wary to doubt even eyewitnesses. But the impersonal testimony of statistics and public records declare them true. The verdicts of coroners' inquests finding death by starvation were returned in batches. Tens and scores mounted to hundreds and thousands until by February, 1847, the police headquarters at Dublin had records of 50,000 such deaths. And this was only the beginning.

The temper of the people hardened. Scornful jokes about "Peel's brimstone" gave way to the words appended to the lists of famine deaths: "Verdict of wilful murder found against John Russell, commonly called Lord John Russell". During the years of the famine the charge lay against the Prime Minister's name like a curse.

O'Connell was willing to drop the demand for repeal in return for aid from the Whig government which he had helped into office. In his increasingly vague state of mind he hoped for who knows what emergency measure to hold the food in Ireland. But Lord John Russell's government was no improvement upon Peel's Tories. It regretted, it deplored, it doubted the necessity of extreme measures, except of course to preserve law and order. It did not deem it advisable to interfere with the normal course of trade.

It continued to provide two measures of relief: the Poor Laws, in other words the Poor House; and Public Works, in other words road building. This help was only for the destitute. To receive it a man had to give up his bit of a farm. He and his family became paupers, part of a landless proletariat for whom in an agricultural country there would never be enough work in the cities.

No wonder many died in their cabins rather than accept the harsh charity of the government. Others, acting before their funds and strength were all gone, emigrated.

Among those who followed Tom Meagher from Conciliation Hall had been a middle-aged, well-dressed gentleman of reserved manner. William Smith O'Brien, a Protestant landlord and member of Parliament, had joined the Repeal Association in protest against Peel's action in dismissing supporters of O'Connell from the Irish magistracy. The man must have had some combination of qualities as oddly assorted as his name for he loyally supported the repeal cause during its decline and in spite of the rowdy side of repeal politics which offended his precise mind. Meagher's Sword Speech was the first occasion on which he openly sided with Duffy and his friends.

Young Ireland was now in a peculiar position. Davis had intended that his young men would revive Irish literature and encourage popular education. But when the famine made survival more important than anything else, Young Ireland had to modify its programme. Whether Davis, with his originality and his ability to inspire those who worked with him, could have made Young Ireland into a national party to replace the decrepit Repeal Association is the kind of question that must go unanswered when a brilliant man dies too soon. As it was, Duffy was glad to have the support of Mr. Smith O'Brien and willingly placed Young Ireland under his hesitant but respectable leadership. The young men then set about forming their own association.

They called it the Irish Confederation and held their first meeting in January 1847. They were old hands at this, having looked after many of the details of O'Connell's mass meetings. This time when they climbed upon the platform —verdantly decked with green and gold flags—to open their own Confederation, nothing had been overlooked.

They had hired space at the Rotunda, a public building consisting of ballrooms and supper rooms where all the important gatherings of Dublin were held. Brawny members of the Dublin Trades Union stood guard. The Old Repealers, who thrust peace resolutions down the throats of others, were not above shying a few brickbats at a rival meeting.

At this meeting Duffy succeeded in disciplining his followers to speak with moderation. Repeal of the union was their goal. While not excluding those who wanted a republic, the Confederation was willing that the Irish should remain under the British Crown provided they had their own Parliament in Dublin. Above all the Confederation stood for the unity that Davis had wanted, the unity of all those who suffered from the country's degradation.

An enthusiastic but orderly audience of about two thousand listened to the speeches. These were long and rhetorical, but thanks to Duffy, free from sedition and libel. Looking over the audience with a sharp eye, he noted that it was made up of working-men, shopkeepers and students, with a sprinkling of professional men and a few of the clergy. They must have more of these last two classes, he decided. He was constantly thinking of ways to attract the Protestant merchants of the north. Fired by his own missionary zeal and the possibilities of Smith O'Brien's support he even hoped to convert to the national cause the most selfish and privileged class of all—the landlords.

D'Arcy McGee, sitting with his colleagues on the stage, believed that he was taking part in a historic scene. Here was the heart and brain of the repeal movement. O'Connell belonged with them, not with the hacks of Conciliation Hall.

Meagher of the Sword longed for a chance to prove his right to his sobriquet by action more forcible than speech-making.

John Mitchel thought of the Confederation as a challenge to English tyranny. Remembering Carlyle's description of the mobs in his *History of the French Revolution*, Mitchel imagined the Irish rising in spontaneous wrath, rifles in hand, barricades for their defence, while Dublin Castle aflame in the background symbolically lit the scene.

To trace the political motives of Devin Reilly, blurred as they were by personal feelings, would be most difficult of all. He responded to the man rather than the cause. He had worshipped Davis from a distance. He could have devoted himself to Gavan Duffy, but Duffy made him mad with jealousy by preferring D'Arcy McGee. The sight of

McGee's homely face, the sound of his flippant tongue infuriated Reilly. He knew he was not as good a worker as McGee. He knew he was lazy, inaccurate and undependable, but the turmoil of discontent in which he lived brought on violent headaches. Under these conditions how could he do his best?

Smith O'Brien presided over this volatile group which for the moment presented a deceptively united front. His reputation stood high. His twenty years' experience in Parliament gave him standing. He was a good man, an ornament to the Society for the Diffusion of Useful Knowledge of which he was a member. His connection with dishevelled Irish politics looked a little like a mésalliance.

The Irish Confederation was not a group to be ignored. O'Connell heard of it. It was what he himself might have done in his younger days. McGee, who was eager for a reconciliation between Young Ireland and O'Connell, claimed to have heard from a first-hand source the effect of the Confederation on O'Connell. His followers had tried to assure him that the meeting would come to nothing. Sure 'twas but a crowd gathered to hear the boys talking. But O'Connell kept saying: No, no, it was a great meeting. They were a great party and he must have them back.

If this was his wish he was not allowed to have it. John O'Connell and the party hacks now had the old tribune under their influence, using him for their own mean ends.

During the winter of 1847 he went to the House of Commons for the last time. In a voice sunk to a rasping whisper he spoke on behalf of the famine victims. In the spring the desire came upon the old man to make a pilgrimage to Rome. He set out with the retinue of friends and relatives that always accompanied him, but he died at Genoa before reaching the Holy City.

Dear to the Irish heart is the infinitely pathetic story of the return to Ireland. As the ship carrying O'Connell's body entered Dublin Bay, it passed an outbound emigrant ship. When those aboard learned what cargo was being brought home a keening rose from the crowded decks such as might have told all Ireland of its loss.

Less edifying is the story of the strange behaviour of the Old Repealers. They held the body of O'Connell from May to August without burial, timing the funeral to coincide with the elections of the summer of 1847. To the country at large they said that Young Ireland had been the death of the Liberator.

They might have spared themselves the disgrace. The elections of 1847 turned on the question of poor relief. Like a malignant growth flourishing with a morbid life of its own in the dying body of Irish society, famine relief had become the principal activity of the country. Those who had votes in many cases were dependent on the jobs as overseers, engineers, paymasters and clerks, that the poor relief and public works provided. Others, out of jobs, hoped to be taken on government payrolls. In 1847, Irish voters with a livelihood to think of elected the government's candidates.

"A whole nation is starving," O'Connell had written a few months before his death. "If any are not they are too few to be mentioned." In terms of stark physical starvation this was an exaggeration. But in the sense that Irish society was perishing from the effects of famine, fever and emigration, O'Connell's words were true.

McGee felt the stultifying effects in his own career, which had looked very promising at the time of his return from London. In 1847 the Library of Ireland had to be dropped. Interest in popular education was dwindling. The Reading Rooms were closed and the readers were joining the exodus to America. McGee's biography of Art McMurrough, King of Leinster, which came out in March, 1847, was the last volume of the series to be published.

The Ballad History of Ireland had to be discontinued. The *Nation* was giving more space to political controversy and efforts to stir up the landlords. Readers who wrote in asking about the Ballad History were told sternly: "What man with a heart would sit down to write Ballad History while his country perishes? We would rather hear of a great league of Irishmen of all creeds confederated together in 1847 to give Ireland to the Irish than all the victories since King Dathy." All that was left for McGee was the barren work of propaganda among the landlords.

This did not mean that McGee stopped writing poetry. He continued to publish short patriotic poems in the *Nation* and other Dublin journals. He also turned his poetry to personal ends, using it with good effect on Mary Caffrey. As he was not handsome and certainly not rich, when he went courting he had to make the most of what he had.

A few of the landlords had shown concern for the state of the country by forming the Irish Council in January, 1847, about the same time as the opening meeting of the Irish Confederation. From the first Duffy worked with the Irish Council, encouraging it in the *Nation*, sending speakers to its meetings to urge it in the direction of tenant rights.

John Mitchel spoke for the Tenant League. D'Arcy McGee also went on these missions to the country. He had a way with him in addressing an audience and could be depended on not to make his rhetorical flourishes at the expense of the final goal, Irish unity.

As a class the landlords played a sorry, not to say villainous part, in the tragedy of the famine. They were not for the most part wealthy enough to forego the profitable market in England in order to keep food in Ireland for starving peasants. Who would pay them? They would be ruined. Neither could the shrewder among them ignore the trend of the times. Now that the Corn Laws were repealed Irish agriculturists would have stiff competition from foreign grain in the English market. Cattle-raising would soon bring larger returns than grain-growing. This meant clearing the tenant farmers off their estates, hiring a few herdsmen and turning the land to pasture.

John Mitchel, never a patient man, soon gave up trying to convert landlords. He began to take up the ideas of a certain John Finton Lalor, who had his own remedy for the ills of Ireland. Lalor wanted to discard the existing social system as having broken down under the famine and to declare the natural right of the people to make a new social arrangement. Put more simply Lalor wanted a new distribution of land. This was to be brought about by a rent strike and, if necessary, physical force.

Duffy had some control over Mitchel's writings in the *Nation* but none over his speeches. At public meetings McGee undertook to oppose Mitchel when he voiced Lalor's theories. The goal of Young Ireland was national unity, he reminded his audience. Lalor was trying to set class against class. Up to this time McGee had worked amicably with Mitchel whom he admired. But from this point he incurred Mitchel's ill will to a degree that did not become apparent till some years later.

For practical purposes the worth or worthlessness of the various plans mattered little. The co-operation between the Council and the Confederation was like a group of people on a heavily listing deck desperately clutching each other. Without self-government they were powerless to prevent their country's disaster. The famine crisis was only part of an old and iniquitous land problem. The propaganda of Young Ireland was futile. The Irish landlords had no tradition of public service that could be appealed to. For generations they had lived by the rule of self-interest. Legislation, not education, was needed. Only action by an alert and courageous government could have reformed them. In the absence of this legislation they were not prepared voluntarily and individually to sacrifice themselves. Inevitably the famine with its attendant fever and emigration had to run its course.

In the end even the landlords did not escape. After the elections of 1847 had put it securely in power the Whig government thriftily cut down on public works in Ireland and increased the poor rates paid largely by the landlords. Thousands of them were ruined.

"The do-nothing attitude of the Irish gentry and land-lords did not save them," wrote Duffy in his memoirs. "Their estates were eaten up by poor rates spent on able-bodied paupers. Before the end of five years, peers, baronets and knights were turned out of their possessions by the Encumbered Estates Court."

Duffy, usually the mildest of men, records their fate with satisfaction.

Chapter Six
ROMANTIC INTERLUDE

ONE CANNOT MOURN a calamity forever, especially when it is a public calamity and one is young. The Young Irelanders did not devote themselves to politics to the point of ignoring the ladies hovering discreetly in the background of their lives. In the spring of 1847 Gavan Duffy took a wife. In late summer of the same year D'Arcy McGee married his Mary.

The years have closed over Mary Caffrey McGee leaving hardly a clue as to what she was like. From the little that is known she appears to have been sociable, in sympathy with the politics of Young Ireland and well-read in a ladylike way. All that we have now is a picture taken after Mary came to America. She is wearing a plaid silk dress with a voluminous skirt and fitted bodice. For ornament she has matching oval-shaped brooch and earrings. Over her shoulders is a black lace shawl, covering her sleeves and folded over the wrists of her shapely hands. She carries herself erect, the head well poised. The face is interesting, although neither pretty nor beautiful—a wide, humorous mouth, a strong jaw line running from ear to chin, good eyes and forehead with delicately arched black eyebrows. Only a woman with well-proportioned eyes and forehead could successfully wear her hair as Mary does, parted in the middle, drawn plainly over the ears and gathered at the neck in a snood.

Looking at that face with its strength and humour one wonders at the obscurity of her life by the side of her more famous husband, and one would like to know more about her.

Wealth courts wealth and the poor man marries the poor

girl. Such is the usual pattern. Such seems to have been the case in this marriage as there is no evidence that Mary brought her husband any dowry. D'Arcy on his part assumed the responsibilities of marriage provided only with pure and fervent patriotism, considerable facility in writing verse and great diligence in the practice of journalism. For many years the McGees depended on this last for their livelihood.

They were married from the home of Mary's mother and disappeared into the neighbouring Wicklow County for their honeymoon. They might have gone half-way across Europe without finding a more romantic spot. Within a day's travel lay an itinerary of streams, lakes, glens and mountains made famous by legend and poetry. Some spots had a kind of private fame for D'Arcy as the places he had visited with Gavan Duffy.

Of course this could not be a walking tour like the other holiday. Strenuous exercise could not be expected of a Victorian bride dressed in full sweeping skirts, many petticoats and thin-soled heelless slippers. Nor for that matter could it be expected of a Victorian bridegroom in his best suit. It is only reasonable to assume that D'Arcy, who is invariably described as shabby, had bought a new suit for his wedding.

If in order to save their finery they proceeded by coach and jaunting car they nevertheless saw all the sights. They visited the Meeting of the Waters and the Vale of Avoca, St. Kevin's Bed and the sites of his ancient churches. They saw ancient towers and stone Celtic crosses with arms joined by a circle, the symbol of eternity. They also saw at the old burial places timelier and sadder sights, the family groups gathered for a last visit to the graves before leaving for the port and the emigrant ship.

Since private life played a small part in D'Arcy McGee's career one would like to think of this honeymoon as a happy interlude. One would like to think that Mary especially found all her heart desired, for she was never to hold first place in the life of the man she had married. Not that D'Arcy would be unfaithful or prefer any other woman to her. But the truth was that she had married a patriot. Love of country would always be greater in this man than love of any creature.

Even after he was forced into exile he simply adopted another country upon which to expend his devotion. As he grew older the idealized figure of Ireland called in his poems his "goddesss", his "idol" and his "soul" tended to fade. In place of the fantasy he found the reality of his own people, the Irish immigrants of the New World. To their needs he gave as careful thought as he gave to the affairs of his own family.

In the first enthusiasm of her honeymoon Mary may have rejoiced in her husband's high-minded patriotism, but one cannot help wondering if in the long run she did not find the constant presence of her shadowy rival somewhat wearing.

Of all the people in D'Arcy's life his mother had influenced him most deeply. He remembered her because of the songs she used to sing to them in the evening and because she had opened to him the world of the imagination and the spirit. This was a country from which he would never be exiled.

He seems to have been on friendly but not intimate terms with the rest of his family. He occasionally visited his father who still lived in Wexford. The elder McGee had remarried and there was a second family growing up. Two of D'Arcy's sisters had died as children. The one who had gone with him to America had stayed there. His elder brother Lawrence was a sailor. His younger brother James had recently come to Dublin where he may have lived with D'Arcy and Mary after their marriage. D'Arcy, using his influence with Gavan Duffy, had found him a place on the staff of the *Nation*.

After the honeymoon the young couple returned to a small house they had rented in Cullenswood, a Dublin suburb. Mary took up her wifely duties, making her husband the first home he had known since he was a boy. D'Arcy resumed his writing for the *Nation* and the depressing grind of Irish politics.

Chapter Seven
NEWS FROM EUROPE

THE NEW YEAR had begun in discouragement. Once in London the Irish Council members, whom Young Ireland had helped to elect to Parliament, forgot the famine and the poor and busied themselves with law, order and safeguarding property. They were especially concerned about cases of agrarian crime among evicted tenants.

John Mitchel not only said, "I told you so"—he left the *Nation,* expressing at the moment of his departure a fleeting regret.

"I am quite certain I could not have worked in subordination to any other man alive nearly as long as I have done with you," he told Duffy, with disarming candour.

Devin Reilly also came to say good-bye. Although protesting with tears his affection for Duffy, he had decided to go with Mitchel. His leaving, he explained, was a matter of political opinion only. Within a month Mitchel and Reilly were publishing a paper entitled confusedly the *United Irishman.* In its columns they attacked Duffy, McGee and other former colleagues with characteristic lack of restraint.

Ignoring the quarrelsome new competitors, Duffy reshuffled the duties of the staff, making McGee his associate editor. In ordinary matters McGee was proving to be a sharp-tongued, impulsive young man. He lacked what he himself would have called the minor virtue of discretion. But in matters of public importance he had a fine sense of the reasonable give and take without which politics becomes a cockfight. The trend of his mind was towards tolerance and moderation. Duffy knew that the policy of the *Nation* would be safe with McGee because he was in sympathy

48

with it. Mitchel's extreme and violent opinions had done
the paper much harm, so that his departure was something
of a blessing. Even so, the staff felt depressed by this fresh
symptom of Irish disunity.

The only bright spot in the drab winter of 1848 was
Tom Meagher who was running in a by-election in Water-
ford. The young parliamentary candidate was enjoying
every minute of the publicity and excitement. He was in
his element parrying his opponent's verbal cudgelling and
"murderer of the Liberator" taunts with gay, quick-witted
repartee.

"Everything goes splendidly," he wrote Duffy. "A
glorious canvass today. All the people—emphatically *the
people*—and the girls and the women. My God! I can
hardly believe my senses!"

Unfortunately the women and girls did not have votes
and Meagher lost the election. But the Young Irelanders
had made a good impression and won supporters in Water-
ford. The times were so bad that they had to be cheerful
on very little. While the election was going on a number of
them went down from Dublin to join in the fun.

This is how it happened that Duffy was alone in the
Nation office when the great news broke. Opening the
exchange papers brought by the London to Dublin mail, he
read the news from France. On February 22 revolution had
broken out in Paris. Street fighting was still going on between the popular voluntary National Guard and the regular
militia with the militia getting the worst of it. King Louis
Philippe had fled. A provisional government had been set
up in the Hotel de Ville.

The news was not splashed in headlines, but given its
proper place under a modest title. Nevertheless the editorial scissors lay unused and the rest of the mail was pushed
aside unopened as Duffy continued to stare at the paper.
A terrible excitement rose in him. It was, as he wrote in
his memoirs, like the thunder that breaks a spell of stifling
weather bringing the relief of the storm.

Was this Ireland's opportunity?

Across Europe, liberals, nationalists, socialists, communists and reformers were asking the same question. Was this their opportunity? Had France given the signal?

In the 1840's news travelled swiftly, but speed was in terms of days and hours, not as in the radio age in terms of minutes. Dublin learned of the outbreak in Paris in the same week that it happened. The next day's post brought news that a republic had been declared. Each day following brought reports not only from Paris but from other centres. The restless capitals of Europe were stirred as they had not been since the unsuccessful uprisings of 1830.

By March revolutions were sweeping Europe like spring storms, boisterous, destructive and full of hope. Old Metternich had been dismissed. Since the fall of Napoleon for nearly half a century the ageing Austrian statesman had dominated Europe, holding Hungary, southern Poland and northern Italy unwillingly in the Austrian Empire. Now he was gone and the web of intrigue and coercion he had woven was broken. The Hungarians were demanding national rights. The Venetians were driving Austrian soldiers from their city. In Berlin the students, emulating the Parisians, had erected barricades.

What was Ireland doing?

Nothing had been prepared. Nothing had been foreseen. The influence of O'Connell was still strong and he had forbidden the use of force. Young Ireland had never been a secret society. It was unversed in conspiracy and underground tactics.

The only man who had foreseen the possibility of a situation like 1848 was dead. Thomas Davis had deduced from his study of Irish history the theory that at certain times when England was hard pressed a show of force quickly gained concessions for Ireland. True, any rebellion that dragged on long enough to bring the full power of England against it was sure to fail. Ireland had had too many mad and cruel rebellions. But Davis had not agreed entirely with O'Connell's non-violence doctrine. He believed that the Irish were justified in resorting to force when a little of it would go a long way.

Was 1848 such a time? Duffy, who remembered all Davis had taught, had to ask himself this question. The answer, he decided, was "Yes". With Smith O'Brien he held meetings to decide on policy and action under the new conditions. The Confederates must agree on what they wanted—an independent Parliament and complete self-government for Ireland under the British Crown. They must agree to use legal, constitutional and peaceful methods. These must not be completely discarded even if for a time force had to be added.

Once again as when the Irish Confederation was first formed, Duffy was able to give the organization a semblance of unity. Even those who wanted a republic were willing to accept the Crown if self-government was conceded. Only John Mitchel, Devin Reilly and a few others stood out. They wanted an immediate insurrection and the declaration of an Irish republic.

During the mad March days political clubs copied from European models sprang up in Dublin, complete with a Technological Society for the Study of Practical Chemistry. The purposes of this Society were obscure but had something to do with the manufacture of gunpowder. Just give the word, cried Mitchel in the *United Irishman*, and a glorious spontaneous revolution would break out. He fervently believed that revolutions followed Carlyle's romantic version in *The French Revolution*.

But the editors of the *Nation* were reasonable men who had read history in a different spirit. They suspected that the fine abandon of the Parisians in street fighting was the result of planning and co-ordination. Before the Irish could act, the flimsy Dublin clubs would have to be united under a central executive. A National Guard would have to be formed. Funds and arms would have to be found.

All this could not be done in a day or a week. The government had added troops to the Dublin garrison. Mitchel's premature cries of "To the barricades!" would only end in massacre. The government also arrested Smith O'Brien, Tom Meagher and John Mitchel on charges of sedition but allowed them bail. Except for these precautions the authorities seemed content to follow the usual policy of wait and see.

The prospects for the success of an Irish revolution were not bright, but they were just good enough that the Confederates felt they ought not to let the opportunity pass. They looked around for allies. They could depend on America for funds. Irish American money was already helping to keep the Irish Confederation and the *Nation* in existence. But communications between Ireland and America were slow. Weeks would pass before the money would arrive. There remained France which had reason to be grateful to Irish exiles for many services.

Perhaps the new French Republic would help—not officially of course, but by encouraging Frenchmen who wished to volunteer for Irish service. Something like Lafayette's mission to America in 1777 . . . Yes, Lafayette was an excellent precedent. The Irish Confederation would send a delegation to Paris to congratulate the new Republic and delicately sound out its leaders.

The executive rented the Music Hall on Abbey Street. There amidst symbolic decorations of lyres and flutes, on the evening of March 15, they unfurled their green and gold flags and held a meeting. The place was crowded. The Irish Confederation, obliged to hold back while the rest of Europe struck great blows for freedom, was desperately in need of emotional relief.

Smith O'Brien moved that congratulations be sent from the Confederation to the Second French Republic. He urged the young men in the audience to enrol as members of a National Guard. Tom Meagher rose to second the motion, allowing himself at the same time one of those bursts of eloquence that endeared him to the populace. "If the government of Ireland insists upon being a government of dragoons, bombardiers, of detectives and light infantry, then up with the barricades and invoke the God of Battles."

To D'Arcy McGee fell the privilege of making the motion that Smith O'Brien and Thomas Meagher be sent to Paris as the Confederation's delegates. He had less prestige than Smith O'Brien and less popularity than Meagher, but he had a better voice than either and in the arts of oratory he was second to none. He faced an audience already aroused, ready to roar or weep at a word, craving a cheer leader. It was an audience to fire the eloquence of a demagogue. But the address the twenty-two-year-old journalist gave that night was not the speech of a demagogue.

He began with a polite reference to Smith O'Brien and the men of the name of O'Brien who had served with distinction in French armies. Then he took up the explosive question of a people's right to resist a tyrannous government. Presenting his case like a lawyer he turned against the Whigs and their government the liberal traditions and teachings of their own party. He recalled the English Revolution of 1688. He quoted at some length from Lord John Russell, Hobbes and Locke on the theory of the social contract and the people as the source of authority. His audience punctuated his quotations with cheers.

He then spoke of unity, a matter to him always of first importance. "Sir, I repeat that it depends entirely on the government whether or not the people openly resist its authority. Resistance I have shown to be of itself just and lawful. To make it so in our case two contingencies are needed—first that we should be united (Loud cheers.)—secondly, that we should demand and be finally refused our rights. No small party or faction or moiety of a people is justified in resisting the established government. Resistance, to be justifiable, must be unanimous or nearly so. Resistance is no faction fight. We must have union before freedom."

Since his audience was Irish he was expected to denounce the government. He disposed of it in a few sentences while his excitable listeners with difficulty kept their seats.

"But we will have union—fifteen hundred or fifty thousand slaves may protest confidence in the government, but

the people have none. Connaught accuses their Premier of
wilful murder—Ulster charges their Irish Secretary with
robbery—Munster points to Bantry and Skull—Leinster to
the ruined factories and deserted homes of Kilkenny, Rath-
drum and Dublin. They are condemned by the universal
voice of Ireland; their party crumbles down, their chief is
sick and weary of office. (Groans.) Yes, the verdicts of
wilful murder hang over his head and sink into his soul. The
fetid air of our pesthouses has tainted his blood, and the
remorse of his own actions has dried up his brain. (Loud
cheers.) Many thousands of men has he sent to the grave
or to exile. (Sensation.) But let him pass."

At the end he spoke of the condition of the country.

"I declare here tonight that I would rather perish by
rope or steel than survive this opportunity. My heart is sick
at daily scenes of misery. I have seen human beings driven
like foxes to earth themselves in holes and fastnesses; I
have heard the voice of mendicancy hourly ringing in my
ears, until my heart has turned to stone and my brain to
flint from inability to help them. I cannot endure this state
of society longer. Nothing green, nothing noble will grow
in it. The towns have become one universal poorhouse and
fever shed, the country one great graveyard. The survivors
of the famine and pestilence have fled to the sea-coast and
embarked for America, with disease festering in their blood.
They have lost sight of Ireland and the ships that bore them
have become sailing coffins, and carried them to a new world
indeed, not to America, but to eternity!"

Smith O'Brien and Meagher were joined by John Dillon
and Richard O'Gorman on their mission to France. Duffy
and McGee stayed in Dublin to look after the paper. They
did not miss much.

Smith O'Brien waited upon the French government and
was received by M. Lamartine, the polite but slightly embarrassed President. He replied to the request for volunteers with a statement so exquisitely correct, non-committal
and ambiguous that it could have been composed only by

an Englishman. The Irish delegation not without reason suspected the British ambassador, Lord Normanby. The men running the month-old Second Republic dared not offend the British government, which was viewing with nervous disapproval the uproar in Europe. But they gave a dinner party for the Irish delegates to soften the disappointment.

Smith O'Brien returned to Dublin by way of London where he took his seat briefly in the House of Commons. Stiff, reserved and proud, he seemed as English as any in that assembly. He spoke against a treason-felony bill under discussion which would make it a criminal offence in Ireland to speak seditiously even if no act followed. He also denied that the Irish Confederation had any intention of asking the French government to interfere in Irish affairs. Members of the House of Commons, who knew the fellow had been to Paris and that he was out on bail under a charge of sedition, listened to his explanation sourly. Unmoved by his arguments they went ahead and passed the bill.

At home the Young Irelanders went up and down the country organizing a National Guard. Smith O'Brien on his return took up this work heartily. But he refused to have John Mitchel as a colleague. In England he had heard Mitchel called a "bloody-minded, treacherous villain" and he believed that they could thank the *United Irishman* for such afflictions as the Treason-Felony Act.

Chapter Eight
THE WIND OF HOPE

A PROTESTANT REPEAL ASSOCIATION had taken form with Samuel Ferguson, a lawyer of scholarly tastes, as its President. At the first meeting his coldly phrased "Ireland has ceased to be a country where a man of spirit, education and honourable ambition could bear to live," echoed McGee's more passionate, "I cannot endure this state of society longer. Nothing green, nothing noble will grow in it." Ferguson shared many of McGee's opinions and admired his poetry. He himself was a poet of some reputation. In this confused year of 1848 the scholarly lawyer and the young journalist who wanted to be a scholar began a friendship that was to last the rest of their lives.

The news from Europe continued encouraging. In France preparations were going forward for an election based on manhood suffrage. The King of Prussia had consented to an assembly to draw up a constitution. The Austrian government was making extraordinary concessions to the Hungarians. The Italians of Piedmont were harassing the Austrian army, apparently making up in tumultuous enthusiasm what they lacked in discipline.

Certain men in public life in England were known to favour repeal of the Union before civil war developed in Ireland. From two or three districts parish priests sent word to the Confederation that their parishes could furnish a hundred to a thousand men each if rebellion were postponed till after the harvest. Were these straws that showed the direction of the wind, or were they merely straws to be clutched at by deluded Young Irelanders? Now groping, now confident, the Confederation went ahead with its plans.

D'Arcy McGee's poetry, which had been growing rather pale and symbolic, took on a more vigorous tone with the promise of action. He wrote marching songs and calls to battle. O'Gorman had remained in Paris to study street-fighting tactics and the training of a National Guard. Two agents were sent to America for funds, their message concealed in a pistol to be fired off in case of capture. There was some talk of sending Tom Meagher to America, an idea which rather appealed to him. But this plan had to be discarded as Meagher like Smith O'Brien was out on bail and had to come up for trial in May.

The wind of nationalism sweeping Europe was by this time blowing strongly in Ireland. Public sympathy was entirely with the defendants. The usual "packed" jury in this case did not favour the government. The verdict of "Not Guilty" was received with noisy delight.

John Mitchel's case was different. He was tried under the new harsh Treason-Felony Act and the jury was picked and packed with unusual care. Certain that his trial would touch off the revolution, Mitchel rejoiced to find himself in a martyr's role. But the Irish Confederates knew that if Mitchel were to be rescued they, and not "the people"— that mysterious entity about which Mitchel was always talking—would have to do it. They were in a cruel position. It was unthinkable that they would desert their former comrade, but they were not ready for open rebellion.

Meagher and O'Gorman, the two most eager to fight, made a tour of the political clubs in Dublin and discovered that they lacked arms, ammunition, food, everything. They also discovered that Dublin was full of British troops. The two scouts had to report dolefully that an outbreak at this time would not have a chance of success. While the Confederation was learning the hard facts of its position, the trial ended with the sentence of transportation to a penal colony for fourteen years. Poor Mitchel was shipped off to Australia.

His "martyrdom" had a good effect, but not in the way he expected. Again his departure from the scene was followed by a feeling of remorseful relief. All the efforts to unite, which various Irish parties had made during the past weeks, now quickened. John O'Connell, the Liberator's son, and the Old Repealers were ready for a reconciliation with Young Ireland. A new party was formed called the Irish League. The Protestant Repeal Association offered to work with it. The Catholic clergy approved it. Even Devin Reilly and Mitchel's followers were willing to join it. For the first time since February the Irish had a solid basis for their hopes. "Resistance is no faction fight," McGee had said. "Resistance to be justifiable must be unanimous or nearly so." This condition was now fulfilled.

But time was running out. Did they dare wait till after the harvest? Would they have had a better chance if they had been able to strike in March?

In France the first elections held by the new Republic were over. All Frenchmen of age had been given the right to vote. They had proved cautious and middle class in their politics. Even the peasants, who owned their farms, were very conscious of the rights of property. The members returned to the new Assembly were all men opposed to the socialists of Paris. They promptly put an end to socialist experiments in government.

The Parisian workers, who had made the Second Republic possible, were disappointed in the new Assembly. In shrill rage they erected their barricades and refused to accept the Assembly. The battles in the Paris streets during the last days of June made the fighting of the previous February look like a tavern brawl. Before the new government defeated the socialists, thousands had been killed including the Archbishop of Paris who had attempted to act as mediator.

The revolutionary turmoil in Europe was stirred up afresh. But this time the wind was blowing from another direction. The world at large could understand a people overthrowing an oppressive government; it could even understand a single class undertaking such action. But in Paris a single class had rejected savagely the expressed will of the rest of the country. This was frightening, a prelude to chaos.

Only one man professed to understand the "June Days". He was Karl Marx. The February revolution, he said, had been certain to fail because the proletariat and the middle class could never have the same interests. The "June Days" had been a true proletarian revolution, the proletariat against all the rest, the forerunner of the classless society. The time had not been ripe for its success. But the time would come. No one else was convinced by this theory, but Marx was absolutely convinced. He prepared to watch and work. The time would come.

The "June Days" had a bad effect on Irish politics. Revolution, it seemed, led only to more revolution. Catholic opinion was shocked by the murder of the Archbishop. Irish unity melted quickly. John O'Connell said he was retiring from public life. The Protestant Repeal Association was no longer heard from. The Irish League never came to life. Young Ireland found itself alone.

At this point the British government, which seemed to understand the art of timing even if it did not talk about it, stepped in. The formation of a National Guard was forbidden. All arms must be turned in to the police. Gavan Duffy was arrested.

On July 9, returning to his home for dinner he found his family trying to appear calm and a detective waiting with a warrant and a cab to take him to the police station. There an uneasy crowd was milling about. D'Arcy McGee and Dr. Callan, a family friend, succeeded in speaking to him. They asked him if he wished the crowd to attempt a rescue. He said that an outbreak at this time would be useless. Before McGee left him Duffy asked him to act as editor of the *Nation*.

THE ARDENT EXILE

The Reaper's Song

The August sun is setting
    Like a fire behind the hills—
'Twill rise again to see us free
    Of life or of its ills;
For what is life, but deadly strife
    That knows no truce or pause,
And what is death, but want of breath
    To curse their alien laws?

Chorus—Then a-shearing let us go, my boys,
      A-shearing let us go,
    On our own soil 'twill be no toil
      To lay the corn low.

"How will you go a-shearing,
    Dear friends and neighbours all?"
"Oh, we will go with pike and gun,
    To have our own or fall;
We'll stack our arms and stack our corn
    Upon the same wide plain;
We'll plant a guard in barn and yard
    And give them grape for grain."

Chorus—Then a-shearing let us go, my boys,
      A-shearing let us go,
    On our own soil 'twill be no toil
      To lay the corn low.

God speed ye, gallant shearers,
    May your courage never fail,
May you thrash your foes, and send the chaff
    To England on the gale!
May you have a glorious harvest-home,
    Whether I'm alive or no;
Your corn grows *here*, the foe comes *there*—
    Or *it* or *he* must go.

Chorus—Then a-shearing let us go, my boys,
      A-shearing we will go,
    On our own soil 'twill be no toil
      To cut the corn low.

Chapter Nine
McGEE JOINS THE REVOLUTION

It was July, the peak of summer, a season to inspire a man to a new poem or a holiday in the country. But these things were not for D'Arcy who was busy organizing a revolution. Since Duffy's arrest McGee had spent his days hurrying from his home to the *Nation*, from the office to meetings, from meetings to the jail, where Duffy under the mildest confinement saw his friends and wrote editorials. Having received his instructions, McGee began the squirrel-run all over again.

The political clubs now had a central executive of which he was a member, but they still lacked arms and supplies. They still waited for funds from America. Then came an urgent message from the *Freeman*'s correspondent in London confirming the rumour that Parliament had suspended the Habeas Corpus Act for Ireland. The authorities now could make arrests without laying a charge.

When this news came McGee stepped out briskly to O'Gorman's warehouse on Merchant's Quay for a final meeting. Only two other members of the executive of five turned up, John Dillon and Tom Meagher, who brought along his school friend Patrick Smythe.

In the gloom of the big warehouse with the water glinting through the riverside entrance, the four looked small and helpless. They had a grave decision to make. They felt that the eyes of Ireland and the world were upon them. Oppressed by the shadows and silence of the place they withdrew to a room on Dolier Street which they used sometimes for small meetings.

McGee's career since coming to Dublin had led him step

by step to this moment. Each step had taken him away from the things he liked and closer to disorderly and violent ways that he would never willingly have chosen. He had come from London and the British Museum with lofty ambitions to serve Ireland as a poet and scholar. Circumstances had made him in turn a political journalist, a propagandist, a conspirator and now it seemed he was to become an armed rebel.

Actually the decision had been made already for him. In the year 1848 a writer did not publish poems calling people to arms without being prepared to take the consequences. On this occasion no one urged McGee to express his opinion at length. He was the youngest present and leadership fell naturally to Dillon who was the senior.

They had three choices. They could submit to arrest. They could go into hiding and wait till the harvest was in and their messengers returned from America. Or they could make a stand and fight. Dillon settled the matter quickly.

As men of honour there was only one course open to them, he said. If after all this talk of resistance they let themselves be arrested or went into hiding they would be discredited in the eyes of the people. He, for his part, refused to skulk from place to place like a criminal. He intended to join Smith O'Brien immediately and call out the political clubs.

Meagher of the Sword, his eyes dancing at the prospect of asserting his right to his title, declared that even though they were unprepared, the God of Battles would nerve the unarmed hands of peasants in defence of freedom.

D'Arcy McGee and Patrick Smythe said nothing memorable.

The question of resistance being settled, they next considered how it was to be done. The Young Irelanders had great experience in drawing up paper plans. The four evolved a bit of strategy which, if American supplies had been on hand, the clubs armed, the time March instead of July, and a number of other conditions favourable, might have succeeded.

They decided to make a stand at Kilkenny, which was on the border of three good fighting counties, Tipperary, Wexford and Munster. The only road by which troops could be brought from the railway into the town passed between high banks and could be ambushed.

A message had come the day before from Irish Repeal Clubs in Scotland advising the Confederates that arms and men could be sent to Ireland if required. The four conspirators, their minds warming to the work, discussed landing a small force from Scotland somewhere in western Ireland, where it would serve to divert the militia and allow the uprising in the south to get under way.

The delicate task of going to Scotland to arrange for these reinforcements was given to D'Arcy McGee. John Dillon and Tom Meagher urged it on him, assuring him that he would be a patriot as notable as Paul Revere if he succeeded.

There must have been a strong inclination at this desperate moment to stay together and face the uncertain future in each other's company. It is typical of his career with Young Ireland that at this point McGee was the one chosen to be sent off alone. He had never shared in the common background, family connections and student friendships that held the Young Irelanders together. Having spent three years in America he had come among them too old in experience to fit in with the younger ones, too young to be accepted as an equal by the seniors. To the end he remained the odd one.

He cheerfully agreed to go to Scotland. It was not his nature, when once he had accepted a cause, to make difficulties or lay down conditions. The Young Irelanders clasped hands and wished each other Godspeed. Dillon and Meagher took the night coach to Limerick. Smythe remained in Dublin to notify the clubs before following them. The same night McGee went north by stage coach.

When he arrived in Londonderry on Sunday morning he remembered that the packet for Glasgow did not leave till Monday. He spent the day tramping about the bogside outside the walls of the city as he wished to avoid recognition. Before leaving Londonderry he remembered to write to Mary. Worry might be bad for her as she was expecting a child. It might not be reassuring to learn that her husband had gone to Scotland on seditious business but it would be better than imagining worse. D'Arcy felt better when he was again on his way. Brooding was useless, only action endurable.

The political clubs of Glasgow, Edinburgh and Newcastle drew their membership from the Irish labourers working on railway construction in Scotland and northern England. Having escaped from O'Connell's doctrine of moderation and the numbing effects of the famine they were full of fight and more than willing to help old Ireland and in this case Young Ireland, too. For a year they had been training and arming for this opportunity. McGee found four hundred men supplied with arms and pledged to make the expedition.

He spent a week visiting the clubs. At Glasgow they gave him £12 to help him with his expenses. Elsewhere he accepted no money, only making certain what supplies each club would be responsible for and if it knew where to send them. These conferences alternated with long hours of travel or waiting to travel.

As much as possible he avoided the streets. As a speaker at numerous political meetings he was known by sight to many people and his was a face not easily forgotten. Between journeys and conferences he killed time in Repeal Reading Rooms (they had almost ceased to exist in Ireland), turning over the English newspapers. In Paisley he had the curious experience of reading a police description of himself in *Hue and Cry*: "Thomas D'Arcy McGee—connected with the *Nation* newspaper—23 years old, 5 ft. 3" in height —black hair, dark face, delicate, thin man—dresses generally black shooting coat, plaid trousers, light vest."

By Tuesday of the following week he was in Ireland and learned that on Sunday the people had been warned in some of the Catholic churches to have nothing to do with the threatened rebellion. But this did not tell him what the conspirators were doing in the south.

And now he came to the country of Sligo and Donegal, a land of sombre mountains and bristling coastline worthy to share with the Hebrides their ancient title, Ultima Thule —the end of the earth. Timelessly the headlands face the storms of the North Atlantic as though nothing lay beyond but space and eternity. Into this country, so remote that the writ of English law scarcely ran there, came D'Arcy McGee to stir up a rebellion.

There was no Repeal Association in Sligo and nothing so recent as political clubs. McGee's cautious questions uncovered a secret society called the "Mollie Maguires". He met the leader by night in a deserted house. The man told McGee that he could call out a thousand men. The local garrison was small and had grown careless. With reinforcements and arms from Scotland his boys could make a good showing.

Here as elsewhere the people hoped that there would be no trouble till after the harvest. For the first time in three years the prospects for the potato crop were good. In a country that had suffered from famine as Ireland had, a harvest was not to be taken lightly. The leader of the "Mollie Maguires" said that if the south rose he would call out the boys. He even went further and offered to send a messenger south to find out what was happening.

McGee stayed at the inn in Benbulken where he could pose as a student on holidays, coming and going freely. The miserable days dragged by while rumours persisted that Smith O'Brien had been taken before he could put up a fight. Not daring to wait any longer McGee tried frantically to start the rebellion in the north. But the local people would have none of it. Unless the south rose they would not bring the law on their heads to no purpose. McGee pleaded and persuaded. He thought up schemes, each wilder than the last.

It was incredible that Young Ireland, having risked everything, could not succeed in even a gesture of defiance.

What a humiliation! What an absurdity! Like one possessed McGee hurried hither and yon about the countryside, scarcely bothering to keep up the pretence of the carefree student, driven by his responsibility to his friends and a growing sense of failure.

From the waters of Lough Derg rose a rugged island called St. Patrick's Purgatory. All day long during the pleasant summer season pilgrims came to the lake and were ferried to the island shrine by several boatmen who kept craft on the lake for that purpose. D'Arcy McGee watched this coming and going for a while, then being a devout man, felt impelled to visit the shrine himself.

The boatman talked cheerily as he rowed. There was no end to the wonders of the shrine, with people coming to it from the four corners of Ireland, even from Dublin. And this was nothing to its former glories. For in the olden days pilgrims came from distant parts, from Spain and even Italy; that was but natural and the shrine as old as the Saint himself.

McGee paid his guide and went up to the chapel where he made his confession. He prayed with his fellow-pilgrims, following the words haltingly as they prayed in Gaelic. His mind grew quiet as the spirit of the ancient place gathered him to itself. What was time but a prelude to eternity, a little space in which man groped for the knowledge and joy that would break upon him in full glory only in the hereafter? When he left he could face his failure with reasonable calmness.

Beyond doubt Smith O'Brien was in jail. (In fact, he had been captured on July 29, before McGee returned to Ireland.) News came successively of the capture of Tom Meagher and two other Young Irelanders, McManus and Leyne. John Dillon and Richard O'Gorman were said to be in hiding. The rebellion had never come off. Famine and emigration had thinned the manhood of the country. The Irish for once had no fight left in them.

A visitor from Scotland sought out McGee at the Benbulken Inn. He brought a message from the executive in

charge of the expedition from Scotland. Since the failure
in the south had made the expedition useless, the executive
advised McGee not to risk capture any longer but to get
out of the country quickly. The local people were of the
same opinion. They had no ill will toward him, but his
presence, now that there was to be no fighting, endangered
them all.

What was he waiting for? As a man of impulse and
action he had endured torments dawdling about Sligo and
Benbulken while the "Mollie Maguires" hedged and hesitated. He longed for the free air of America. In this stifled
country the memory of its raucous shouts of liberty echoed
gloriously.

Taking to the road once more he made for Londonderry
and the protection of Bishop Maginn, reputed to be sympathetic to patriots. The Bishop lived up to his reputation.
He sheltered McGee and undertook to arrange for his passage to America.

The news that came to the Bishop's palace was more
accurate and frequent than the rumours circulating in the
country places. Revolution had suffered setbacks throughout
Europe. The French courts were passing savage sentences
on the insurrectionists of the "June Days"; the Italian revolutionists had been utterly defeated by the Austrian army.
The Pope, who earlier in the year had looked favourably
on reforming movements, had grown displeased with the
irreligious attitude of the Liberals. He ended by strongly
disapproving of the Italian nationalists and their war with
Austria which he regarded as a danger to the peace of
Europe and Catholic unity.

Suffering from frustration and failure McGee could not
bring himself to believe that the glorious promise of 1848
was not to be fulfilled. Why had the clergy turned the
people away from Young Ireland's effort to make them
assert themselves? Why should they be starved and driven
overseas as if they had no rights in their own country?

To which there was the clerical retort: Poor men should

not be asked to lose their lives to please vainglorious young radicals who did not know how to hold a gun much less marshal and direct a rebellion against England.

This was the result of O'Connell's policy of peace and moderation, came the counter argument. Irishmen no longer knew how to fight.

This kind of recrimination could go on endlessly. In the stagnant years following the famine, the Irish kept it up with irritable persistency.

For D'Arcy the last stage of waiting was the worst for he had to keep to the house. Mary came from Dublin to see him, bringing fresh linen, clothes and whatever small comforts and necessities wifely solicitude suggested might be useful on a long journey. They embraced in an ecstasy of unhappiness while Mary wept. She must lose her husband, although not yet a year married and the child unborn.

But their time was too short for grieving; there were many practical matters to settle. Some arrangement had to be made for Mary until D'Arcy could send money from America. She would not want. His family and her own would see to that. And the child would be born in Ireland. In the spring when there was good sailing weather they should both come to him in America where he would have a home for them. So he cheered her.

She brought him news from Dublin, any scrap of which he was avid to hear. Duffy was strictly guarded and no longer permitted to see or write to his friends. The *Nation* for a while had struggled along. Seventeen-year-old James McGee had brought it out once almost single-handed. Another time Duffy's sister-in-law, Mrs. Callan, had gone to the office and prepared an issue for the printer. But the police at last had locked the premises and carried away the files. James would have to look for other employment. Who knew how long Mr. Duffy's trial would last? People said that Smith O'Brien and those who had been taken with him in the south would be sentenced to death.

At this time no one knew for certain what had happened

in the south, for those taken were not allowed to communicate with their friends and those who had escaped were in hiding. But stories of Tipperary and Ballingarry were already forming in the minds of those who had been there. Perhaps even now they were being told by fugitive Young Irelanders who sheltered in friendly cabins or in disguise sailed for foreign ports.

Through the tears of rage and shame which would always accompany the telling of this story glanced the rapier flash of Irish laughter. For surely no rebels in all the annals of revolt ever had so much trouble finding someone to fight with.

Had not Charlie Kickham, the son of the grocer at Mullinhone, seen Dillon mounting a barricade with his pikemen, a fine rifle in his hand,—indeed it seemed to be the only one in the company—a plaid scarf across one shoulder over the all-black suit in which he invariably clad his handsome person? But there had been no one to oppose him and the boys, who were willing to stay out all night, had a way of melting out of sight about breakfast time.

Did not Terence McManus a little later find Dillon atop another barricade at Killemaule, offering defiance to a troop of cavalry? But the officer politely requested that he and his men be allowed to pass, since they were upon their lawful occasions and intended no molestation to Dillon and his barricade. Two reasonable men do not fight each other. What could Dillon do but wave the captain and his troop on?

And was not McManus with Smith O'Brien himself at Ballingarry? Three times did the rebels demand the surrender of the police barracks where a sergeant and six men were stationed. The first time the sergeant said, faith, there was no need for the like of that and them all peaceable one with the other. Later Smith O'Brien and a delegation came again for they needed such arms as the police had, being very short themselves. And the sergeant pulled a long face and said 'twas disgraced entirely he'd be if he surrendered to such a poor handful. Would the gentlemen return in larger force so that the surrender might be made with decency? But when Smith O'Brien came with a larger force, the sergeant and his men had made off for a neighbouring police barracks, taking the arms with them.

When the bullets did fly from a farm-house in Ballingarry which the police had taken over, did not Smith O'Brien insist on staying within range of them, even though there was none to support him? It was not as though he had had the lust of battle upon him. There had been no fighting. But there was a great, stiff pride about the poor man that made him prefer being dead to being ridiculous.

His friends succeeded in saving his life, but were not able to spare him the indignity of arrest.

There was not much of all this that Mary could tell her husband at the time. He heard the whole story much later. Before half the things they might have told each other were said her visit was over. There was no use prolonging farewells. One last embrace, a fervent "God be with you, love!" and Mary was on her way back to Dublin.

Bishop Maginn had provided for his refugee's moment of danger which would come when he attempted to board a ship leaving the country. D'Arcy was supplied with a suit of clerical black with a Roman collar. In this disguise he proceeded sedately and confidently to a point of embarkation on the Foyle. There a tender carried him to a waiting ship, the *Shamrock*, bound out of Londonderry for Philadelphia.

Others besides D'Arcy escaped from Ireland during the last months of 1848 under circumstances that made good stories afterwards. On board a brig sailing out of Galway a roughly dressed countryman edged up to a tall young priest, who was gazing sadly at the fading coast, and muttered: "Haven't I seen you before?" Dillon, stiff with caution in his borrowed clericals, turned and recognized in the peasant the debonair Pat Smythe.

Richard O'Gorman in whose warehouse the rebellion

had been hatched, escaped on a vessel which he discovered was bound for Odessa in Russia. This country, he was reliably informed, was an outlandish place where he would be expected to have a passport. As O'Gorman had no such document he left the ship at Constantinople and from there found passage to New York.

Thus deviously the rebels who escaped capture found their way one by one to America.

The Wild Geese

"What is the cry so wildly heard,
    Oh, mother dear, across the lake?"
"My child, 'tis but the northern bird
    Alighted in the reedy brake."

"Why cries the northern bird so wild?
    Its wail is like our baby's voice."
" 'Tis far from its own home, my child,
    And would you have it, then, rejoice?"

"And why does not the wild bird fly
    Straight homeward through the open air?
I see no barriers in the sky—
    Why does she sit lamenting there?"

"My child, the laws of life and death
    Are written in four living books;
The wild bird reads them in the breath
    Of winter, freezing up the brooks—

"The spring, that makes the poets sing,
    Will whisper in the wild bird's ear,
And swiftly back, on willing wing,
    The wild bird to the north will steer."

"Will *they* come back, of whom that song
    Last night was sung, that made you weep?"
"Oh! God is good, and hope is strong;—
    My son, let's pray, and then to sleep."

Part Two

EXILE

Chapter Ten

THE EMIGRANT SHIP

I~N~ 1848 a man wishing to leave Ireland in a hurry could travel as far as Newfoundland for as little as five dollars, provided he was willing to sleep on the deck of a fishing ship and live on salt cod. Few emigrants made the voyage so cheaply and rigorously, but even under the best conditions no one enjoyed much comfort. The emigrant could expect cramped quarters and a diet of salt pork, ship biscuit, molasses and oatmeal.

One emigrant agent in a printed circular assured his prospective passengers that they would find their health improved by forty days of rest and sea air. The circular did not go on to explain that this beneficial effect would depend on good weather permitting the passengers to leave their stifling quarters in the steerage and take the air on deck. It neglected to state that a prosperous voyage would depend on favourable winds bringing the ship to port before the food went bad and the drinking water gave out; it would depend above all on the absence of cholera, ominously known as "ship fever".

The best that could be said of emigrant travel in the nineteenth century was that fares were cheap and ships plentiful. The usual fare for steerage passage was twenty-five dollars. For forty-five dollars an emigrant could travel on a ship offering "intermediate" or private accommodation for family groups. For sixty dollars he could cease to be an emigrant in the ordinary sense of the word and become a cabin passenger with eggs, butter, oranges and bottled ale added to his bill of fare. But as emigrant families had to save their money for a start in the New World most of them risked the cheapest passage.

Every ship crossing the Atlantic from the ports on the Irish Sea during the 1840's was an emigrant ship. Some were built and operated solely for this trade, others carried passengers in the hold side by side with the cargo. Owners of lumber ships, carrying their heaviest cargo from America to the British Isles, found it especially profitable to carry a full load of emigrants on the westward trip.

It was a simple matter to rig a dormitory between decks, hammer together wooden bunks, whitewash them and furnish them with straw-stuffed sacks as mattresses. The law required that the emigrant quarters from time to time must be fumigated with vinegar as a protection against cholera. The prudent captain usually issued instructions that single women were to be quartered at one end, single men at the other and the married couples and families in the centre. Thus the rudiments of health and decency were maintained. To these arrangements were added a supply of the usual ship's food and a couple of live pigs kept under crating in the longboat as provision against shortages—and the emigrant ship was equipped for the voyage.

Few restrictions hampered the traveller at either end of his journey. Passports were unnecessary, immigration quotas unknown. Ship fever was the only impediment to landing. Since in spite of the vinegar fumigation some ships were floating pesthouses by the time they reached America a minimum regulation required them to put in at quarantine stations where the sick were taken to hospitals, more accurately called "fever sheds". The well were then free to land at the nearest port and make their way in the New World.

If the best feature of emigration was cheap fares and lack of restrictions, the worst was the cost in human suffering. Of the million or more who left Ireland between 1845 and 1854 one out of five died before the end of the journey.

D'Arcy McGee was spared the more harrowing experiences of emigrant travel since he endured only the normal hardships of a normal forty-day crossing before the autumn storms set in.

Life at sea left him plenty of time to brood, especially in the long night watches when the sounds on board sank to a murmur—the creak of timbers, the restless stirring of the sleeping and the sleepless in their crowded bunks, the clang of the bell and the voices of the sailors as the watch changed on deck. Then he would reflect bitterly on the hard fate that was driving him and his fellow-passengers from their country.

All across the north Atlantic ships were sailing westward crowded with emigrants. Thousands had gone before, hundreds of thousands were to come after. D'Arcy McGee had been caught up in one of the great migrations of human history. But this tremendous and dimly realized fact was of less interest to him than the reasons that had led to his flight.

He had dreaded this so deeply that he had thought his very fear might hold back the calamity. "Then, indeed, I knew all was up. Then indeed I felt the force of what I had long before prophesied: 'What if we fail?'" Even now he could hardly believe that Young Ireland had failed. It was unendurable to recall the English papers boasting that Ireland would become a completely English country when emigration had cleared out the native population. He writhed when he thought of his friends in jail or refugees like himself.

At this time the failure of the revolutions of 1848 on the continent was not fully apparent. To McGee it seemed a shameful thing that Ireland alone had failed to strike out for freedom because the people had rejected the leadership of Young Ireland. It might have eased his bitterness a little if he had known that in many parts of Europe in the next few months young men would be hiding out and making hazardous night journeys to slip over the border or to take ship for any country other than their own. McGee travelled with the spearhead of nineteenth-century migration that was to bring from Europe multitudes of the dissatisfied and ambitious and the hard-pressed, all seeking the fabulous freedom of the New World.

But as he stared into the shadows these larger issues brought little comfort. His thoughts were painfully taken up with himself and Mary and Duffy and his friends. Especially with himself. His poems written at this time show that he was depressed because he feared that with the failure of the rebellion he had lost his claim to fame. He worried during the long nights, not over his situation—a price on his head and less than one hundred dollars between him and destitution—but because he had failed to achieve glory for Ireland. Viewed in this light, exile became a fate more grievous than death.

It was better in the daytime when the passengers could take a turn on deck and watch the sailors go aloft to trim the sails. As the long afternoon wore on, if the weather was fine, someone might bring out a fiddle and the young people would dance a jig, each couple taking their turn as there was not space enough for general dancing. Among the passengers there was a great deal of amateur interest in charting the course and observing the weather; much visiting back and forth and discussion of the future. Hope travelled with the emigrants, even the most wretched, even on the fever ships.

McGee suffered as little as any from the physical discomforts and irritations of ship life. He could retire into the world of his poetry, putting his gloomy, angry night thoughts into verse, perfectly happy as long as he was writing.

A boy and girl sought him out as he bent over his book, the girl blushing and backward, the boy resolute. They had a favour to ask his reverence. They were promised to each other and intended getting married when they reached America, but with his reverence aboard they had a mind to wed now and set foot on new sod as man and wife.

Sharply reminded of his clerical costume, McGee hastily

told the couple that this was no time for marrying. They must wait till they landed.

But presently they were back again, even the girl no longer coy, both urging him. D'Arcy was quite moved by their pleas and would gladly have married them on the spot, but he was obliged to send them off.

His faculties, he said, were suspended while he was at sea.

The incident left him somewhat disturbed. Who knew what might happen on this crowded ship? Suppose he were called on to administer the sacraments to the dying. The most dismaying possibilities occurred to him and he decided that he must lay aside his priestly disguise and tell the captain who he was.

The captain, a good Galway sailor, far from being upset on learning he had a political refugee on board, clapped McGee on the back and entered into conversation with him. It was grand luck to have someone to talk to, a man like Mr. McGee who had travelled and taken part in public affairs.

The life of an emigrant ship's master was full of trouble. A man who followed the hard and dangerous life of the sea might expect at least to escape the landsman's domestic vexations. But the captain of an emigrant ship had the worst of both worlds. He had the weather to reckon with, the responsibility for the ship and crew with all the crises of family life added, old people dying, children falling sick, babies being born and women everywhere.

If he chose, the captain of the *Shamrock* could tell grim stories of winter crossings which he knew either at first hand or from accounts of other ship masters told at the ports.

Winter storms invariably delayed a ship, while among the emigrants, practically imprisoned below decks, food and water ran short and sickness spread. It was a harrowing task to unload a group of fever-stricken people at a quarantine station, poor creatures who would find a grave instead of a home in America. Beside the fever sheds at Grosse Pointe, the quarantine station for Quebec, was a graveyard that grew and grew like a city. But burial at sea was even more dreadful. It was not so much the fear of death as the thought, as one poor soul put it "that the minute the breath is out of our bodies we're flung into the sea to be eaten by them horrid sharks".

Oh yes, the seawise captain from Galway could vouch for the hazards of winter travel. Even intermediate or cabin accommodation was no guarantee of safety or comfort. Mr. McGee would do well not to send for his wife till late in the spring.

The *Shamrock* stoutly tacked and buffeted her way against the prevailing west wind and early in October approached the coast of North America. Excitement mounted daily among the passengers. At some undefined line in the coastal waters their status changed. They were no longer emigrants, people leaving a country, but immigrants, people coming to live in a country. Subtly their attitude changed with their status. By the time they took on board the pilot who was to guide them into harbour all, even the most homesick, were looking forward to the moment of landing.

From time to time they sighted other ships engaged in the commerce of the New England ports. A high-masted Boston clipper with towering tier on tier of white sails for a short time disdainfully shared the ocean with their dumpy, wallowing vessel. These clippers, the ultimate perfection of the shipbuilder's craft, even though they were already doomed by the greater speed of the new steamships, in the 1840's still sailed the seven seas, swift and beautiful. The emigrants, while such a ship was in view, glimpsed for a moment the horizons of the world; saw India and the Orient, spice islands and the palm-fringed atolls of the South Pacific.

The passengers of the *Shamrock* now scoured and tidied their dingy quarters so as to make a good impression on the doctor who came aboard from the quarantine station. Then with a clear bill of health they sailed, agog with interest, up the Chesapeake to their harbourage at Philadelphia.

All wore their best clothes. Was not this one of the most important days in their lives?

McGee could not avoid being infected by the excitement of the rest, even though he had been through all this before. He saw the joyful reunion of the family with the son or brother who had come to America ahead. He saw the bewilderment of those who had no one to meet them and the human sharks, smiling and sharp, who descended on them. He noticed that by their faces and voices the rogues were undoubtedly Irish. Some of the newcomers eagerly accepted them as friends, all unknowing that tomorrow they would find they had been cheated and robbed by these waterfront operators. D'Arcy McGee was older now and noticed many things that as a boy he had missed.

Chapter Eleven
THE CANADIAN SCENE

Aمerica was very much as McGee remembered it except that life was faster and louder. New states had been added to the Union, new railways were being built, good prairie land was drawing pioneers to the west. Smart men were growing wealthy. This did not mean that everyone was getting rich, but to a newcomer it seemed that everyone talked and thought of nothing else.

The revolutions of 1848 had aroused little interest in the United States. Walt Whitman, the carpenter-journalist who wrote gusty poetry about democracy, hailed the men of 1848 as brothers. In unrhymed, reverberating stanzas he praised their efforts and sympathized with them in their failure.

The enterprising editors of the dailies, who had rushed aboard ship to interview Dickens, still sent their reporters to meet incoming ships and learn the news from Europe. Not that Europe was of much interest to their readers, but a war, an assassination of royalty, the failure of an international bank was fresh saleable news especially for the paper that told it first. Revolutions in Paris, like Paris fashions, were recognized as having special dramatic quality. But apart from France, Americans were not concerned with the political turmoil in Europe.

They hardly had time for their own politics. Although the abolitionists still demanded freedom for the slaves with unremitting energy, slavery as a political question involving state rights was met by a series of compromises that permitted the expansion of slavery into new territories. No major political party took a firm stand against it till the formation of the Republican party in 1857.

North of the border the situation was different. In 1849 a mob burnt the Parliament Building in Montreal. This, however, was not revolution but counter-revolution. The Canadians had made their attempt at revolution by force in 1837, eleven years before the European outbreaks.

The Canadas were only two of a group of colonies which included Newfoundland and the three Maritimes, each treated as a separate entity by the Colonial Office in London. But in political matters these British American colonies, if not mature, were certainly precocious. Connoisseurs of government in the Colonial Office were becoming interested in them. And they were very much interested in themselves.

Canada East and Canada West, prodded into an unwilling union after 1837, developed more slowly than the United States. Canadians could not go west in covered wagons because the great prairies were cut off from them by a thousand miles of rock and forest. In this northern wilderness was gold beyond the riches of California, but it did not float in the sands of rivers running through a summer country. The gold of Canada was buried in rock hundreds of feet deep and sealed in for eight months of the year by ice and snow. Generations would pass before it would be discovered.

During the winter the farmers, sitting around their stoves, had time to think about taxes and the government, while lawyers and journalists discussed these matters publicly and at all seasons. Lord Sydenham, one of a series of governors sent to straighten out affairs after 1837, was astonished at Canadian preoccupation with politics. Speaking as a good administrator and sound business man, he exhorted the people to stop bothering about abstruse constitutional questions. They would do better to take example from their American neighbours, attend to their own business and get ahead in the world.

He might as well have asked George Stephenson to leave

his steam engines or William Morton to stop experimenting with ether as to have expected the Canadian Reformers to give up examining the workings of the British Constitution, a blessing they possessed without enjoying. It was a riddle they were reluctant to leave, especially when the answer was beginning to grow clear.

Had not Lord Durham in his brilliant "Report on the Affairs of British North America" said the very thing that the Reformer, Robert Baldwin, was trying to make the Colonial Office see—namely, that in England the government or executive was responsible to the elected Parliament and the Crown did not interfere?

If the majority in the British Parliament voted against the government the Prime Minister and his Cabinet resigned. Victoria, when a young queen, might weep and sulk when she lost a favourite Prime Minister, but she never refused to accept the one chosen by Parliament to take his place. When Sir Robert Peel was defeated by a majority in Parliament, even though his victory in repealing the Corn Laws was still fresh in the public mind, he and his Cabinet resigned as a matter of course.

But governments and ministers of the Crown did not behave like that in British America. No majority in Parliament could put them out; they clung to office even when an angry Parliament refused to vote them money. As to the colonial governors, they believed, not unreasonably, that they had been sent out to govern. The Queen, as a constitutional monarch, bowed to the will of Parliament, but when a colonial governor and Parliament disagreed they defied each other.

The task of Robert Baldwin was to make the Canadians on one hand and the Colonial Office on the other see that the colonies would never have parliamentary government after the English fashion until certain conventions were observed and the game played according to the rules. It was not a question of passing laws and changing institutions. It was a question of practice. The British Constitution was something of a lawyer's riddle, but the Reformers who had brooded long and earnestly on it believed they had found out how it worked.

The Colonial Office, well versed in politics and law, saw the point of their recommendations quickly, but since it was a typical British institution it made changes only under great pressure. When it finally sent Lord Elgin to Canada as Governor with instructions to act in every respect as the representative of a strictly constitutional monarch, the Reformers had won their point. All was now settled except for the Tory office holders. Without the backing of the Governor or the Colonial Office, under the new rules they had to give up to the Reformers the prerogatives of government which they had held for so long. They felt very bitter about it.

John Alexander Macdonald at the age of thirty-three was the quiet, knowing kind of man whom older successful men do not disdain to take into their counsel. He represented Kingston, Canada West, the town in which he had grown up the most promising member of a rather shiftless family. As a youth he had borne a heavy load of family responsibility added to long hours of work and study as a lawyer's apprentice. In later life he sometimes said that if he had had the advantages of a university education he would have chosen to follow a literary calling. This was mere romantic imagining. Under any circumstances John A. Macdonald would have been a politician. His natural inclination towards politics was so pronounced that once his law practice was established, inevitably, almost without effort, he entered upon his political career.

John A. watched the Reformers' hard-won struggle for responsible government without taking part. He had been elected to Parliament as a Tory, therefore it was no business of his to follow the Reformers in their analysis of the Constitution. On the other hand he was not an extreme Tory nor one of the colonial gentry. He had never held a government office for so long that he felt it belonged to him. Consequently he was able to take the defeat of his party more calmly than some.

Although Parliament met in Montreal which had become the capital of the two Canadas under the union, Macdonald still had his home in Kingston. His private life was not particularly happy. His two-year-old son had been killed in an accident. An air of chronic sickness hung over his household; his mother was an invalid and his wife often ailing. At its best social life in Kingston was hardly stimulating. Like many others in the hard, practical America of the nineteenth century John A. was starved for intellectual nourishment. He tried to form a literary society in the colonial town and gather together a little library for its members. But even as the project showed some promise, Charles Stuart, his closest friend and the liveliest of the group was stricken with tuberculosis.

"Though I am yet a young man," Macdonald wrote at this time, "many, very many of my companions have disappeared and my firmest and best friend is about to leave me."

It is not surprising that he turned from his chill personal life to find a substitute for warmth and friendliness in the lobbyings and committee meetings, the late-sitting sessions and heated debates of parliamentary life.

He was in Parliament when the Reformers brought in the Rebellion Losses Bill, intended to compensate those whose property had been destroyed in the rebellion of 1837. The bill excluded any who had been convicted as rebels, but Macdonald, who thought Lower Canadians too prone to call rebels "les patriotes", voted against it as did all the Tory party. But he did not go as far as the extremists who, after the bill had been passed, tried to force the Governor to quash it. Macdonald had nothing to do with the Tory-inspired rowdies who booed Lord Elgin as he drove away from Parliament and pelted his carriage with rotten eggs. He certainly was not one of the persons of Tory sympathies who harangued the same mob on the Place d'Armes. But he and other law-abiding men of his party were too late, when the mob got out of hand, to prevent it from setting fire to the House of Assembly. The building itself, a converted market, was not particularly valuable, but the early records of the city of Montreal destroyed with it were irreplaceable.

The burning of the Parliament Building was a disgrace which the Tory party tried with some success to foist onto the anonymous mob. The Tories, now alas, merely Her Majesty's loyal opposition, even undertook to implicate the Reform government, declaring it should have had the building guarded. They remained in a dangerous mood. These men, who had energetically put down the rebellion of 1837, had lived to see the Reformers pass the Rebellion Losses Bill. Their excessive loyalty to England had won them no consideration when their commercial privileges were wiped out by the repeal of the Corn Laws. Quite at their wits' end a number of prominent Tory business men drew up a manifesto approving annexation to the United States.

John A. Macdonald was invited to sign this document but refused. In his slow, canny way he decided that matters had gone too far. To have mobbed the Governor, burnt the Parliament Building and sought annexation to a foreign power was enough to discredit any party, even the loudly loyal Tories. John A. undertook to bring them to their senses. He was not sufficiently important to take the lead, so from behind the scenes he instigated the British America League and moulded its programme which favoured Canada remaining under the British Crown and a federation of British American colonies with protective tariffs.

In face of the Reformers solidly in power he was not disheartened. A political situation does not remain static and Macdonald was sharper than most at seeing the possible moves ahead. The very pre-eminence of the Reform party might prove a weakness. There was a noisy editor in Upper Canada who published a Reform paper called the *Globe*. Already he was forging ahead of the leaders of the party, demanding instant changes where they wanted to proceed cautiously, undermining by his appeals to prejudice the basis of the Reformers' strength, their alliance with the French Canadians. George Brown and the *Globe* could be depended upon sooner or later to split the Reformers.

In the meantime Macdonald was using his influence to prepare his own chastened party for better times. It dropped the worn-out "Tory" title and used its other name "Conservative", later changed to Liberal Conservative, a term of Macdonald's invention. He had slowly maturing plans for usurping the Reformers' alliance with Lower Canada, appreciating better than George Brown the wisdom of Sir Charles Bagot, a recent governor, who had summed up Canada in the single shrewd dictum: "You cannot govern this country without the French."

Macdonald was not yet the Conservatives' leader. There were older politicians more important in the public eye. But within the party men were impressed by instances of his foresight and his ability to take advantage of an opponent's mistakes. More and more they looked to him for guidance, and the sense of power exhilarated him.

At this point D'Arcy McGee makes a brief, jarring entrance on the Canadian scene. From New York where he was living in 1849 he issued a manifesto calling Canadians, especially Irish Canadians, to revolution:

"This combination of events (the revolutions in Europe) cannot but increase the hopes of revolution among you, and in God's name, do not let it come on you unprepared . . . Never had men holier cause. England has ruled you for a century and at the end of it you find yourselves ruined. Are you content? Are you happy? Are you not slaves?"

The manifesto drops into the stream of history with a splash and disappears. Its author, in view of his later life, steps onto the stage like an actor who has mistaken his cue, begins the wrong speech and quickly backs off.

He might have been excused for ignorance of Canadian affairs because they were intricate and understood outside the country only by a few. But oddly enough, the manifesto shows that he knew that the disorders of 1849 were not a popular outbreak but reaction against a popular government. The natural moderation of his character shows strangely here and there. "We do not counsel you (the Irish

Canadians) to originate a revolution. It is neither our business nor our place to offer such advice." He urges understanding between the French- and English-speaking populations. These bits of McGee's real thought run through the exaggeration of the manifesto like words of sense spoken in delirium. Had D'Arcy in crossing the Atlantic suffered a sea change or had he fallen a victim to a new form of ship fever?

Chapter Twelve
McGEE v. THE BISHOP

O F ALL THE immigrants who came to the New World the Irish were the most home-sick; at least they were most articulate in their home-sickness. Their songs, deeply sentimental and pathetic, rivalled the lilting, sweetly sad melodies of the South in popularity. The fact that many of the immigrant songs were imitations written by people who were neither Irish nor immigrant only proves the strength of the original inspiration. Kathleen Mavourneen was everyone's sweetheart and Erin a kind of universal homeland. Before the end of the nineteenth century they were becoming part of American folklore.

Unlike the negroes who were the source of the southern melodies, the Irish were assimilated rapidly into the new country. Within a generation or two the Irish family had become American. The tears were dried, the heart comforted with new loves and with the boundless nostalgia for the old land passed the inspiration of the songs. The negro out of his sorrow continued to give form to the music of the New World, while the Irish influence faded.

Although D'Arcy McGee's songs were not set to music, he constantly wrote down his thoughts in verse and made of his hopes and sorrows poetry that belongs to the literature of exile. Much of it was personal and very likely included in his letters home.

Mary must have had her heart ravished by the poems in which D'Arcy imagines one or the other of them as dying and leaving the survivor in a pitiable state. She must have read with mixed feelings the poem dedicated to D'Arcy's two loves, his wife and Ireland, with Ireland coming out

90

somewhat the better. But other poems were more flattering and consoling. He sent her verses for St. Valentine's Day and many poems urging her to come to him and recalling the happy hours they had spent together.

For the most part D'Arcy's poems of exile describe home-sickness as anyone might feel it—a bit of scenery or a sound suddenly reminding him of the old land, the dreams more vivid than reality in which he talked with Mary and Duffy, the bleak awakening, the tears shed in secret.

His experiences were not all on this level. At the time he was writing his emotions into his poems he was leading a busy life as editor of a newspaper.

The world of journalism was changing as the penny dailies grew to skyscraper proportions overshadowing the old-fashioned weeklies. The dailies were more interested in news than in ideas. They dealt in crimes, disasters and political scandals—all of which had a definite commercial value when served to the reader hot and strong.

Since his training was journalistic D'Arcy McGee turned naturally to the career of an editor. It offered the best opportunities to one who had little capital but a great deal to say. He did not even consider the field of the ignoble dailies. An editor, in his opinion, should be dedicated to a cause and should be responsible for forming public opinion.

Very little equipment was needed to start a paper. A desk, a supply of paper, ink, a paste pot and shears and a few ideas. A printing press and some knowledge of the printers' trade was necessary for the editor in a small town, but in the cities there were plenty of printers' shops which would undertake at reasonable rates to set up and bring out the paper. A weekly could be started with as little as $150. McGee did not have that much when he arrived in New York, but within ten days he had borrowed enough to establish his own paper.

It was called the *New York Nation* in compliment to the Dublin *Nation* and, according to the prospectus, was to be devoted to "Ireland, her emigrants and European democracy". It contained editorials, essays and poems, mostly written by McGee. The tone of the articles had the same wild exaggeration, the same glimpses of half-submerged sense already noted in McGee's strange manifesto to the Canadians. In transferring his efforts from Dublin to New York the judicious side of his nature suffered an eclipse and all that was impulsive and hot-headed swayed his opinions.

The reason lay not in delirium or mysterious sea change. It went back to the meeting in O'Gorman's warehouse with Dillon and Meagher when he had decided for rebellion. That afternoon he had taken a road from which he believed there was no turning back. He had left Ireland an avowed revolutionist; he was accepted by Irish Americans as a revolutionist. Very well, he would be one. He did not stop to consider that he was a radical by accident and not from conviction. Instead he started a newspaper to give public expression to his confused state of mind.

At first radicalism came easily. Like other refugees of 1848 he could not believe their cause had failed. Karl Marx seems to have been the only one to realize that 1848 was already history. There would be other revolutions, Marx said, but they could not be expected for fifteen or twenty years, perhaps not even in a lifetime. This cool detachment was quite impossible for McGee. Day by day, week by week, he continued to seize on every word of news from Europe and Ireland, hoping for new uprisings or some happy accident.

The only news from Ireland was the trial of the rebels taken in Tipperary. They were well defended; the money from America which had arrived too late for the rebellion was used for lawyers' fees. Except for Duffy, who was tried separately, the insurrectionists, in spite of the efforts of their lawyers, were quickly disposed of. In an atmosphere of gloom the country learned that Smith O'Brien and Thomas Meagher had been condemned to death. But on the advice of the British government, which was reluctant to provide the Irish with more martyrs, the Queen commuted the sentences to transportation for life.

At this point Smith O'Brien made a sensation by refusing the royal pardon. He preferred death to a lifetime in Australia. Tom Meagher, who could not resist a dramatic gesture, followed his example. Between them they created a situation without precedent in British law. The Queen was shocked at this fresh evidence of the persistent wickedness of Her Majesty's Irish rebels and she urged Parliament to pass without delay the necessary legislation to enable her to enforce the pardon. Parliament acted with unusual speed with the result that Smith O'Brien and Meagher sailed on the prison transport with the rest.

In New York McGee fiercely and loyally defended everything Young Ireland had done, even the Tipperary fiasco. When his own ideas failed he used the phrases and ideas of Meagher and Mitchel as a man in battle might pick up the rifle of a fallen comrade. He denounced England for the whole course of her dealings with Ireland, an attitude generally accepted as proper to an Irishman. He also denounced the Irish clergy for opposing Young Ireland's attempted rebellion and here he was on more dangerous ground. Before long McGee and the Bishop had discovered each other and were head on in opposition.

John Hughes, Bishop of New York, had risen by strong will and ability to the administration of an unruly diocese. During the Know-Nothing riots which had broken out in New England as an expression of fear and prejudice roused by the enormously increased Irish immigration, he had not only to keep his parishioners from taking the offensive against their persecutors, but to secure protection from municipal authorities that were, at best, indifferent.

"Do you fear for your churches, Bishop?" the mayor had asked.

"No, sir, it's your buildings I fear for," had been the Bishop's reply. If the city of New York could not avert the threatened disorders, he continued, he would be obliged to allow his parishioners to organize for their own protection.

The hint was taken; there was no mobbing of Irish

Catholics in New York. The authorities might not love the Bishop nor the Church he represented, but they had a certain respectful fear of him and knew that he would stand no nonsense.

His Grace had shown interest in Young Ireland and even some sympathy. But the reckless speeches and writings of Mitchel, Meagher and Finton Lalor had left him, like others, doubtful as to what the movement really stood for. The affair in Tipperary convinced him of its folly. The man who fought his own battles skilfully, who understood to a nicety the diplomatic use of the threat of force, had no patience with the sorry mess the Young Irelanders had made when they had finally gone into action. They were a disgrace to the fighting tradition of Ireland. The Bishop said so in an article published in the *New York Freeman*. He advised Irish Americans to waste no more money on them.

The publication of a newspaper by a Young Ireland refugee right in his diocese could hardly appear to the Bishop as anything but an annoyance, especially when the Young Irelander countered the Bishop's criticism with a general attack on the clergy. As for Bishop Hughes, McGee wanted nothing to do with him. When the Bishop accused him of being a bad Catholic, he retorted:

"My crime is not that I do not believe in the creed of my fathers and my affections, but that I have failed to pay my court to some great unknown who sits chafing on his chair, impatient of his daily dose of honied praises."

McGee was mistaken in his man. The Bishop was neither expecting nor dispensing honey. Furthermore he had no intention of ignoring D'Arcy McGee. Here was a trouble-maker to be dealt with firmly.

McGee had already drawn attention to himself by his talk of revolution and his attacks on the Irish clergy. As he went between Philadelphia, New York and Boston arranging for the printing and distribution of his paper, he saw the wretched condition of the immigrants and the low esteem in which they were held. He spoke out freely about this too. His bitter criticism of the position of the Irish in

America and of the whole idea of immigration had stirred up controversy in all the Irish American papers.

It would be pleasant to record that in contrast to the lurid penny dailies the weekly journals pleaded their cause on a high plane. But this was not the case. The tone of several of the weekly journals equalled in scurrility anything found in the daily press. The Bishop had only to glance over the pages of these Irish American papers to learn that McGee had made enemies. One paper was running a series of articles on him called "The Traitor". Just wherein he was a traitor was not very clear, except in so far as he was a wretch capable of betraying anything— "This creature is a horrid hunchbacked, half-breed specimen of a viperous, slanderous, lying race, that in the first place should never have been born."

Bishop Hughes at least recognized the young man as intelligent. There was force and point to the rashest of McGee's writings that could not be countered by drivelling insults of this sort. The Bishop decided that he himself would take up the Young Irelander's challenge. He published a series of letters in the *New York Freeman*, signed simply "An Irish Catholic". He arranged to have McGee informed privately as to the identity of his opponent.

It was most unfortunate, because McGee felt forced to keep up an argument started in anger and disappointment. He had already begun to grow a little tired of it, to return instinctively to his earlier interests, history and literature. He was writing a history of the Irish settlers in America from the earliest times. He had also published a memoir of Gavan Duffy which helped to focus public interest on Duffy's trial then going on.

In the spring of 1849 Mary sailed from Ireland. She was bringing the baby, a girl whom they named Martha Dorcas, and with them came D'Arcy's brother James to try his luck in the New World. With the last letter written from Ireland to say that they were setting out all communication ended. D'Arcy reckoned the probable length of the voyage in weeks

95

and days. He wrote poems saluting the ship and her passengers and imploring heaven's protection. No vessel ever crossed the Atlantic more lavishly hung round with poetical prayers and good wishes. He was among the crowd waiting at the dock for the gang plank to be lowered and the immigrants, dressed in their best, to land. He shared with hundreds of others the high moment of recognition and welcome that almost compensated for the sorrow that had gone before and the disappointments that were to come.

Shortly after the arrival of the family the good news came that Duffy's trial had ended favourably. After nearly a year in jail he was a free man. McGee celebrated by writing a poem to Duffy and a letter full of congratulations and projects.

As soon as he was free Duffy began planning to revive the Dublin *Nation*. Many difficulties lay in the way. The files and lists of subscribers had been taken by the police. The staff had been scattered into forced or voluntary exile. Duffy wrote more than one letter to McGee inviting him to return to Dublin and offering him a quarter share in the paper. He wrote that he would rather work with McGee than any man he knew. He reminded D'Arcy of their comradeship and the rambles in Wicklow. They were affectionate letters, but McGee felt too deeply involved in his own paper and immigrant affairs to accept the offer.

"Seven months ago I entered this city with £11 in my purse. Since then I have received $5,000 all of which has been sunk as it came in their *Nation*. I therefore feel myself bound to our outcasts at the same time my heart longs and strains after Ireland and you."

This was one of the few times McGee talked about money. Considering that the prevailing spirit decreed that the poor man should strive to make money and the rich man to become richer, McGee's attitude was rather unworldly.

"My little *Nation* in 1850 will give me personal independence, all I want or wish for . . . As it is, half of it is at your service at this hour and if you refuse it I have a mental reservation to devote so much of its gains to whatever Irish enterprise you originate at home."

Duffy wrote again urging McGee to return. He and his family were but sojourners in the New World, the green isle called them back. Still McGee chose to stay by the work that circumstance had thrust on him. Although, as he told Duffy, he believed that the Irish cause in the grand sense could best be served in Ireland, there was a whole world of Irish immigrants around him and whatever he had of intelligence and talent now belonged to them.

It was a sound decision, but strange for a patriot who a short time before had been writing of Ireland in terms of passionate idolatry. McGee was in the position of the lover who discovers to his secret astonishment and embarrassment that, although separated from the mistress he had vowed he could not live without, he not only continues to live but to be interested in living.

When he recovered from his first loudly expressed shock at the condition of the immigrants he wanted to do something about it. Many of them were not only poor but illiterate. The New World could give them work as manual labourers. Why should it not help them to an education? McGee became very active in starting night schools, which in time played no small part in the process of making an American.

Into a drab gas-lit schoolroom, still unaired from the children's classes, came the young labourer, the big, uncouth boy from some primitive farm in Roscommon or Meath. Arriving in America with nothing but his strength and native wit, he became one of an army of ants, the day labourers, digging canals and building railroads. He fought those who laughed at his ignorance and called him "Paddy" and "bogtrotter". Thinking over his plight he decided there was no future for him except as a drudge unless he had an education. While various of his countrymen went to the grog shop for the evening, he went to night school.

Wedged into a narrow desk, bent over a child's slate, he sweated more profusely forming letters and figures than he ever did over a pick or shovel. Within six months he was sufficiently literate to understand and draw up a simple contract for his first job on his own. The qualities that had led him to seek aid in the classroom carried him on to success. Within ten years he was a prosperous contractor. Within twenty he was rich and his daughters went to the convent school to be educated as ladies.

His story had the merit of being true and of presenting simply, even starkly, the ever popular drama from rags to riches. Passing in legendary form back to the old land the story led simple folk to believe that they had only to go to America to become rich.

D'Arcy McGee worked whole-heartedly to organize the night schools. The enthusiasts and reformers of his time believed that universal elementary education, or the ability to read and write, would advance the whole human race, not only to a higher standard of living, but also to a higher state of life. From McGee's later statements on education it seems unlikely that he ever considered literacy the answer to all the problems of humanity, but he certainly considered general education as a need that was practical and urgent.

He soon found his efforts blocked by the Bishop. The combination of D'Arcy McGee and a night school suggested only one thing to the episcopal mind—a political club. And the Bishop knew all about political clubs, rifle clubs and technological societies for the manufacture of gunpowder. "The Irish do not require the strong doses of patriotism which Mr. McGee administers. His countrymen here should mind first their duty to God, to their families and to the country in which they live."

The Bishop made no distinction between the moderate and extreme opinions in Young Ireland—they were all wild fellows like John Mitchel. Many of the furious articles in the *New York Nation* during McGee's first months in America did nothing to modify this impression. Even Duffy was dismayed to find the brightest and—he had hoped—the steadiest of his young men publishing the opinions which appeared in McGee's paper. A shrewd old lawyer, who had eased Duffy and his paper out of more than one tight corner, once told him: "Never beat your head against a wall, especially a church wall." This advice Duffy now passed on to McGee.

"You do not act wisely in attacking the bishops and priests in that style. They are not to be *written* out of their position of political authority, but you are to be driven from yours for you are but one man. Besides, you are not strictly just . . . If they preached against all editors how would we regard them? My friend, your anger is misleading you."

But McGee was too deep in the controversy to withdraw gracefully. Also the ease with which he had started his paper, the many plans on which he was constantly working, the satisfaction of having Mary with him all helped to conceal from him the fact that his affairs were not as prosperous as he thought.

Bishop Hughes's disapproval was not to be lightly dismissed. He was expert in controversy, experienced in dealing with bigotry and political chicanery of the grossest kind. His articles in the *New York Freeman*, under a pseudonym that only partially concealed his identity, were trenchant and unsparing. He had his opponent at a great disadvantage in that many of his arguments were ones with which McGee ordinarily was in sympathy. Having disproved McGee's case by argument, the Bishop now stepped out in his official capacity and warned against a paper edited by one "whose heart had apostasized from the honoured creed of his country while his lips had not yet mustered the bad courage to disavow the faith of his forefathers".

This was hardly true to the facts, although it may have been a logical conclusion from the Bishop's arguments. But since the Bishop's prestige stood high, the controversy had a disastrous effect on the circulation of the *New York Nation*.

Bishop Hughes may have been responsible for the paper's failure. It might have failed in any case. Although McGee started several papers—some with, some without, episcopal approval—none ever became firmly established. As a journalist he was sufficiently outstanding to be both praised and damned by his contemporaries. Journalistically he was a success; his financial success is more doubtful.

McGee moved from place to place, sometimes transferring his paper, sometimes starting a new one. He liked to be out and around, taking part in public life as well as passing judgment on it. He used his desk for writing editorials and poetry oftener than to keep accounts or for work on routine details.

The *New York Nation,* his first independent venture in journalism, did not reflect his real mind. Along with the rebellion of 1848 it was an erratic episode in his life. Even without outside opposition, in its original form it could not have lasted long.

Verses from

To Duffy, Free

Through long sorrows and fears,
And past perilous years,
And darkness and distance,
And seas, where the mists dance,
    I see a new star!
Not a comet, or wild star,
But a radiant and mild star,
Still shining as Venus,
Still bright'ning like Sirius,
On a night in July,
Is the star I descry!
And though myriads of miles and of waves intervene,
Admonish'd, I worship the star I have seen.

'Tis thy star, oh, my friend,
That doth shine and ascend
    On the night of our race;
Thou art the appointed,
By affliction anointed,
    As through grief cometh grace;
Born heir to the planet,
See now that you man it
With the heroes whose worth
Hath made this round earth
    A circular shrine;
For the sun hath not shone

On such work as, when done,
 Will be thine.

The fate of our land
God hath placed in your hand;
He hath made you to know
The heart of your foe,
And the schemes he hath plann'd;
Think well what you are,
Know your soul—and your star;
Persevere—dare—
Be wise and beware—
Seek not praise from today;
Be not wiled from your way
By visions distracting;
Heed not the detracting
Of souls imbecile
Who your mastership feel,
Yet hate you, as pride hates the sky-piercing spire,
Because than its own gaudy dome it springs higher.

Go forth, knight, to the altar
 With bold heart and holy,
And fear not, nor falter,
 But ask, and ask solely
The might and the grace
 To redeem our fall'n nation
 From its deep desolation,
And lift up our race;
 Let your vigil be long,
 For prayer maketh strong
The arm of the weakest,
And the will of the meekest,
 To wrestle with wrong;
Born heir to the planet,
See now that you man it
With the heroes whose worth
Hath made this round earth
 A circular shrine;
For the sun hath not shone
On such work as, when done,
 Will be thine!

Chapter Thirteen
McGEE MAKES UP HIS MIND

B Y THE SUMMER of 1850 McGee's *Nation* had petered out. His efforts in New York on behalf of the immigrants, the poor outcasts, had not been well received. It was necessary to look elsewhere for a fresh start. He thought of returning to Dublin where Duffy's offer to share his paper was still open. Even as he was making preparations for the voyage, he received a letter from a friend in close touch with public affairs in Ireland, reminding him that the ban against him had not been lifted and that he might be arrested if he returned, especially if he took any part in politics. This was a point both McGee and Duffy had overlooked. Once it was brought to his attention McGee realized he had no choice but to stay in America.

He moved with his family to Boston where he accepted lecture engagements to meet expenses. As long as he retained his eloquence and the Irish of New England were willing to listen to lectures the McGees need not starve. But lecturing was an uncertain source of income and D'Arcy inevitably started another paper.

This was the *American Celt*, which advanced the idea that since the Celtic race included large numbers of Scots, Welsh, French and Spaniards, not to mention the Celts in America, they should cultivate a brotherly feeling for each other. Apart from this the new paper was not unlike the *New York Nation*, although it did not run into the *Nation's* difficulty with the clergy.

James Fitzpatrick, Bishop of Boston, was the episcopal cousin claimed by the Morgan side of D'Arcy's family. He acknowledged the relationship and accepted McGee as a kinsman. Of a more sympathetic nature than Bishop Hughes, he looked on McGee as a hotheaded young man who would cool off more quickly if not badgered, and in this opinion he was not wrong. Now that his anger had burnt out and there was no Bishop Hughes to pile on fresh fuel, McGee was more disposed to reconsider his position.

Perhaps he had been wrong in thinking that the part he had taken in the rebellion of 1848 made him a radical for the rest of his life. The career of a revolutionist was sordid when there was no inner conviction to elevate it. He would end by becoming a mere agitator, or even a hack writer, hiring out his talents to whatever party paid him to express its opinion. A depressing prospect and for a man like McGee an impossible one.

Far from being a genuine radical he could not conform even to the milder tenets of nineteenth century liberalism. To be sure, it stressed the importance of humanity and the individual, but it was hazy about the existence of God and the nature of the soul. It had as its core a philosophy of rationalism that was too cold and restricted for D'Arcy's temperament. Since his most brilliant faculty was his imagination, he saw more clearly in his moments of inspiration than by the steady but limited light of reason. Intuition as well as logic formed his thought. Nor could he accept the division which liberalism made in human affairs, keeping economics, politics, philosophy, religion and art separate in the life of society, as though each were isolated and complete in itself. To McGee's mind religion bound the other parts together making life, as far as was possible in man's fallen state, all of one piece. He himself had what a psychologist would call an integrated personality. Put more simply he had faith; put more definitely he had what a Catholic would call the Faith.

As he had always expressed his opinions in print, it was not long before he found an opportunity for summing up the course he had followed since 1848 and making his present stand clear. The opportunity came with Tom Meagher's arrival in New York in May, 1852.

Meagher had escaped from Australia to California. From there he travelled to Panama, crossed the isthmus and took ship again for New York. In the course of his adventures as state prisoner and fugitive he had travelled around the world and acquired a wife in Australia. His arrival in New York caused great excitement among the Irish Americans who had always considered him a romantic figure and who had largely provided the funds that had made his escape possible. Now they feted him at public dinners and made a great fuss over him.

Although McGee was not in New York to take part in the celebration, he added his greetings to the rest, saluting his colleague of 1848 in a short poem with a Gaelic title and addressing to him a letter of advice which he published in the *American Celt*. In this letter he stated his own conclusions on the liberal philosophy of Young Ireland:

> Permit me, as one who has been over the ground of this inquiry, to tell you what discoveries I made upon it. This I will do as candidly and plainly as if I were dictating a last will and testament, for in this case all plainness is demanded.

> I discovered at the very outset of the inquiry my own ignorance. This I discovered in a way which, I trust in God, you will never have to travel—by controversy and bitterness, and sorrow for lost time and wasted opportunities. Had we studied principles in Ireland as devoutly as we did an ideal nationality, I might not now be labouring double tides to recover a confidence which my own fault forfeited . . .

> Having discovered by close self examination that the reading chiefly of modern books, English and French, gave very superficial and false views of political science, I cheerfully said to myself: "My friend, you are on the wrong track. You think you know something of human affairs, but you do not. You are ignorant of the primary principles that govern and must govern the world." . . . Thus I reasoned with myself, and then, setting my cherished opinions before me, one by one, I tried, judged and capitally executed every

one, save and except those which I found to be compatible with the following doctrines:

1. That there is a Christendom.
2. That this Christendom exists by and for the Catholic Church.
3. That there is in our own age one of the most dangerous and general conspiracies against Christendom that the world has yet seen.
4. That this conspiracy is aided, abetted and tolerated by many because of its stolen watchword—Liberty.
5. That it is the highest duty of a Catholic man to go over cheerfully, heartily and at once, to the side of Christendom—to the Catholic side—and to resist with all his might the conspirators who, under the stolen name of Liberty, make war upon all Christian institutions.

It was a strangely blunt statement from a man who understood the arts of persuasion. In an effort to be perfectly sincere, McGee seems to have deliberately laid aside all arts and graces and to have spoken with awkward, penitential plainness. From this letter, he seems to have chosen a narrow, rigid frame in which to work. But for him it was the only one. He required a positive creed and the vague agnosticism of liberalism baffled him. It may be argued that the philosophy of liberalism is not inconsistent with religious belief, which is as it may be, but from this point in his life McGee looked to the creed and not to the philosophy for guidance.

Actually the field in which he exercised his talents proved much broader than it appeared. Although he turned his back on the liberalism of Thomas Davis, it was McGee, Duffy said, who of all the Young Irelanders most resembled in his later career the originator of the movement.

The open letter to Meagher caused much comment in the Irish American journals. Some considered it a very manly stand, greatly to McGee's credit. Others regarded it as merely pretentious, but said this in more insulting language.

McGee did not remain long in Boston. There were too many Irish American papers there already snapping at each other. Also McGee's changed attitude soon showed strongly in his paper, even before the letter to Meagher. His subscribers who had helped him to a start, expecting a rousing, radical, anti-clerical paper like the *New York Nation* were dissatisfied with the *American Celt*'s increasingly conservative and responsible tone. Finally, there was something unsuitable about Boston for making a new start. Early in 1852 McGee moved his paper to Buffalo.

Iona to Erin

(What St. Columba said to the bird flown over from Ireland to Iona)

Cling to my breast, my Irish bird,
    Poor storm-toss'd stranger, sore afraid!
How sadly is thy beauty blurr'd—
    The wing whose hue was as the curd,
Rough as the sea-gull's pinion made!

Lay close thy head, my Irish bird,
    Upon this bosom, human still!
Nor fear the heart that still has stirr'd
    To every tale of pity heard
From every shape of earthly ill.

For you and I are exiles both—
    Rest you, wanderer, rest you here!
Soon fair winds shall waft you forth
Back to our own beloved North—
    Would God I could go with you, dear!

But you will see what I am bann'd
    No more, for my youth's sins to see,
My Derry's oaks in council stand
By Roseapenna's silver strand—
    Or by Raphoe your course may be.

McGEE MAKES UP HIS MIND

The shrines of Meath are fair and far—
    White-wing'd one, not too far for thee—
Emania, shining like a star,
(Bright brooch on Erin's breast you are!)
    That I am never more to see.

Be thou to them, O dove! where'er
    The men or women saints are found,
My hissop flying though the air;
My seven-fold benedictions bear
    To them and all on Irish ground.

Thou wilt return, my Irish bird—
    I, Columb, do foretell it thee;
Would thou could'st speak as thou hast heard
    To all I love—O happy bird!
  At home in Erin soon to be!

Chapter Fourteen
TO BUFFALO AND BACK

Nothing but a fresh start was possible in Buffalo; the town itself had no background. It had grown in a few years from a muddy little frontier village to an ambitious city funnelling traffic from east to west. Lake shipping was the reason for Buffalo's existence and dominated its life. The long, narrow harbour was filled with ships—machine-driven steamers, as well as the slower, cheaper and still serviceable sailing ships. Their crews thronged the streets, hotels and places of entertainment. Irish labourers were everywhere in evidence. They had come with the building of the Erie Canal, literally digging their way, yard by yard. When the canal which connected the Lakes with the Hudson River was completed most of the Irish remained in Buffalo to work on the waterfront as stevedores. The others scattered to new construction jobs or moved into Canada to take up land.

Boundless optimism inspired the new city. Smart men made fortunes. Some, it is true, reached heights of success only to fall ignominiously—like the contractor who built ninety-nine business houses, but ended in jail because his practice of higher finance included forged cheques. Or the city's most prosperous hotel man, a personage as gilded and sparkling as his own premises, a millionaire at forty, who went down in the real estate scandal and ultimately died in the poorhouse.

But the others secured their gains and lived in mansions close to the business centre. The craze for ostentation had not yet corrupted architecture. The mansions were solid and handsome, showing the proportions and good taste of an earlier period. Inside, the signs of new wealth were more evident. Velour portières smothered doorways and windows and hung down to thick-carpeted floors. Marble statues and suits of armour purchased in Europe flanked elaborately upholstered American-made furniture. At night, gas jets concealed in intricate chandeliers shed a glaring light on all this opulence.

D'Arcy McGee's course did not take him into the homes of the rich but into the bustling world of the hotels and boarding-houses. These were the real heart of this trafficking city. Their hospitality was indispensable, especially at the season when the ice jams at the lower end of Lake Erie held up the shipping. Then those hotel and boarding-house keepers, who had laid in plentiful supplies of food for a houseful of guests who would be with them till the crisis in navigation passed, grew prosperous.

The city prided itself on its entertainment. All the fashionable lecturers, imported and native, visited it, including Mr. Dickens, Mr. Thackeray and Mr. Thoreau. An English lady wrote of witnessing from a box in the theatre a performance of *Romeo and Juliet* during which the audience held her attention as much as the play. The pit was filled with labourers and lake sailors in shirt sleeves and straw hats following the play with vociferous attention and refreshing themselves between the acts from bags of cakes and bottles of whisky.

Culture did not stop with the lecture hall and the theatre, but could be carried from the book auctions into the home, the ship bunk and the hotel room. McGee, grandson of a Dublin book dealer and a great reader all his life, must have given at least passing attention to Buffalo's book stores. Visitors, accustomed to the venerable atmosphere of European book shops, marvelled at the boxes of books looking as enticing as sugar plums in gay bindings, wonderfully embossed and gilded. They listened in amazement to the glib-tongued auctioneer who daily ran the sale and when they saw some prosperous farmer leave with a gaudy volume of Thucydides or Shakespeare tucked under his arm they asked themselves was it possible that the common people of America had such solid reading tastes? McGee, from his wider knowledge of the country, could have told the European visitors that the book was bought to decorate the parlour table and rarely would anyone be bold enough to look into it.

One form of art was not imported but belonged especially to the lake city. This was carried on by the steamboat artists who decorated the lounges and salons of the lake ships. An example of their art could be seen in an immense mural covering the flat front of several buildings in downtown Buffalo. It depicted a steamer full size, complete in every visible detail, ploughing its way through the waves of Lake Erie.

The paintings in the salons of the real ships, though necessarily on a smaller scale, were even more gorgeous and imaginative. The subject of the painting was usually taken from the name of the ship. If the name was classical, the painting would run to mythological ladies suitably draped and cupids floating in clouds; if Indian, very likely Sioux warriors, befeathered and mounted, would be shown charging over the heads of the passengers at dinner.

The steamers of the Great Lakes and the waterways of the New World, prototypes of the modern luxury liners, were planned as floating hotels. Even travellers of moderate means, who had never been inside a mansion, and who possibly could not afford the best hotels, could command the splendours of the lake steamers. For the price of their tickets they were sustained with lavish meals and, when they withdrew from the promenade deck, were surrounded with upholstered furniture, carpets, carvings, fittings of gilt and rosewood and the sumptuous steamboat murals as the final, unsurpassed touch of elegance.

McGee lived in Buffalo for over a year publishing the *American Celt*, officially a resident, really a transient, as it is doubtful whether he brought his family there. He moved in the flamboyant world of the Great Lakes without becoming part of it. But like London it influenced his life deeply because while he was in Buffalo he first became acquainted with Canada.

The residents of Buffalo, looking across the Niagara River, could see on the opposite shore another country. Even in quiet times this gives a slight feeling of exhilaration and in the 1850's this position on the border had unusual and dramatic significance. In Buffalo the abolition movement went underground and did real work. Runaway slaves did not always come to the city itself, as agents of the slave owners waited along the waterfront to capture them. But from secret stations along the lake shore they were smuggled aboard ships which obligingly swung over to Fort Erie before docking at Buffalo and landed the trembling, anxious, exultant refugees in Canada.

The Canadian border and the slave smuggling helped to preserve the frontier spirit of Buffalo, in spite of its wealth and pretensions. Even after the frontier proper had moved farther west, the people continued forthfaring and adventurous.

D'Arcy McGee also looked across at the other country with feelings peculiar to himself. Yonder was a country that lived under the British flag, that motley pirate rag of a government that had banned him from his own land. Only a narrow strip of water separated him from British America. People from either side passed back and forth freely. He knew that Irish labourers moved into Canada to pioneer in the bush. Under the loose and easy organization of the British Empire the law that banished him from Ireland did not hold in Canada. Nothing prevented him from travelling there as freely as anyone else. He could, if he wished, promote the sale of his paper in Canada. He could lecture there. Before long the fascination of this country proved too much for his curiosity. He boarded a lake steamer calling at Canadian ports and set out on a tour of observation. In time, he had correspondents in several Canadian towns, where the *American Celt* had fairly large numbers of readers. Canadian audiences heard him lecture.

111

This interest in Canada developed only very gradually as a result of his more pressing concern for the state of the immigrants. They were going through a stormy period of adjustment. Too many had crowded into the eastern cities during the famine years. They became citizens with the right to vote without even faintly understanding the political life of the country to which they had come. Demagogues and ward bosses exploited their ignorance and their votes. Prejudice against them took the form of the Native American Party usually called the Know Nothings, because of its secrecy about organization and membership. The remedies it demanded were as crude as the evils it opposed. In a country that was drifting towards civil war because of its inability to solve the problem of negro slavery the Know Nothings proposed to make another class of helots by depriving immigrants of citizen rights. Although America claimed to lead the world in civil and religious liberties, the Know Nothings wanted to prevent Catholics from holding public office.

McGee had a sensitive understanding of the inner tragedy of emigration. Something was always lost when people were uprooted from their ancestral soil and transferred to a new environment. Nor was the tragedy less in the case of emigrants like the Irish leaving a poor country for a rich one. It did not matter that they exchanged a land where they subsisted on potatoes and went barefoot for one where they ate meat and wore shoes. The loss was spiritual and was rarely made good in the new country, at least in the first generation.

This was why McGee, although he devoted himself to the emigrants, rarely spoke in favour of emigration. This was one reason he became a devout and militant son of the Church. The Faith was in many cases the only possession left to the Irish from the wreck of their fortunes. It was one of the few traditional loyalties they could honourably adhere to in their new country. Here was soil in which the transplanted people could take spiritual root and become whole again. It was inevitable that the emigrants would change; new duties and loyalties claimed them. But in the matter of religion they must not change.

McGee met the challenge of the Know Nothings by a series of five lectures which struck directly at the core of nativist prejudice—the fear that Catholic immigrants were importing into the Republic an alien institution. McGee countered with the general argument that the Church was not an alien institution but had come to the New World with the first explorers and colonists. "Why be at war with history?" he asked the Know Nothings. "The Jesuits are there at the outer gate of all our chronicles."

Extensive reading went into the preparation of the five lectures. Histories of America in two and three volumes, personal narratives of the missionaries, solid biographies of famous persons were rigorously searched for the facts on which he based his case. When he later printed his lectures in book form he cited his authorities in precise footnotes that would not disgrace a modern Ph.D. thesis. Study for D'Arcy McGee was a labour of love. In preparing his lectures on "The Catholic History of America" he must have experienced again the pure joy of scholarship he had known in the British Museum.

The lectures were delivered during the winter of 1853-54, so that the preparation for them must have been made during the period when McGee was leading a very active life, travelling between Boston and Buffalo, visiting Canada, moving his paper in June, 1853, from Buffalo to New York. The quiet atmosphere of a library like the British Museum was not conveniently available. Whether the volumes of history and biography weighed down his portmanteau and were read in the sociable surroundings of trains and steamboats, whether they slid heavily from his bed late at night in hotel or boarding-house, or provided Mary with a taciturn evening in his company when he was at home, the long hours of reading were worked in somehow. Such was the catalyst of his imagination and eloquence that when he presented it to his audience the heavy matter of history had taken on the easy grace of an old story and the freshness of a new one.

At the beginning of America's story stand three figures, a sailor, a lady and a monk. With this introduction, having shaken the dust of pedantry from Columbus, Isabella of Spain and Dom Peres, the Dominican, McGee went on with his seemingly artless narrative. The lectures were singularly free from exaggeration or controversy. McGee at his best was moderate in thought and expression. His purpose was to set the record straight. He avoided the rut where other historians had trod monotonously and repetitiously and carried his listeners along new paths. He presented history from unusual angles, for example from the viewpoint of the missionaries. He brought to light little-known facts—the tolerant policy of Washington and the Founding Fathers that would have won the French Canadians to the Republic as contrasted with the bigoted manifesto of the First Congress that scared them off.

McGee did not neglect, in following the broad course of history, to work in here and there the names of distinguished Irishmen. He was Irish himself and with his audience enjoyed lingering over a fine name as much as over a fine sentence.

The last lecture of the series was on the recent Irish Catholic immigration. To these immigrants, despised because of their poverty and misery, McGee gave the tribute that the Republic had withheld. They were the cheap, unorganized labour that dug the canals and built the railroads, manned the factories and the mines. Subordinates in power, they were principals in labour.

The growth of the Catholic Church as a result of Irish immigration McGee considered a glorious achievement, whatever fear and dismay it might cause in certain quarters. He recognized it as a kind of poetic justice that the Irish, who out of their poverty were building the wealth of the New World, were also the humble means of moulding American civilization by bringing to its harsh materialism the culture and philosophy of the ancient Faith.

The lectures did not attempt to meet the practical problems of the immigrants, but they did something which a discussion of merely practical matters could not have accomplished. McGee took his listeners from the confusion of the moment, from the squalor of slums and the brawling of ward politics to a point where they could view the subject in historic perspective. He gave to an uprooted people going through a period of many hardships and humiliations a reason for pride, a sense of background and of belonging to the new land to which they had come.

The reasoned, artfully simple presentation of his theme rises at times to heights of glowing eloquence. Passages, somewhat rhetorical when taken alone, in the context grow gradually and richly from the cumulation of fact and argument. Even today, read in the brittle, yellowing pages of an old book, the lectures have lost none of their dramatic force and movement. Given by McGee with his particular gifts of voice and expression it is not hard to imagine them delighting and enthralling the habitual lecture-goers of the 1850's.

The lectures reached a large audience. They were given in New York, Boston, Philadelphia, Baltimore, Washington, St. Louis and Cincinnati. The common folk of the Irish communities filled the halls, while more distinguished people and clerical dignitaries shared the platform with the speaker. In Washington, senators and members of Congress attended.

Besides the audiences who heard the lectures, an even larger group was reached by reports given in the *American Celt*. Finally, in 1855, the lectures with footnotes and appendix were published in book form entitled *The Catholic History of North America*.

For his times D'Arcy McGee was well skilled in the arts of publicity.

Chapter Fifteen

THE FATE OF UNSUCCESSFUL REVOLUTIONISTS

New York in the 1850's was a centre for Young Ireland refugees. They were constantly coming and going and usually not without drawing attention to themselves. When Tom Meagher arrived in May, 1852, Richard O'Gorman and John Dillon were there to greet him. Devin Reilly, moody and unhappy, had moved on to Washington where he secured a minor appointment in the Land Office. The irrepressible D'Arcy McGee was in Buffalo. Pat Smythe, who had gone to Australia with the plans and funds that had accomplished Meagher's escape, returned to New York with him. There is a picture still in existence of Smythe at this time, a young man with a small pointed beard, cloak thrown back, silk hat in hand, the very personification of romantic adventure.

Meagher's arrival started a round of entertainment to which all sorts of people were invited. Thackeray, the English novelist, who was in New York at this time, met Dillon and Meagher on one occasion. Although like Carlyle he had no sympathy for the Irish cause, he told Duffy later that he had found his friends delightful, Dillon modest and agreeable, and Meagher quietly amused by all the fuss being made over him.

Whether or not the letters written to him by Duffy as well as McGee influenced him, Meagher avoided taking part in public life during his first months in America. Like McGee on his arrival, Meagher was repelled by the condition of the Irish in the coastal cities and he was slower than McGee to identify himself with them. It was they, rather, who insisted on identifying themselves with him. When finally he was induced to undertake lecture engagements his speeches, according to O'Gorman who later wrote his biography, lacked the fire and intensity of his Irish days. He spoke like one who no longer had a cause.

Irish Americans had to wait for John Mitchel to bring them an injection of what Bishop Hughes called "red-hot Irishism". He reached New York in November, 1853, another fugitive whom Smythe had helped out of Australia. Under his influence loose strands of what had once been Young Ireland were gathered briefly into a hard knot of conflict.

He started a paper called the *Citizen* with Meagher and Reilly, who wrote from Washington, as occasional contributors. Dillon, who was practising law in partnership with O'Gorman, did not write for the *Citizen*, but at this time he was a close personal friend of Mitchel. All these men had an ingrained antagonism toward England, the result of their own experiences and the traditions in which they had been brought up. But Mitchel had a capacity for hating which the rest of them lacked. His hatred of England remained the one steady factor in the course of a long and often eccentric life. The others came to look upon him as a symbol of opposition.

This was not the sole reason for his influence. He could be a most diverting companion. His home life had an easy, hospitable quality quite different from his controversial public career, while his *Jail Journal*, the memoirs of his exile written in impeccable prose, charmed even his enemies and assured his memory to posterity. He also had a curious, unexpected sense of humour rarely found in a fanatic. He enjoyed the reaction of the outraged abolitionists when he publicly stated that far from opposing negro slavery he would like nothing better than to live on a plantation like a southern gentleman, and if his slaves were lazy he would certainly beat them.

His paper the *Citizen* was for the moment a sensational success, with a circulation climbing rapidly to 50,000. But its career was bound to be stormy. Its editor took an extreme stand on every subject he discussed, embarrassing the Irish Americans by supporting the slave owners, bringing down the wrath of Bishop Hughes by trying to revive the revolution of 1848 and arousing his old friend and enemy the Dublin *Nation* in the person of D'Arcy McGee. It was difficult to ignore Mitchel and impossible to agree with him. After some weeks of courteously and objectively reporting banquets, meetings and ovations in the fugitives' honour, McGee finally came out with an editorial against Mitchel's quite open attempts to start revolutionary activities among the Irish Americans. Then the fight was on!

The articles in the *Celt* were written with reasonable restraint, but Mitchel's paper plunged directly into offensive personalities. No gratitude was shown for the reckless loyalty with which McGee had defended Mitchel at a time when the "martyr" of 1848 had not been able to speak for himself. The only recognition given was to declare it all part of McGee's false, scheming nature. The *Citizen* maliciously distorted everything he had done or tried to do in 1848 as well as the interest that by 1854 he was beginning to show in Canada. In short with fine disregard for the libel laws, the *Citizen* called McGee a liar and a hypocrite.

From London, where he was serving as a member of Parliament for Ireland, Gavan Duffy watched with sorrow the quarrel between the men who had once worked together on the *Nation*. He had given up all idea of armed rebellion, a course he had always considered more a counsel of despair than a practical policy. He was now trying to form an independent Irish party in the House of Commons and a new Tenant Right League to help the Irish peasants to keep their farms. But he had not lost interest in the aftermath of 1848 and could observe close at hand among the quarrelling political refugees from the continent as well as among his own friends in America what happens to those who serve lost causes. "It seems the eternal fate of unsuccessful revolutionists to fly at each other's throats," was his comment. Perhaps because his own feelings were most deeply involved with the Irish refugees he considered their recriminations the bitterest.

A few months after Mitchel's *Citizen* was started Duffy again wrote to Meagher, this time a public letter reviewing the Irish political scene. He begged Meagher to break his connection with the *Citizen* and take no part in the attacks on McGee, a man who "had been slandered to an extent that would have blackened a saint of God".

It may have been the effect of Duffy's letter or merely coincidence; whatever the reason, Meagher did stop writing for the *Citizen* and took up the practice of law which he had been studying since coming to America. Later he retracted many of the harsh things said against McGee to which he had indirectly given support by his connection with the *Citizen*. But by the time the retraction was published in his biography both he and D'Arcy McGee were dead.

In less than a year the *Citizen*, after a rocket-like success was falling to pieces. Mitchel, having praised the policies and institutions of that part of the Union, decided to go south. The paper continued in existence for a short time after he left and Devin Reilly still wrote for it. In a frenzy of long-gathering resentment he started a series of articles against D'Arcy McGee, which he hoped would drive his former colleague from public life. Scurrilous and overloaded with extreme and indiscriminate insults, they were of such a character that only someone lost to decency and common sense could have imagined them being taken seriously.

Reilly had the poor satisfaction of having done his worst against a man for whom he had always felt enmity. But he had no way of knowing how deeply his words had cut, or how long the poison of his slanders would work, or if McGee had even bothered to read them. The *American Celt* continued to be published. McGee continued to lecture about the country.

Dissatisfaction with life weighed upon Reilly. Men like

119

Davis, Duffy and Mitchel whom he would have followed had failed him. In his letters to Mitchel he speaks of "long ill-health, fretting, poverty and accumulated sorrow". The old headaches persisted. Mitchel, although protesting in his memoirs his good intentions, had not found time to look up his friend and disciple when he was in Washington. The ties with Irish politics were weakening and the dull security of a civil servant's position did not compensate for the lost excitement. Some time toward the end of 1854, Devin Reilly, clerk in the Land Office, graduate of Trinity College, Dublin, one-time writer on the Dublin *Nation,* journalist and patriot, committed suicide.

Chapter Sixteen
DISCOVERY OF CANADA

WHAT KIND of a country did McGee find when he came to Canada? Unfortunately he did not leave an account of his travels. In a few letters that remain, in his poems and in the *American Celt* there are references to visits to Canada and to lecture engagements, especially in Montreal and Quebec. By the time he moved the *Celt* from Buffalo to New York in 1853 he already had correspondents in Montreal and in towns in Canada West, places in the neighbourhood of Buffalo which he likely had visited when he first crossed the border.

The world of the Great Lakes and the St. Lawrence to which all these places belonged was changing rapidly. If we would see it as McGee saw it, we have to turn to the accounts of his contemporaries. Those who visited Canada ten years earlier found a primitive, pioneering country depending on ox cart, stage coach and a few sailing vessels for travel. Those who came ten years after McGee found a railroad running the length of the St. Lawrence valley and the Great Lakes with branch railways being built into the back counties. But the decade of the fifties was the heyday of the steamboats. Canada was a lake-and-river world with canals bearing the steamers inland through miles of country that after a few years would never see the strange invaders again.

Travelling was becoming a fashionable adventure and quite a number of people thought it worth while to publish their experiences. The amount of good travel writing in the world's literature is small and these pushing Victorian tourists added little to it. The several accounts of Canada written in the 1850's suggest that their authors stared without comprehension and felt curiosity without sympathy. They returned home with a hodge-podge of impressions and no clear ideas, their prejudices strengthened by their ill-digested worldly experience. Under the illusion that they were helping to spread useful knowledge they added their volumes to a mass of indifferent travel writing, some of it published under such distinguished names as Dickens and Thackeray.

Happily, Canada in the fifties was described fairly thoroughly and with good judgment by Johann Kohl, a well-educated German with a fluent command of English and French and a background of travel in Europe, Russia and Central Asia. When in 1860 the Prince of Wales's visit awakened general interest in Canada, Kohl's book *Reisen in Canada und durch die Staaten von New York und Pennsylvanien* was translated into English as the best contemporary account of that country.

Johann Kohl travelled through Canada in October of 1854 and it so happened that D'Arcy McGee made one of his visits just one month later, covering practically the same route. We can follow from his own account the observant Mr. Kohl steaming up the Great Lakes in an autumn of great beauty and serenity. Then, withdrawing to a point of historic perspective—a viewpoint McGee himself was very fond of—we can see him following the same course, enjoying a season that still remained unusually open even though the first snows were swirling into the St. Lawrence valley in the vicinity of Quebec. They not only followed the same route, they had the same purpose. Great numbers of Irish and Germans were coming to America. Johann Kohl and D'Arcy McGee shared a common interest. Both wanted to know what Canada had to offer the immigrants.

Mr. Kohl took the usual route from New York to Canada, up the Hudson valley to Montreal. Here at the conjunction of three water-ways he had a choice of going down river to Quebec, up the Ottawa following the route of the fur traders and lumbermen, or through the locks of Lachine into the spacious region of the Great Lakes. Mr. Kohl followed each in turn, going down the St. Lawrence first to Quebec. French villages lined the shore in sight of the commerce passing up and down the river but remote from it, deeply coloured by their own traditions and drawing a modest prosperity from the land. In these villages, Mr. Kohl found an ideal rural simplicity such, he declared, as he had never expected to find in real life. His ability to speak their language gained him a welcome among the habitants. He made numerous notes on the difference between the language of the New World and the speech of Old France. But he found these differences no greater than the variations from the mother tongue of "Yankee" English prevalent both north and south of the Great Lakes.

He had the German's fondness for voluminous information given in meticulous detail and he tabulated geological formations and flora and fauna with as much interest as he described the social life. The Great Lakes and the St. Lawrence fascinated him. They were like a great arm of the sea, an American Mediterranean extending far into the continent. Deep-sea life was found in the St. Lawrence; seals, more common in the North Atlantic then than now, were occasionally seen in the river and in rare cases were said to have reached Lake Ontario, where the astonished inhabitants took them for sea serpents. On the other hand, the Lakes were undoubtedly a fresh-water system draining an immense territory from lake to lake, from level to level down to the sea. "Like a great brewery," wrote Kohl, "where the liquor was funnelled from vat to vat by connecting valves and pipes"—an extraordinary simile probably chosen by the German because of its homely significance for his own people.

He did not confine his travels only to those parts of the country served by the luxurious steamers. He ventured into the back country, jolting over abominable roads in groaning stage coaches, which in some cases were only wagons fitted with benches and a canvas top. In order to see more and to distract his mind from the hardships of his journey, he would climb in front and sit beside the driver. From this position he could watch the dexterity with which the ungainly equipage was handled and admire the horses, sturdy thick-set beasts, a different breed from the animals on the American side of the border, reminding Kohl of the indestructible horses of Poland and Russia.

In his precise, accented English, he asked questions. Was this boulder-strewn terrain of the Ottawa valley fit for farming? What skills and trades were most useful to a settler? What about the winter? The driver explained that this was good pasture land; the boulders protected a growth of lush grass about the base long after the grass on more open pastures had dried up. Almost any skill or craft could be put to profitable use in a new community. Regarding the Canadian winter Mr. Kohl could find no one who would say a word against it. Roads were better when packed with snow and sleighs glided over them more smoothly than wheels in the summer. The winter season was healthful and stimulating. Canadians considered the climate of their lake and river country much superior to that of the valleys of the Missouri and the Mississippi which they spoke of as little better than fever swamps. The vital statistics of the country throw some light on this robust attitude. The adult population was made up largely of people between twenty and thirty, the numbers for each decade over forty decreasing sharply. They were a young, pioneering people who took every hardship in their stride, even the climate.

Then too, there was something about the long golden autumn, day succeeding perfect day, that made even the native forget the coming storms and cold. Such a season had lured the first explorers to their deaths. Mr. Kohl, who was not running a similar risk, often found himself content to drop questions and criticism and just enjoy the weather.

As he drove north from Toronto to Lake Simcoe, the forest closed in around him, splendid with colour. Never had he seen such colour. People assured him temperately that some years the hues were even more vivid, nevertheless everyone agreed it was an unusually fine fall; seldom did the leaves remain so late. Mr. Kohl drove hour after hour through the windless forest that blazed quiet and still like a painted fire. His orderly mind tried to sort his impressions. Which trees turned russet and which yellow? Was it the species of tree or the way the light fell that made some look rosy pink and others ruby or scarlet? When he arrived at the inn where he was to pass the night he was still too drunk with colour to make his usual factual notes. Instead he was led into artistic speculation on the subtle range of shades to be seen in a single tree and why a sugar maple flaming red should retain a wreath of perfectly green leaves among its foliage and how it happened that even on a cloudy day the grey light reflected from countless translucent red and yellow leaves filled the forest with a strange radiance.

In the course of his excursions inland, sometimes in public coaches, sometimes in privately hired conveyances, Mr. Kohl made passing acquaintance with a number of drivers. These handymen had to know more than the road and the management of horses. Their duties included mending the harness, mending the carriage, mending the road and reaching a tavern by mealtime. It was well also that some tried to keep up the spirits of their passengers, for the road was rough and the hospitability of the taverns nothing to boast of. Poor food, either fried and greasy or boiled and tasteless, was indifferently supplemented by whisky made from mouldy barley and rotten potatoes.

Ingenious and resourceful people like the Yankees and Irishmen proved best fitted for this arduous business of travel in the bush. Mr. Kohl, who seems to have been cheated by an Irish cabby in Montreal, afterwards avoided Irish drivers, thereby missing some rollicking company. One traveller describes an Irish driver who could mend a wheel, carpenter, play the fiddle, drink and converse in the most sociable fashion. It is to be feared that their Yankee competitors encouraged Mr. Kohl in his doubtful opinion of the Irish. Irishmen, they told him, were quarrelsome fellows given to whisky.

The French, Mr. Kohl's other source of information, when on the subject of the Irish shrugged their shoulders and raised their eyebrows to imply that words were inadequate to describe this odd race. "Les sans bas," "the no-stockings", they called them among themselves. It was generally known that many Irish, men and women, arrived in the country without these warm and decent items of clothing. Modesty forbade one speculating on what other portions of underwear they might also lack. The good habitant, warming his own well-encased calves before his Quebec stove, could not imagine poverty as dire as that. It must be lack of foresight. An improvident people.

Still the Irish came in great numbers and in spite of their odd, difficult ways they settled down and prospered. Why did not more Germans come to Canada? Mr. Kohl wondered. With their thrift, skill and industry they would do well.

To leave the rough country of the back settlements; to come again in view of the great, shoreless expanse of Lake Ontario, or Erie, or Huron; to step up the gangplank of a garish, bedizened steamer stocked with solid comforts, was to enter another world. At this season the nights came early and the mornings were cold. Even the smell of hot lubricants from the engine room pervading the ship took on a new significance of warmth and well-being.

A spirit that Kohl called Yankee enterprise set the pace for both American and Canadian lake shipping. It was an ambitious and competitive spirit. It built and overbuilt, launching fleets of steamers, each lot speedier and more ornate than the last. It won and lost fortunes. It showed itself in the bravado of the sailors, who yielded nothing to salt-water mariners. The hazards of navigation and the ferocity of the storms, they maintained, were as great as on the Atlantic—exaggerations with which travellers were inclined to agree, especially those who struck bad weather on treacherous Lake Erie. Nothing but choice, the sailors implied, kept them and their vessels on fresh water. Ships built on the lakes and manned by lake crews had more than once ventured into the ocean and sailed as far as Australia.

The spirit of daring and emulation inspired both captains and crews and caused them to invent hazards when natural ones was lacking. This took the form of impromptu steamboat racing, which in Canadian waters was forbidden by law. Most vessels had a supply of colophene on board. If a rival showed interest in a contest the colophene was sprinkled on the engine room fires which flared up, sending yellow smoke in place of black belching from the smoke stacks and raising the steam pressure dangerously. The ship shot forward at new speed while the rival using the same tactics did likewise. The steamboats, moving perilously close to each other, raced for the same goal. On deck the hardier passengers shouted encouragement and defiance.

Mr. Kohl had one experience of steamboat racing and thought his last hour had come. There was not only the danger of collision, but the fear of bursting boilers, a fairly common disaster before the invention of safety devices for steam apparatus.

A passenger who travelled frequently on lake ships declared racing was a most dangerous practice. Only recently there had been a case of bursting boilers on Lake Erie—a shocking affair, with good men killed in the engine room and families left widowed and orphaned. Truly the fun was not worth that. But the same passenger admitted that he liked a speedy ship. It would be irksome to travel on a laggard boat. Any captain and crew, if they were men of spirit, would accept the challenge of a rival, especially approaching the entrance to a canal or harbour. Everyone raced coming into Buffalo.

Johann Kohl left Canada with the conviction that his countrymen would do well to consider its advantages when they thought of emigrating. Many of them knowing it to be a "monarchy" imagined that they would find there the same restrictions and taxation from which they were trying to escape. On this point Mr. Kohl gave them the strongest assurances. Taxation was light and Canada paid no tribute to England. He also came out strongly on the matter of

127

political freedom. Like many conservative-minded visitors he had found the highly organized political parties of the American cities and the emphasis on "majority" rule oppressive. "There is more real freedom in Canada than in the United States and people may express their opinion with far less restraint. In the States they are afraid of the majority and their own party . . . Many of the educated and truly enlightened Americans will talk much more freely in Canada than in their own country."

Not long after Kohl had returned from his tour D'Arcy McGee hurried into Canada with a long list of specific questions about land grants, rates of wages, seasonal employment and suitable districts for settlement. Several letters reporting his findings appeared in the *Celt* addressed from Quebec, Montreal and—rather surprisingly—from St. Louis.

He did not make so prolonged a tour as Kohl's, but whereas Johann Kohl came only once, McGee made several visits to Canada and travelled extensively through the country after he came to live there. No place, no mode of travel, no situation or type of person mentioned by Kohl but sooner or later was thoroughly familiar to McGee. In spite of the difference in national temperament and Kohl's broader experience and greater formal education, they tended to observe the same things because of their common interest in the immigrant.

The Irish had been coming to all the British American colonies since the beginning of the century. During the years of the famine in Ireland the largest and most disastrous immigration had taken place. The wretched people had brought cholera with them and carried it wherever they went. Their graves marked the country from end to end, from Grosse Pointe at Quebec to the newest townships in Canada West.

Montreal suffered the worst visitation as the largest quarantine station was outside its port. In the emergency, civic officials, doctors, priests, nursing sisters and volunteers had laboured courageously, even in many instances sacri-

ficing their lives. The city was aghast at the calamity un-
deservedly laid on its doorstep, and the habitants in the
countryside whispered that it was all a plot of the English
to kill them off with pestilence. But their mutterings were
worse than their behaviour. In the matter of the immigrants
they showed their charity by adopting with effortless good
nature the orphans of the fever victims into their own
large and flourishing families. Time quickly repaired the
effects of the cholera. When McGee came, grass covered
the graves, the orphans had found homes and the widowed
were remarried.

Going between Montreal and Quebec he saw from the
deck of the steamer the numerous villages strung along the
shore, each centred around the spire of the parish church.
In both cities he saw the great stone houses of the religious
orders and the schools, often of venerable age. Lower
Canada was predominantly Catholic and D'Arcy McGee
had a sense of home-coming such as he had felt nowhere
else in America.

Upper Canada he had first visited when he crossed from
Buffalo. There he found a rawer pioneering country, a
population largely Protestant and the mellow note of
Catholicism absent. Nevertheless this country rather than
Lower Canada was the goal of the Irish immigrants. They
did not stay in the cities, of which there were few, but
spread into the villages and the country where they settled
on farms.

In Hamilton, McGee met Bishop Farrell and his coadju-
tor Father Gordon, an Irishman from McGee's own town,
Wexford. They had seen the diocese grow from a mission
and had organized parishes out of the wilderness. Father
Gordon made the parochial rounds on horseback, travelling
from farm to farm in the back townships of Adjala and
Tecumseth where the settlements were largely Irish Catholic. Where there was no chapel he said Mass in the largest
farm-house and bonfires on high points of land notified
Catholic settlers for miles around of his arrival. After Mass

there was a great festal breakfast that in summer overflowed out of doors and became a picnic.

Of course this was in the early days. As soon as possible they had a church, hand-wrought from the bush by community effort—a "bee"—and strictly temperance. The drinking and unseemliness incidental to a barn-raising must have no part in a church raising. Father Gordon made this point clear and the settlers conceded that was as it should be. The log chapels of Adjala and Tecumseth were built with no other stimulant than pious enthusiasm and scalding hot tea.

On various occasions during his travels McGee visited some of these backwoods settlements and learned about them at first hand. He visited Peterborough, about thirty miles inland from Lake Ontario, a pioneer community which for rather obscure reasons seems to have been considered the quintessence of Upper Canadian rural settlements. A few half-pay military and naval officers had come there with their families and attempted to make farms. An occasional young Englishman with an income from home and guns and fishing tackle in his baggage posed as a settler. None of these people were fitted for the backwoods and eventually they found a more congenial life in the towns. But their presence gave a little air of "society" to Peterborough County and was one reason for the settlement being mentioned frequently in diaries and letters.

The backbone of the community was a group of two thousand very poor Irish settlers who came to Canada in the 1820's, through the good offices of a Canadian, Peter Robinson. He had obtained from the Imperial government passage, livestock and supplies for a year and a half for each family. The government of Upper Canada supplied the land. All this added up to unusually generous provision for immigrants. Although not regarded exactly as a model community,—it was hard to be model in the bush and the Irish were notoriously untidy—Peterborough came to be looked on as an experimental colony. This, rather than the half-pay officers, led to its entertaining more than the usual number of distinguished visitors.

It was much stared at and commented on. Some, and they were of the housewifely sort, saw in the uncouth stump-choked farms nothing to justify the expenditure of public money. Peterborough looked, if anything, slightly worse than the usual straggly pioneer settlement. Others, more aware than the critics that no settler established himself in the bush without funds of his own or someone's help, found in this community people who, broken by hopeless poverty in the old land, had transplanted successfully and were thriving wholesomely.

The attitude of the settlers themselves was the best proof of the colony's success. They were grateful—a state of mind that does not always follow upon government help. They had been given a chance to be independent and in a modest, unspectacular way they had clung to it. The name of the settlement, Peterborough was their gesture of thanks to their sponsor.

The hardships of their first years had not depressed them—certainly not in retrospect. "We were far happier then," said one settler who lived to reach prosperity and old age. "No fashion—no style—no doctors to pay, and when Sunday came all you did was to take a walk in the bush. Consolations of religion? We did without them! In the spring we made maple syrup and with that and potatoes and wheat we lived like fighting cocks."

This Spartan and primitive life was not as completely agreeable to the settlers as the old-timer chose to remember it. In 1826 shortly after the settlement was started, the Governor, Sir Peregrine Maitland, visited it and received an address in which the settlers, having offered to fight for the king in defence of the colony, asked for a priest, a schoolmaster and a grist mill. The point of the grist mill was driven home by one of the welcoming committee stepping forward and telling the Governor and his entourage that he had to stay up at night to chew the grain for the children's porridge.

When D'Arcy McGee visited the settlement some thirty years later it possessed these amenities and in addition stores, four churches, a post office, a circulating library and several distilleries. By 1855 a little railway, one of the first in Upper Canada, connected Peterborough with Port Hope on Lake Ontario.

But the stamp of the backwoods remained on the settlement. One reason was that the district, which was not the best for farming, was a fine hunting and fishing country. The good things that nature refused in fields she gave generously in the forest. When the hunter's moon shone through the last rags of leaves in the late fall, the settlers returned from a day in the bush with the stiffening carcases of deer. Their families feasted for days on princely venison, and the branching antlers were hung over the hearth.

Johann Kohl had marvelled to see hunting trophies such as these in a farmer's house. Who but a noble had a right to hunt deer in Europe or Russia? The antlers meant nothing to D'Arcy McGee. No one in the memory of living man had hunted deer in Ireland. But the firm, sweet lake salmon served on the settler's table drew his attention. Poaching? No, the game and fish in this country was for those who could take it. The young gentleman on the other side of the bush with his fine guns and rods sent by his family in England could try his luck with the rest, but they all had the same rights.

His visits among the Irish Canadians affected McGee deeply. Everything he heard and saw was enhanced by his imagination and enthusiasm. Yet it would be wrong to assume that he was deceiving himself. He was a journalist and, thanks to his correspondents, better informed than most about Canadian affairs. He did not imagine he had found a paradise.

He was aware that recent incidents in Lower Canada were not in keeping with the benign scenes that had delighted him there. He knew about the Tory riots that had lasted for days after the burning of the Parliament Building in 1849, and the lectures of the apostate priest, Gazazzi, in Quebec and Montreal, which had caused more riots in which lives were lost. He had only to read the files of his own paper for lurid accounts of these last episodes. He knew that Upper Canada could hardly be called a picture of harmony. George Brown and the *Globe* saw to it that the tone of politics was raucous. The Orangemen had come with the other immigrants from Ireland—Irish, or Scotch Irish as they sometimes preferred to call themselves—who supported the policies of England and a militant form of Protestantism. They transported to Canada the provocative memory of King William and the Battle of the Boyne as piously as Aeneas conveyed his household gods to Latium.

But McGee was not in search of an idyll but of a land where the immigrant might find a decent life. What he saw in Canada was always contrasted with what he had seen in the cities of the United States. There the frontier had moved so far west that immigrants, who had spent their last penny to reach America, were virtually trapped in the slums of the ports where they landed. The official reports on the tenements of New York in the fifties and sixties are nightmares in cold print. The shock of what he had seen with his own eyes was something that McGee never forgot. He came to the sound conclusion that people of rural background adapted themselves more successfully to their new life if they settled in the country. Under all the stories, visits and incidents that made up his Canadian experience were the solid statistics of settlement. In the United States seventy-five per cent of the immigrants stayed in the cities; in Canada seventy-five per cent went on the land.

The *American Celt's* advice to prospective emigrants more and more stressed the advantages of Canada and frankly propagandist poems appeared in its columns dwelling on the charm of country life.

Chapter Seventeen
HAIL AND FAREWELL

Many times D'Arcy McGee had stood at a ship's rail and watched the shore receding or approaching. This time he saw the lights coming on in the dusk off the south coast of Ireland as the ship approached Cork. He recalled, or someone near him recalled, that in the old days hermits had lived along the shores and a passing ship would dip its sails in salute to the holy men. D'Arcy's thoughts began to fall into rhythmic patterns and the facile verses took form ready to be transferred to paper as soon as he went to his cabin. It was a sad poem about the dear, lost days, but the occasion that had inspired it was joyful. McGee was returning to Ireland for a visit.

After Meagher and Mitchell had escaped from Australia, the British government forestalled further flouting of its authority by setting free Smith O'Brien who obviously was the next to be rescued. It then wrote the whole affair of 1848 off the books by granting a general amnesty to everyone concerned. O'Brien, Dillon and Pat Smythe returned to Ireland. The others remained where they were, contenting themselves with a visit when they could afford it.

McGee's opportunity came when he was invited to lecture to certain young men's societies on the question of emigration. In this way some of his expenses were met. While keeping his lecture engagements, he also had time for a holiday. It was early spring, the Irish air damp and tender, the country poignantly green. He went to see his father at Wexford, and visited the graves of his mother and sisters near his old home. While he was in Cork he had visited the grave of Gerald Griffin, an Irish writer of bril-

134

liant achievement who had turned from literary ambitions to enter a religious order. At one time, when the Dublin *Nation* was at its height, McGee had hoped to bring out a new edition of Griffin's works. Now, he marked the visit to the grave with a poem, taking great pains to discipline his usually too copious verse into the more restrained form of a monody.

He might have lingered in the south of Ireland, communing with the dead and enjoying life half in this world, half in the next, had not Dublin lured him and the promise of a visit with Duffy.

Even here McGee found the past and post-mortems awaiting him. Duffy was eager to tell him all that had happened since he had gone to America, filling in the gaps left by their letters. After he came out of prison, Duffy had drawn up a programme to form an independent Irish party in Parliament and to build up the Tenant Right League. With this programme he had attempted to unite the north and south and to secure the support of the rural clergy who were in close touch with the largest section of the population. After the first encouraging response this support was not forthcoming. Duffy blamed the papal legate, Dr. Cullen, the Archbishop of Armagh, an Irishman educated in Rome who, in Duffy's opinion, knew as little of Irish ways and politics as a foreigner. He believed Duffy to be an extremist like John Mitchel and used his great influence against him.

McGee from his own experience could sympathize with his friend. He too had had trouble with the ecclesiastical authorities and he too had been identified with the radicalism of Mitchel.

When the whole course of Young Ireland after Davis's death is summed up, Mitchel is seen as the guiding spirit, not the hesitant Smith O'Brien to whom Duffy had given the leadership. Mitchel was the bright but evil genius of the movement. This was something that Duffy, faithful to the memory of Thomas Davis, would never admit. But if ever he realized that Mitchel as his friend had done his cause more harm than as his enemy, it must have been in the course of his conversations with McGee at this time.

He told the story of his disappointments and failure for the most part calmly and with detachment. He had determined to withdraw from Parliament and from Irish public life. Duffy was planning to emigrate with his family to Australia. His position as editor of the Dublin *Nation* and his various imprisonments and trials had made him a public figure for years. This decision to leave the country caused something like consternation as it became known.

So Gavan Duffy despaired of Ireland, did he?

To which Duffy replied: No, he did not despair of Ireland but only of his ability to serve her usefully.

It seemed like talking around the question, but Duffy meant it quite simply and sadly. He had spent his small inheritance in the Irish cause; he had impaired his health and broken his heart, although he himself would never have put it in just those words. At thirty-nine, neither old nor young, he felt he owed something to himself and his family. He had completed his law studies at an earlier period and, although he had never practised law, he could fall back on this qualification to start a new life in Australia.

McGee, an emigrant too, could hardly argue with Duffy's determination, however much he might be taken aback. He did not even feel justified in speaking for America against the choice of Australia. In his lectures to the prospective emigrants he had advised them if they *must* emigrate to avoid the cities and go on the land, and also to go to Canada rather than to the United States. But Duffy was an emigrant of a different type. His experience and inclination would almost certainly involve him in the public life of whatever country he moved to. McGee, discouraged with the trend of affairs in the United States at this time, could not conceal his attitude from anyone he talked to freely. He was discouraged by the frank materialism, the obsession with making money, more specifically he was disgusted with the Know-Nothing Party which in 1855 was at the peak of its strength and following policies close to persecution. And always, in the background, was the danger of civil war. The general public gave no thought to this possibility. Ominously, only the well-informed feared that the break between the North and South would come. It was impossible to foresee what might be the results of an upheaval such as this in the new, undisciplined society. It is significant that, although McGee had been publishing a newspaper in the United States for nearly seven years, he had neither joined a political party nor taken out citizenship papers.

The grave and disturbing topics they discussed did not prevent Duffy and McGee from enjoying each other's company. The nine years' difference in their ages seemed less than it once had, and the older McGee was more presentable than the boy whom Duffy, just a little embarrassed, had taken one morning ten years before to meet Thomas Davis.

True, no tailor McGee could afford could do much about changing his short stature and stooped shoulders into a figure of fashion. But more than the mere matter of clothes, the prestige of his recent successful lectures gave him poise and maturity. His homely appearance had an arresting quality. Pomade could not keep his thick black hair in order for long and usually it stood up fiercely like a black cock's crest. He wore a fringe of beard reaching from ear to ear as though to round off or balance the unruly mop of hair on top, or perhaps add dignity when he still might be thought too young for the influence he was attempting to exert. An age less devoted to classic regularity of feature than the Victorians might have found McGee's ill-assorted features attractive—the wide forehead and fine, dark eyes, offset by the short blunt nose and the thin mobile mouth with an out-thrust lower lip. The poet and scholar were in that face and the aspiring plebeian also.

Duffy took him to dinner parties where his wit flashed out bright and ringing as a new minted coin. Compared with McGee's repartee, Duffy noted that the efforts of some of the practised raconteurs and diners-out sounded studied and a little dull. In this way and with plentiful conversation McGee passed the time of his visit. He was not averse to prolonging it since it was doubtful whether he and Duffy would ever meet again.

Chapter Eighteen
THE FATE OF THE IMMIGRANTS

ALTHOUGH most of McGee's American experience was acquired in the cities of the New England states, he was alert to the importance of the frontier in American life and the opportunities it offered to the settler. The term "frontier" suggests a line of settlements facing the wilderness. Actually in the 1850's it was a condition of life found anywhere on the continent west of the Mississippi and north of the Great Lakes. The frontier was huge and indefinite. It was referred to in a general way as "going west". For some the lure of the horizon was so great that they never settled anywhere but kept "going west" until the last journey over the last horizon took them west in a figurative and final sense. But most of those who went west settled on the land and established communities. The real frontiersman was not the adventurer with a rifle, but the farmer with a rifle and a plough.

McGee came to the conclusion that the frontier was the proper place for the immigrant. He recommended Canada because reasonably close to the ports of debarkation was the cheap, uncleared land that immigrants in the United States had to go hundreds of miles to reach. This interest in Canada on the part of an editor of an American paper and one, moreover, who freely criticized conditions in the United States, left McGee open to misunderstanding. His enemies, voluble journalists for the most part, misunderstood and misinterpreted him with the greatest malice. When criticism became too oppressive he answered in defiant editorials.

"We will serve the Irish in America only as a free man,

as one free to speak the truth, pleasant or bitter, free to suggest, blame, to retract, to correct, defend or denounce. Such a service, honourable to the people and glorious though exhausting to ourselves, we chose in early youth and would fain hope to combat in till the very last."

To understand his American career it is necessary to see it as a whole, free from the noise and confusion of controversy in which he worked. When he first came to America at the age of seventeen, he had accepted the noble words of the Founding Fathers and the sentiments of the patriotic songs quite literally and with all the intensity of his nature. The Know-Nothing Party soon disillusioned him—not utterly, but sufficiently to cause his attitude toward the country of his exile to change from affection to cool objectivity.

This did not mean that he had turned against it. He supported immigration to the new western states as heartily as to Canada. Later, when the Civil War began and there was secret rejoicing in many quarters because the dangerous American experiment seemed to be crumbling, McGee, as will be seen, deplored this attitude. But he personally preferred the political institutions of Britain to those of the American Republic, and one of his most reassuring discoveries about Canada was that these gnarled and hoary institutions had been transplanted successfully and were showing signs of new life and growth. He was doubtful about constitutions "fabricated in one's study", and he held that "all states have natural constitutions which grow up with them and are not made to order". He was at some pains, however, to make clear that he believed republican and democratic institutions the right ones for the United States and that, even though the Republic's constitution was a committee-made, paper one, the Founders had produced something of permanence.

The *American Celt* which aroused indignation by advancing these opinions was a respectable-looking weekly which had been enlarged to eight pages and improved in format and typography when McGee moved it from Buffalo

to New York. The front page was taken up with a sentimental novel of Irish-Victorian flavour, continued from issue
to issue. Then followed news from Ireland, England and
any part of Europe where something of note was happening. All this news was taken from the *Celt's* exchanges and
was several weeks old by the time it reached the readers,
but even so they were kept reasonably well informed about
the world at large. Correspondents from Canada contri-
buted special articles on the political history of that country.
Advertising (at reasonable rates, but cash down) was re-
legated to the back pages. Tiny scraps of news tucked in
here and there gave a dash of the pathetic or shocking. A
young lady (no name) in Louisville, while dressing for a
ball, had dropped dead. In New Orleans a German immigrant girl (no name), finding she had been betrayed,
had committed suicide. Poetry served to elevate the feelings. All the features of a modern newspaper were present
with varying emphasis, except sports and the comics. The
topics of American life most vitally interesting to the readers
were dealt with in the editorials.

The *Celt* claimed 10,000 regular subscribers apart from
the advertisers and general sales. At the rate of $2.50 a
subscription this promised a gross income of at least $25,000.
However, the contention that the Irish American, in spite of
having more money, was less prompt than the Old Country
man in paying his debts, had some justification. As many
as a third of the listed subscribers were sometimes in arrears
at the end of the year, and the editor had to resort to
threats of cutting off their papers or publishing their names
for all to read.

After all the expenses of publication, distribution and
incidental fees to correspondents and contributors had been
paid, four people had to make a living from what remained.
By 1854 McGee had on his staff two associate editors and
his brother, James, as a travelling agent. It is difficult at this
point of time to know what kind of a living they made from
the *Celt*. It is possible that they may have been uncertain
about the matter themselves. Certainly, McGee, who had

his lecture engagements as well as the *Celt* as a source of income, never became rich.

All this made up the exhausting side of journalism. The glorious aspect which sustained them in their labours was the cause they served—the cause of the immigrants. McGee acted on their behalf vigorously and constantly. He promoted the night schools in a more favourable atmosphere than formerly as a result of a more or less tacit reconciliation with Bishop Hughes. In his most brilliant and congenial effort he had given the immigrants a claim to the past as well as the future in his lectures on the Catholic History of North America. He now began an audacious campaign to clear the slums by inducing the Irish to go west into the new states beyond the Mississippi, or north into Upper Canada.

By 1856 the *Celt* had exhorted and persuaded to such purpose that a loose organization, called the Irish Emigration Aid, came into existence on both sides of the border. In February, eighty delegates from this organization were sent to a convention at Buffalo to discuss the possibility of an Irish settlement.

Establishing new communities was not an unusual activity in North America so that the delegates had many precedents to guide them. These ranged from communities based on extreme social and religious theories like New Harmony, Indiana, and the Mormons in Utah, to conservative undertakings like the government-aided Peterborough colony and settlements sponsored by the Canada Company in the Huron district. The Buffalo Convention favoured the more conservative types.

McGee submitted a plan in broad outline for a joint stock company to purchase a tract of land in Illinois or Missouri sufficient for the settlement of 200,000 people. Settlers without private capital were to be furnished with loans repayable on easy terms. The stock company was to be responsible for providing each settlement with a school and a church.

The Convention approved the plan, but the catch was

to induce enough investors to finance the settlement. The finance committee, appointed to attend to this, proved ineffective. At this point the project broke down.

The campaign carried on by the *Celt* was not without results. The existence of the frontier was brought to the attention of immigrants who still had to decide where to settle. Influenced by McGee's editorials, one hundred families with enough money to finance themselves moved into Canada West and bought farms; an undetermined number of others went homesteading in Illinois. But the shift of destitute immigrants from city to farm did not take place. The volatile Irish preferred the hazards of city life to McGee's advice to "pluck the primal forests up and sow their sites with corn". Instead, they became cab drivers and policemen. Their zeal in fire-fighting created for them permanent jobs on what had started out as volunteer fire brigades. If they were literate they usually had something to do with newspapers.

The more astute went into the liquor trade as tavern and grog shop proprietors; or acted as agents and middlemen for the exploitation of their simpler countrymen. They developed a lamentable talent for petty, scheming ward politics and the manipulation of votes.

The simple and humble became servants in hotels and boarding-houses where their country-bred decency compensated for the clumsiness of their services. McGee deplored their lack of "cleanliness, sobriety, caution, perseverance and the other minor morals", but went on to point out that they were endowed with rarer qualities, "spontaneity, delicate discrimination and moral enthusiasm". Their various adaptations to their new environment were often rapid and amazing. The mistress, who trusted her lace curtains and accumulated bric-a-brac to the Irish hired girl who had never known anything but a dirt floor and a thatched roof, might, in a few months, observe her peasant wench stepping out on Sunday rustling a silk petticoat and unfurling a frilled parasol with more airs than the lady herself. A people too quick, too imaginative. No wonder McGee believed they needed steadying influences.

His crusade had failed. The slums remained clogged with human wastage. The Irish, undertaking a change more drastic than any experienced by former emigrants, passed abruptly from primitive agriculture to an advanced urban industrial society. The loss, body and soul, was beyond reckoning. Most people preferred not to think of it; but those who did were agreed that the family of rural background did better when transferred to a rural community. Even if the children of the second generation responded to the pull of the cities, the transition to American urban life was less extreme for them than it would have been for the generation fresh from the old land.

> In the valleys of New England,
>   Are you happy, we would know?
> Are you welcome, are you trusted?
>   Are you not?—Then RISE AND GO!
>
> Ye are toiling, toiling ever,
>   Toss'd like sea-waves to and fro;
> Up at sunrise, up at sunset,
>   Still detested—RISE AND GO!
>
> As ye act, or as ye falter,
>   We will deem ye men or no;
> For the homestead, for the altar,
>   Take advice—ARISE AND GO!

So wrote D'Arcy at the height of the *Celt's* campaign. After the failure of the Buffalo Convention he was in a mood to follow his own advice. Several delegates from Montreal called on him at the *Celt's* office in New York. They had certain suggestions which they presented in the course of a long conversation. McGee had made a favourable impression on his audiences when he lectured in Canada and on his part had formed a very good opinion of them. He therefore listened with close attention to the proposals made to him by the gentlemen from Montreal.

Part Three

LAND OF MY ADOPTION

Chapter Nineteen

MONTREAL

THE McGEES were moving to Canada. There had been an impermanence about their several homes in America. Could they expect something better from this new move? D'Arcy seemed to think so. He left for Montreal to start a newspaper in the spring of 1857. The drift of talent from Canada to the United States has always been considerable. D'Arcy McGee's supporters in Montreal had succeeded this time in reversing the trend by inducing the most outstanding of Irish American editors to transfer his activities to Canada. Not only was financial support forthcoming, but more than a hint given that a political career for McGee was in prospect.

He had written his farewell editorial in the *Celt* the previous Easter week and sold his share in the paper before leaving New York. That summer he spent in Montreal setting up another paper, the *New Era*. It was a tri-weekly and, although it proved short-lived, was in some respects his most ambitious journalistic attempt. With McGee was associated Michael Hickey, an Ottawa Valley lumberman, co-founder with John Egan of the village of Eganville, where he had supervised the building of saw and grist mills. During a depression in the lumber trade he turned to journalism, an interest closer to his heart. He was easily persuaded to give up a small paper he had started in Ottawa to go into partnership with D'Arcy McGee. Here was a happy combination of McGee's wide journalistic experience with a partner of sound business background and a Canadian into the bargain. The prospects for a permanent and successful career in Canada were so good that in the fall McGee sent for Mary to join him.

The family had remained in Brooklyn partly to avoid travel in the summer which was the fever season, and also because Mrs. McGee was expecting another child.

The years in America had not been kind to Mary. Little Irish-born Martha Dorcas, the "blue-eyed, prattling daughter" of D'Arcy poems, had died at the age of four. Two other children had also died in babyhood, a daughter, Rose, and the son whom they had named splendidly Thomas Patrick Bede. In 1857, of the four children Mary had borne her husband, only one, Euphrasia, survived. The loss of their children was a grief they shared, as several plaintive poems testify, but it was felt by Mary in its most intimate sense. She nursed the children during their illnesses and faced the loneliness of the house after they were gone. The baby born in August, 1857, was their last child. They called her Agnes Clara and she thrived reassuringly. With her two children, Mary was probably well content to leave the sad memories of her first years in America and join her husband in his Canadian venture.

It is difficult to say precisely who besides D'Arcy, Mary and their two daughters made up the McGee family at the time of its removal to Montreal. James apparently felt sufficiently well launched to remain on his own in the United States. John McGee came from Ireland to join them about this period. He was one of the second family, a half-brother, although D'Arcy always referred to him simply as "my brother". Mary's mother, Mrs. Caffrey, also lived with them in Montreal. Certain sisters or half-sisters are vaguely mentioned as belonging to the household from time to time. The elder member of an Irish family in America could expect such visits and additions, especially if he was established as an editor, a well-known lecturer and an author. Even granting his considerable prestige, McGee was probably not as prosperous as the family in Ireland imagined. But he had a strong family feeling and did his best for all of them.

MONTREAL

The road between New York and Montreal was one of the most travelled in North America. Railroads were still used largely for portaging between the water-ways so that the journey was made by a series of steamboats, trains and stage coaches. There was singularly little complaint about this disjointed way of travelling; the variety of locomotion was accepted as a sign of progress. An early type of baggage express operated along this route. Travellers from Europe and England, who were accustomed to spending most of their journey collecting and distributing their baggage about them, felt dispossessed and lost when it was whisked away and they were left with a cardboard receipt as a flimsy substitute. But when it was restored to them intact at the other end, their confidence was secured and they were loud in praise of the system.

Conditions of travel in America were in many respects superior to those on the other side of the Atlantic, especially in the matter of handling crowds. But the lack of privacy was a great trial to the fastidious. On steamboats the bunks might be comfortable and the sheets fresh and spotless, but the passengers shared common dormitories. In the dining-rooms of hotels and ships the lavish meals, deftly served and properly supplemented with damask, silver and glass were eaten at long tables accommodating the maximum number of guests. One was even expected to pass one's leisure time in the ornate public parlours and salons with everyone else. The private rooms of even the best hotels were mere sleeping cells and room service was practically unknown. The American mode of travel was quite acceptable to the not-too-exacting McGees. They travelled for the practical and ancient purpose of getting from one place to another and not from the new-fangled tourist motive of amusement. They expected inconveniences and were well pleased with whatever luxuries and comforts came their way.

Proceeding by boat up the Hudson as far as Albany they passed the night at one of the city's many flourishing hotels. At a disconcertingly early hour they took a stage

149

coach to Lake Champlain where they embarked on a
steamer, a trim little ship without the splendours of the
Hudson River boat, but nevertheless very comfortable and
so fresh with paint and polish that it seemed the very origin
of the word shipshape.

Then followed the pleasantest and most leisurely part
of the journey. Even the preoccupied mother of two
children would have time to sit quietly in a sheltered spot
on deck and watch the scenery. For one startled home-sick
moment the noble contours of the Adirondacks, the curving
line of shore and water, might have reminded the Irish-
woman of the Old Country, but only for a moment. The
barbaric colours of these autumn hills had little kinship with
the muted blues and purples of Wicklow or the sharp,
sparkling blue of sky and lake with the quiet black bog
water.

The early fall evening was setting in when the steamer
reached the border at Point Rouse. After the merest token
inspection by the customs official the McGees transferred to
a train covering the portage between Lake Champlain and
La Prairie on the St. Lawrence. The little wood-burning
engine rattled and chugged through the deepening twilight,
a great trail of sparks streaming from the flaring stack. The
trimly painted doll-like dwellings of New England had been
left behind and instead the travellers saw the solid stone
houses of the seigneurs and habitants, with high steep roofs
and overhanging eaves; houses with deep foundations,
looking as much a part of the landscape as if they had grown
there. The travellers from the United States now heard
French spoken by the local passengers and at the stations
they saw the country people, some wearing the typical
dangling woollen tuque, greeting each other exuberantly.
Could this half-foreign country ever be their home? Mary
McGee may have wondered.

Another stop, another change, this time to a ferry crossing the St. Lawrence to the island of Montreal. Once more
into a stage coach and this was the last lap of their journey.
It was night now. Mr. Kohl, that indefatigable traveller,

when he had arrived at this point in his journey, had hung over the rail of the ferry and craned his neck out the window of the coach to catch a glimpse of the distant city, silvery and dreamlike with the moonlight on its tin-covered roofs. But the weary McGees, like most travellers arriving by night, probably waited for another day to form their impressions. At one point the coach took on a smoother motion. This and the sight of houses and gas lamps at regular intervals informed them that they were in the city streets. Presently they were alighting once more and D'Arcy was telling them that they had arrived; they were home.

It was unfortunate that travellers should enter Montreal at night as the city was so situated as to offer itself dramatically to view from several directions. It was built facing the river and by the fifties was already extending upward to a series of natural terraces which finally rose abruptly to a mountain of no great height, flanked by a twin mountain at that time still in the country. The present metropolis of Montreal has grown round both Mount Royal and Westmount and extends across the island to Rivière des Prairies. But in the McGees' time the city was contained between Mount Royal and the St. Lawrence.

Then as now the mountain was a pleasant place for drives, rides and rambles and the best spot from which to contemplate the scenery. The old city had not yet been submerged in the shadows of skyscraper office buildings. The strong square towers of the Parish Church of Notre Dame dominated the scene, with the slender spires of St. Patrick's and Christ's Church as graceful variants.

It is the nature of a city to grow and extend itself in layers, encircling and penetrating the original city which remains as a core and exists here and there in bits that have survived change. A city in time becomes a succession of cities, like ninefold Troy discovered by the archaeologists. Montreal was experiencing a period of growth in the fifties and sixties. New buildings were going up, banks, business houses and rows or terraces of dwellings.

But the old city was well built and not easily obliterated. The early Montrealers had used stone even as far back as the Indian wars, protecting the town with stone ramparts in place of the usual palisades of stakes. They built Norman fashion and their gabled houses and deep-walled hospitals and convents had massive dignity.

The new city fortunately looked to the past rather than to the bad taste of the later nineteenth century for architectural inspiration. True, Molson's Bank, under construction in the neighbourhood of Notre Dame was hideously large and ornamental, but the new houses on the upper levels of the city had an agreeable classical plainness, a nice proportion and balance in the arrangement of doors and windows so that the symmetry of the whole afforded joy and refreshment to the eye. The McGees had their first home in Montreal on St. Antoine Street, at that time considered very much in the suburbs. In the older part of the city there was no space between the house and the sidewalk, while on St. Antoine Street there were little gardens in front.

Montreal had always been a city. It had been founded as the mission station of Ville Marie with a church, a hospital and a school dedicated to Our Lady and the greater glory of God. But even the austere intentions of seventeenth-century religious leaders could not prevent a spot so suitable for all purposes attracting the types of people who make a city—the traders and adventurers, the artisans, the soldiers, the lawyers and officials of government, even the farmers, who profiting by the island's exceptional fertility, supplied the city markets.

The completely urban character of Montreal gave it tolerance and a capacity for accommodating diverse elements which was all to the good. After the middle of the eighteenth century, French and English had to live together in the city and make shift at getting on under circumstances that were not always harmonious, as the English inclined to arrogance and the French were intractable. The Scots added a particular quality of their own. They were mostly business men, hard-working and hard-headed, very able in the management of people. In their shipping and fur-trading enterprises they employed numbers of French Canadians with whom they got on very well. Historic connections existed between the French and Scottish people. Old, tenuous and half-forgotten as they were they still exerted a subtle influence and made the Scots in a measure a lubricant easing the relations between the two language groups.

But these larger issues were not the daily life of the Montrealers. That was more likely to be set to the tune of the regimental band that played nightly in Barracks Square while people strolled in twos and threes in and out the old grey streets; or to move in winter with the glinting feet and swooping curves of the skaters circling around the rink while the still obliging military band, in greatcoats, puffed and tootled energetically against the cold; or to jostle at all seasons in homely fellowship at the Bonsecours Market where everyone was to be seen at one time or another and the ladies, defying fashion, carried enormous muffs in which they stowed away unbelievable quantities of provisions.

The constant presence of the religious orders had always indirectly encouraged a cosmopolitan appearance in Montreal crowds. Where such unusual costumes as those of the nuns and the clergy were freely accepted, many individualistic people tended to dress in character. In the fifties the unassimilated Scot clung to his tam and plaid; the habitant, bringing in his eggs and chickens to sell at ten cents a dozen and twenty-five cents a brace, still wore his woollen tuque and girded his waist with a woven sash; the raftsmen in town from a lumber drive down the Ottawa flaunted their loud-checked shirts; and liberally sprinkled through the market crowd were the poor, stockingless, shabby Irish, the hardy survivors of the famine and the fever ships.

On first thought it might seem dangerous to add these immigrants to the city's uneasy balance of forces, but Irish turbulence did not prevent them from finding, like all the others, their place in the life of the city. As one Irishman put it: "We feel at home here. There is no city in the States in which we occupy a more favourable position. We are not foreigners here as we are sometimes considered elsewhere."

This proved to be very largely D'Arcy McGee's feeling. It was a relief to belong to an Irish community that was not overwhelmingly composed of the poorest, most battered and shifting of the working-class. There were people here with whom he could form friendships, professional and literary people. There were, for instance, the Sadliers; James, a publisher who had printed some of McGee's lectures, and his wife Mary Ann, a novelist, one of those remarkable Victorians who succeeded in coupling a prolific literary output with a sizable family (Mrs. Sadlier had six children). She was also a lively conversationist and D'Arcy admired her greatly. The two families were soon on most neighbourly terms.

All this does not mean that people like these were not to be found among the Irish of the United States and in greater number; but in Montreal the famine immigration had not come in the avalanche that had descended on the American seaports and it scattered more quickly to the new settlements of Upper Canada. As a result the balance of social classes among the earlier Irish immigrants had not been destroyed.

D'Arcy McGee's constant and sincere interest in the immigrant was not strictly democratic and not at all socialistic. In the American cities he had glimpsed the beginning of the new masses, the city proletariat for which Karl Marx was industriously writing a philosophy, and he had found it monstrous. There is no evidence that he knew anything of the still obscure Marxian doctrines of the classless society. He preferred to regard the immigrant as a person in a social class rather than as a unit in the mass. In coming to Canada McGee may have been only retreating before the advance of industrialism which would in time overtake that country also. On the other hand, he believed that in Canada there was a better chance to preserve the values especially of family life and traditional piety that industrial democracy was threatening to destroy.

The prospect of a public career implied by the Montreal delegates at the time of the Buffalo Convention was now made good. The Irish in Montreal had grown to one-third of the population. It was not unreasonable that they should consider running a candidate for one of the three seats allotted to Montreal in Parliament. Their active St. Patrick's Society was well equipped for electioneering. D'Arcy McGee shared their aspirations, but was not involved in their local jealousies. While each officer of the Society was prevented by a sense of equal merit from yielding a position of special honour to another, all were willing to stand aside in favour of the newcomer. In the fall of 1857 McGee was chosen unanimously by the St. Patrick's Society as its candidate in the forthcoming election. The Society advanced the interests of its man so energetically that McGee not only won his seat in Parliament, but polled the largest number of votes in the city of Montreal—a heady victory for his supporters and something of a shock to political veterans who found their calculations thrown out by the Irish vote. After having for years lived on the journalistic fringe of public life, D'Arcy McGee now became directly active in politics.

Chapter Twenty
POLITICS AS SPORT

Several members from Lower Canada stood on the newly built station platform of the recently completed Grand Trunk Railway and denounced the weather in voluble French. Toronto was having a February thaw; rain melted the snow and stirred up the mud; clammy mist blurred the lake to an indeterminate grey.

The Quebecois, weighed down by mountainous bearskin coats and sealskin caps designed to look opulent in the biting zero weather of their native city, were at a loss to understand the unnatural climate of Upper Canada. It only proved the folly of allowing Parliament to meet in such an unwholesome part of the country. They continued to grumble until a more suitably clad friend joined them and rallied them into a better humour.

Since the burning of the Parliament building in 1849, Parliament had met alternately in Quebec and Toronto. This was a temporary arrangement that satisfied no one and the question of a permanent capital for the united Canadas was of public concern. Quebec, Montreal, Kingston and Toronto all claimed the honour. Each at one time or another had been a seat of government, each felt it had some especially good ground for its claims.

A fifth town also had forced its way into the competition. This was Bytown on the Ottawa. Whatever the four original claimants thought of each other's qualifications, they agreed that Bytown was quite unacceptable. It was a new and unimportant place. No one went there but military engineers; no one lived there but lumberjacks. Furthermore, the place had a disorderly reputation, the lumber trade being infested with Irishmen and Yankees. Indeed, only people like the Yankees would have the effrontery to enter the place into competition with the noble cities of the St. Lawrence and Great Lakes.

Ignoring all objections, Bytown went ahead with its plans. It had itself incorporated as a city and changed its name to Ottawa, more suitable for the capital of a potentially great country. If enterprising Yankees were pushing the claims of the new city they were at least loyal Yankees. One of the arguments they advanced was that the place was far safer from attack by the United States than the other Canadian cities. The Royal Engineers had already started certain military installations in Ottawa for that very reason. Also its position on the Ottawa River made it almost as much a part of Canada East as of Canada West. Finally, when four cities contended with equal urgency for the honour was it not simpler to chose a fifth? This last argument carried some weight with the leader of the Conservative government, John A. Macdonald.

He was further inspired to place the choice in the hands of the Queen. Carried through the proper diplomatic channels the matter was brought to the royal attention; and after due consideration Her Majesty was pleased to choose Ottawa as the capital of the united provinces of Canada.

This choice was known to the members of Parliament when they assembled in February. Most of them were furious except, of course, the members from the Ottawa valley. The Queen was not blamed. It was most unlikely that Her Majesty had ever heard of Bytown-now-called-Ottawa. Clearly she had received advice on the matter from the Canadian Prime Minister, John A. Macdonald. He liked to take the easiest way out of a difficulty.

This was one of the subjects agitating the Parliament to which McGee came as a new member in the winter of 1858. The other questions before the House were also somewhat parochial. McGee had received instructions from his constituents as to what stand he was to take on each of them. He was to support the separate schools, oppose the Orange

Order and have nothing to do with the electoral principle of representation by population, commonly called "Rep. by Pop."

"Fail in this," warned the *True Witness,* an Irish Catholic Montreal paper, "falter for one moment in your allegiance to the great and holy cause which we have chosen you to advocate and you will find us as prompt to pull you down as we have been to raise you up . . . No excuse will be accepted, and no pardon or indulgence extended for the slightest deviation from the paths of rectitude."

In spite of this threat, which was all the more ominous in that he was not a man to accept dictation and was certain sooner or later to "deviate from the paths of rectitude", McGee started out on his parliamentary career confidently. When he took his place in the House of Assembly he could reflect on how far he had come since his first experience in the British House of Commons. Then he had been only a reporter, now he was one of the legislators.

In this Canadian Parliament the setting was familiar. There was the same oblong room; the Speaker's chair on a dais; the mace, the symbol of office on the table before it; the seats of the government party on the right and those of the opposition on the left. A gallery for the public and the press extended around three sides of the House. The one hundred and thirty-three members were less than a third of the number in the British House, but the Canadian legislators had made better provision for their own comfort. The floor, padded and carpeted from corner to corner, absorbed all incidental noise. Boys in Eton suits acted as messengers, lolling alertly on the steps of the Speaker's dais, ready at a nod or the snap of the fingers to perform small services. The traditional benches of the British House of Commons took the form in Canada of a cushioned chair and a desk for each member.

McGee had been elected as an Independent, but as the men with whom he had joined forces during the elections were of the Reform party he sat with them in the opposition. While the session was getting under way, he and other new members had an opportunity to observe their fellow legislators.

On the government side of the house with the members of his Cabinet about him sat John A. Macdonald, Attorney-General for Canada West, leader of the Conservative party and head of the government. He was of medium height, a loose-jointed man with a great Scotch nose and a great deal of dark curling hair which he wore rather long. He was supposed to resemble Disraeli, perhaps because of his great nose and the curls, or perhaps by reason of their common reputation as schemers. D'Arcy McGee considered the possibility of a resemblance until he heard Macdonald speak. The flat, nasal voice and gauche mannerisms of the colonial statesman completely drove from his mind the image of the suave and subtle English Jew.

Sitting beside Macdonald and working very closely with him at every point was the leading French-Canadian Conservative George Etienne Cartier. He controlled a solid block of French-Canadian votes in the House and his support made it possible for Macdonald to remain in office. Macdonald's alliance with Cartier had been, up to this time, the most foresighted move of his career.

The members who sat to the left of the Speaker were almost as numerous but less united than the government party. The largest group was that section of the Reform party nicknamed the "Grits", who rallied around George Brown, the formidable editor of the Toronto *Globe*. He was a giant of a man, six foot two and built in proportion, with an austerely handsome and humourless face. As an editor he was very influential in Upper Canada; as a parliamentarian he was inexperienced and easily outmanoeuvred by the more skilful Conservatives. But such was his arrogance that he dared to tell Parliament that his paper could make or break any government in Canada. He was one of the few men who could put John A. into a temper. A brisk and affable young lawyer, Oliver Mowat, new to the House that session, acted as Brown's second in delicate situations, undertaking to mitigate his chief's tactlessness.

Like the Conservatives the opposition also had a Canada West and Canada East combination, although less effective. George Brown had in uneasy alliance a French Canadian, Antoine Aimé Dorion, who had been elected with McGee as one of the three members for Montreal. His heavy-lidded eyes, sallow complexion and regular, clear-cut features made him more Latin in appearance than most of his compatriots who were Norman and Breton types, and suggested physical sluggishness and intellectual activity. He had advanced ideas on democracy and the value of making all public offices elective and was reputed to be anti-clerical. But he was a philosophical radical rather than what at a later date would be called an activist. By temperament and intellect he was better suited to the company of his equals than to the coarse encounters of popular politics. His courteous manner, his mastery of both French and English were in marked contrast to Cartier, his compatriot on the other side of the House, a little man of fierce energy whose fluent English was strongly flavoured in idiom and accent by his Gallic origin. But even greater was the contrast between Dorion and George Brown, who had very few intellectual interests—in spite of owning a newspaper—and no manners to speak of.

Another member of the House who briefly attracted McGee's attention was William Lyon Mackenzie, who had led the Rebellion of 1837 in Upper Canada. At sixty he seemed of venerable age in an assembly of men who were for the most part in their early forties or even, like McGee, in their early thirties. McGee felt he ought to pay some graceful compliment to Mackenzie when he made his first speech, even though the tide of public affairs had swept on, leaving the old rebel in a backwater. There he sat at his desk taking little part in the debates but often working on his *Weekly Message*, a paper which he brought out at irregular intervals. The habits of a lifetime had made him an inveterate journalist. His desk was crammed with newspapers and littered with shears and paste pots as he worked over his clippings. His shoes, which he removed for greater comfort, stood on the floor by his desk. When he did break into speech it was sudden like a thunderbolt or cryptic like the warning of a prophet.

McGee had had time to look over his new associates. Then early in March it was their turn to sit back in their chairs and look him over. It was the occasion of his maiden speech. He had come among them with a curiously varied record which lent itself to distortion. He had been a rebel. He had been called an apostate by the Bishop of New York and a traitor by some of his Young Ireland companions. After residing less than a year in Canada he had been swept into Parliament on a tidal wave of Montreal Irish votes.

The wave of Irish enthusiasm which had borne him to triumph, had washed under George Etienne Cartier, who had previously sat in Parliament as one of the members for Montreal. Cartier's party, which could not afford to lose him, had arranged for his nomination for the County of Verchères where he was elected by a narrow majority of thirty votes. The success of the "Irish adventurer" at his expense had unpleasantly jolted Cartier's vanity. McGee did not lessen the irritation when, in a badgering mood—he hated being called an adventurer—he pretended not to remember the place Cartier represented, but referred to him with well-simulated vagueness as the "honourable member from some county constituency".

Besides the showy triumph of his first election, McGee had more permanent qualifications with which to impress Parliament. He was a poet of some standing. It is difficult at this date to explain precisely the kind of prestige that this conferred because in the mid-nineteenth century poetry was still regarded, even in popular estimation, as the supreme form of literature and the poet as much superior to any other kind of writer. More than one of his contemporaries in Parliament had attempted to mount the winged horse themselves and had hidden away in their desks and among their private papers poetic efforts which commendable prudence forbade the light of day.

McGee also had a reputation as an orator who could

captivate any audience. Those who had heard him said that one forgot he was a homely little man in listening to him and watching his face, expressive and mobile as an actor's.

On the whole the members of the Canadian House of Assembly did not pretend to oratory, satisfied that honest manliness made up for this deficiency. But they were quite prepared to appreciate eloquence in someone else. Their experience in making and listening to indifferently good and bad speeches qualified them as fairly competent judges. Therefore when D'Arcy McGee, after being formally presented to the House, arose to address it for the first time they watched him with guarded curiosity.

He stood quietly and used his hands very little. This alone was noteworthy in an assembly where some awkward and unconscious mannerism marred the delivery of nearly every member. Since a sonorous voice was greatly admired they were a little surprised that McGee's voice was higher and lighter than they had expected. But it was expressive and singularly clear, capable of reaching a much larger audience than the group he was addressing. Before he had spoken long they had ceased to listen critically. He had won them and they were attending to what he said.

He spoke on the Address to the Throne, the opening speech in which Macdonald had set out the government's policy for the coming session. This he criticized in a general way as not coming to grips with the real problems of the country. He then touched on some incidental matters that when read now are only faintly amusing, but which the House found highly diverting—a reference to a member of the government who was not present because he was still about the country seeking election. ("Hear, hear", from the opposition.) It seemed he had presented some of the electors with Bibles. McGee expanded this bit of news. (Laughter.) He gave it a little twist and presented it from a new angle. (More laughter.) He added a few more touches, (loud laughter), and finished off with a mock serious moral. (Both sides of the House rocked with laughter and the Speaker had to request the Sergeant-at-Arms to restore order in the galleries.)

Nevertheless, when the newspapers commented editorially on the speech they stressed its balanced and judicious qualities rather than the merely amusing. He had made his stand as an Independent clear on all the principal issues. He supported the Reform opposition on most points but on the question of the separate schools and representation by population he parted company with them. He forbore making any rousing peroration to his speech. The pedestrian politics of the session of 1858 did not inspire the higher forms of eloquence. But he did remind the House that "politics are not the tricks of a trade, but the great science of affairs, the science of peace and war".

There is no doubt that McGee's speech was well received by both sides of the House. John A. Macdonald was one of the first to cross the floor and shake hands, congratulating him. The *Globe*, which during McGee's election had committed itself no further than to say "Mr. McGee is a doubtful personage but he sometimes speaks the truth", now went a little further:

"His speech was a decided success. It is seldom that a popular orator makes so splendid a hit in first appearing before a legislative chamber. It was proof of his rare tact as well as talent."

On the seventeenth of March, St. Patrick's Day, the Irish of Toronto held a parade and the Orangemen attacked them. The one was as much a feature of the celebration as the other. Brickbats flew and clubs and pitchforks came into play. One of the participants was killed. This, too, was not unusual. The Orangemen attacked the cab carrying D'Arcy McGee from Parliament to his hotel and wrecked the first floor of the National House where he was staying.

McGee deplored the violence and suggested a startling remedy. Let the Irish give up street parades on St. Patrick's Day and celebrate indoors; the feeling between the Orangemen and the Catholics made parades an incitement to disorder. McGee knew that he could do nothing about the twelfth of July celebration of the Orangemen, but he was prepared to test his influence by trying to prevail upon the Irish Catholics to set them an example of restraint.

At this point McGee turned back to the influences of his earlier life—to O'Connell and his policy of non-violence, to Thomas Davis and his theories of political education. To give these ideas weight a newspaper was necessary and this meant starting a new one. The existing Irish Catholic papers in Upper Canada believed in meeting their opponents on their own ground by keeping up a constant exchange of insults and laying heavy stress on the fighting spirit of the Irish. They were useless for political education of a more advanced kind.

D'Arcy's paper, the *New Era* of Montreal might have served the purpose but it was already on its way to the limbo of defunct newspapers. His new parliamentary duties did not leave him time to edit a tri-weekly paper and he had no one to act for him. The partnership with Michael Hickey had not turned out well. Hickey was in favour of Ottawa as the capital; McGee stood out for Montreal. They dissolved the partnership amicably but it meant giving up the paper. Hickey went back to Ottawa where he entered a law office. McGee also associated himself with a lawyer, Thomas J. Walsh of Montreal, and planned during intervals between parliamentary sessions to study law.

The *New Era*, now passing out of existence, was the last paper McGee edited personally. In Toronto he and his political sponsors were successful in finding a man with the necessary experience and qualifications who would manage a paper for them. Towards the end of 1859 the *Canadian Freeman*, a weekly edited by James G. Moylan, made its first appearance and was known familiarly as D'Arcy McGee's paper.

The session during which McGee acquired his first experience as a legislator was unusually long, lasting from the end of February to the middle of August. A variety of

situations occurred, from which McGee learned a great
deal about politics carried on at a rather low level. There
was no great national issue to challenge the members to
their best efforts. The major problem—the union that had
failed to unite Upper and Lower Canada—was carefully
shelved by the government. John A. Macdonald preferred
to believe that the union could be made to work and that
he was the man to do it.

The government and the opposition wrangled over the
choice of Ottawa, which many including adherents of the
government did not want to accept in spite of the royal
decision. They also discussed education and the separate
schools. This was a question of considerable importance;
McGee made an excellent speech on it, but it was to be
several years before any legislation was passed on the school
question.

In this atmosphere of frustration, trifling matters took
on false importance; interest focused on personalities. The
give and take of parliamentary debate was carried on more
to keep in practice than for any better purpose. Referring
to each other formally as "the honourable member from—"
or the "honourable Attorney Canada East", the members
exchanged the most scathing remarks, the bluntest and most
unvarnished rudenesses.

McGee was well equipped for this kind of verbal sniping.
His tongue was as quick and sharp as the best of them and
his wit brighter than most. He proved rather dangerous
because he could invariably raise a laugh that left his
opponent disarmed and helpless. The House of Assembly
enjoyed his thrusts, but as unkindly as it was high spirited
it scored off McGee by giving him a reputation for being
frivolous, a slight man of less merit than many had at first
believed.

In any situation where friction developed George
Brown's dominating and uncomfortable personality was sure
to make itself felt. This time he took the limelight in a more
heroic fashion than usual, defending himself against an old,
often-repeated accusation of having left Scotland under a

charge of embezzlement. This scandal was all the more painful and embarrassing in that it really involved Brown's father and not himself. Brown's forthright character showed to exceptional advantage in his defence of himself and his father. The members of the House were moved by his frank appeal to their sense of fair play. Even the government party newspapers responded by declaring Brown's speech manly.

McGee, who was forming his opinion of the members of the House, was favourably impressed by Brown's behaviour on this occasion and also by his frequent denunciations of the government party. In politics one cannot play a lone hand for long, so he was looking about for allies. There was a certain link between McGee and Dorion as they had both run against government candidates in the Montreal elections; and since Dorion was more or less in alliance with Brown, McGee's attention was directed toward the Grits' leader.

As a political ally Brown had certain disadvantages. He was a man of strong prejudices and great fighting qualities, who would never be content with a paltry opponent. He had to have something large to contend with; so George Brown went after the Pope, the embodiment to him of all tyranny. Since His Holiness was too remote for the Upper Canadian editor to come to grips with, in practice this meant bedevilling his Catholic fellow-citizens.

Having suffered from the *Globe's* bigotry, McGee's Irish Catholic constituents were made very uneasy by his attitude towards Brown. The *True Witness*, his self-appointed instructor, disapproved in its loudest tones. But McGee continued to act according to his opinion. He believed that George Brown, who was ambitious for power, would need the support of the Catholic electors even more than they would need him. He believed that, now that the editor had entered Parliament, the realities of political experience would teach Brown tolerance if only as a necessity. Up to a point future events proved McGee right, although, as a tolerant man himself, he underestimated the granite quality of George Brown's prejudices.

As much concerned as Brown about the corruption of the government, McGee saw no hope of remedy until Macdonald and his party were run out of office. They had enjoyed the powers of government for five years and in the opinion of their opponents had grown old in iniquity. Corruption! The word was in every mouth:

"The present government is a government of corruption. Their hope is in corruption. Their creed is corruption. They endeavour to corrupt every class in the country—every power in the country, the executive, the judicial and the popular power. And they draw into partnership a corrupt governor-general." This is what McGee told a political meeting and in so speaking would seem to have said the last word on the subject.

It is necessary to look into this ambiguous word, for presumably the government, the opposition and the people knew what was meant by it. Taken by itself the word suggests unmentionable things—the unnamed sins of the cities of the plains.

In reality it implied false election returns, with petitions coming before Parliament protesting crude election frauds such as voters' lists composed of names from tombstones and from the New York City directory. It included the venality of the government in allowing an unreasonably large number of local appointments to go to Orangemen, with the result that petitions came before Parliament, angry petitions, complaining of violence and even murder going unpunished because Orange magistrates dismissed charges against fellow Orangemen.

There is no doubt that McGee took a serious view of the relations between the government and the Orangemen, who were adept at climbing on political bandwagons and at the time seemed to have attached themselves to the Conservative party to a man. Possibly he exaggerated in his own mind the Orange Order's influence. But this was his first session in Parliament and it was not surprising that he failed to gauge all the complex factors accurately.

What else could he think as the petitions piled up; or when the pipe band of the Toronto Orangemen escorted newly elected members to the Assembly and contrary to all parliamentary propriety forced its way onto the floor of the House and saluted the outraged legislators with "The Protestant Boys"?

In addition to these laxities, there were the grants to railways, not the ones passed by Parliament, but extra sums sought by railway directors who were members of Parliament and given by ministers of the Crown who were, or had recently been, directors of railways.

There was the friendship between the Governor-General, Sir Edmund Head and John A. Macdonald, a widower now, who had his bachelor quarters close to Government House. There was informal going back and forth watched jealously by others. The Governor was supposed to be above parties. How could he be impartial if he was the crony of the leader of one party?

In these things lay the corruption of the Macdonald-Cartier administration.

The session was not without unusual incidents. The government resigned and was replaced by another government which was defeated in less than a week, whereupon the original government took over again. This was an occurrence unique in the experience of even veteran parliamentarians.

This resignation was unnecessary in the first place. A majority in the House supported a motion disapproving the choice of Ottawa as the capital. The motion did not automatically defeat the government and when Macdonald made an issue of the matter and called for a vote of confidence he was sustained. Even so, he chose to take the disapproval of the choice of Ottawa as implying the defeat of the government and resigned with his Cabinet.

George Brown and the Reformers were delighted; it was more than they had dared hope for. The Conservative party was in great consternation at Macdonald's strange behaviour, but after a few private conferences among the leaders, the situation was accepted in a resigned and even cheerful spirit.

Before the next day's session began the usually sedate atmosphere of the House was noticeably lacking—the semi-religious atmosphere compounded of the mace on the table and the Speaker, presiding in dignity above, towards whom each member bowed as he took his place while the smooth-faced pages moved silently back and forth at the members' behests. Instead, Macdonald and Cartier and the other members of the executive cleaned out their desks like schoolboys preparing for a holiday, while members drifted from group to group speculating on what was happening between the Governor-General and George Brown, who was absent.

Of course he would be asked to form the new executive as he had the largest following among the opposition. But whom would Brown ask to hold office with him? Dorion, most likely; he commanded the French-Canadian following in the opposition. But whom else?

The members of the retiring government, having finished their chores, were facetiously offering the keys of their desks to this one and that. Perched on a desk the Honourable Member for Berthier sang an interminable folk song with the refrain "Vive les gueux". For some reason everyone found this extremely funny. The House of Assembly was becoming every moment more like a disorderly schoolroom when the Speaker in his robes and looking rather severe entered and called the session to order. Like boys caught out of bounds the members hastily took their places.

A member of the Reform party informed the House that Mr. Brown was still in conference with the Governor about forming a new administration. As nothing could be done till the results of these negotiations were announced he asked for an adjournment of the House till the new government was ready.

In commendably short time Brown and Dorion had formed their Cabinet, but were unable to announce a policy or programme to the House. For, though all the Cabinet were of one mind in accepting office, they were agreed on nothing else. It was a rule of Parliament that any member accepting an executive position must vacate his seat and seek re-election. Brown and his Cabinet returned to their constituencies, explaining that they would announce their policy to the House on their return. But within a day, one might almost say within a few hours of their departure a Conservative member moved an amendment to a motion to make it a vote of want of confidence in the new government. The Brown government lost the motion by forty votes. Brown tried to save himself by asking for a general election, but, when the Governor refused, he had no course open but to hand in his resignation for himself and his Cabinet. They were out of office before, properly speaking, they could be said to have been in. The House was astounded at the rapid movement of events.

The Governor-General now called on Alexander T. Galt, a man of recognized financial ability, to form a government. But he did not have any great following in the House and, taking heed of what had happened to George Brown, he prudently refused the honour. Sir Edmund Head then called on Cartier who promptly accepted and submitted the names of John A. Macdonald and his other colleagues, including this time the name of the astute Mr. Galt.

To the amazement of the House, within the space of a week the Reformers who had been in office were out and the Conservatives who had been out of office were in. But this was not the end of the excitement. The old-new Cabinet members did not choose to risk their seats and reputations by leaving Parliament for the required re-election. Instead, as, with two exceptions, they had all held office recently they took advantage of a rule which permitted a Cabinet minister to change his portfolio or office without seeking re-election. Each minister therefore accepted a different portfolio from the one he had previously held. Then in a few days they all shifted back again. The Legislative Assembly was at a loss as to whether Macdonald and Cartier should be admired for their cleverness or condemned for their trickery.

"Well, the old set is back," was the way McGee described it. "It reminds me of nothing so much as the instructions to his pupils of a dancing master in a country town. 'Grand right and left, turn corners and back to places.' They soon found their way through the last figure—back to places. It is impossible to describe the number of corners they turned!"

The Conservatives, relieved to have their party in power again, were prepared to approve. Beyond a doubt John A. was an extraordinarily clever fellow. If he had made a fool of George Brown it was all part of the game. Brown had never spared the leader of the Conservatives in the *Globe*.

But the country as a whole was scandalized by all this changing of administrations and shuffling of portfolios. Coming at the end of a long session that had accomplished little, it seemed to reduce government to a farce. The incidents of this week continued for a long time to have a strange fascination for Canadians, always an intensely political people. The statesmanlike conferences that brought about the confederation of the British North American provinces were recorded only in the sketchiest and most casual fashion. They are the despair of historians. But ironically, the records of the trivial intrigues of the summer of 1858 have survived in tedious detail. Every manoeuvre may be followed, not only from day to day, but even from hour to hour. With morbid interest each move has been examined and the lengthy memoranda exchanged between the Governor and George Brown commented on almost sentence by sentence. It seems as though once and for all time we see constitutional government carried along a certain path to its ultimate conclusion, stripped of all its greater purposes and significance and reduced to a game. A skilled and formal game, but of no more consequence than shifting counters on a board or jerking puppets.

But it was just those large issues of constitutional change, which Macdonald and Cartier had hoped to bury, that now rose up and marched into the Cabinet in the person of Alexander Galt. His services as a financier were valuable to the administration as well as his knowledge of the rapidly growing problems of railway and long distance transportation. His practical experience had brought him to the same conclusion as the theorists and idealists, the conclusion that Macdonald was trying to avoid, namely the confederation of British North America.

The session was almost over and within the Cabinet the two leaders were prepared to compromise. As long as the constitutional question was not thrown into the political arena they were willing to have it discussed on higher levels. Accordingly, after Parliament had prorogued, in the fall of 1858, George Cartier, then Prime Minister, Alexander Galt and John Ross, also of the Cabinet, sailed for England to lay before the Colonial Office a plan for the confederation of all the British North American provinces.

Chapter Twenty-One
THE ROYAL VISIT

Among the many object lessons in politics which the members received during the session of 1858, none was more striking than the manner in which Alexander Galt, who had previously sat with the Reformers, was scooped up into the Conservative government. It must mean either that the Conservatives were going to adopt some of the Reformers' ideas—a move not unknown in political tactics—or that they were making another attempt to smother them. McGee thought the latter most likely. "It will not avail the party of expediency, the party of corruption," he said, "to affect regard for one of the principles of the statesman who prefer to remain in opposition."

The session was over and Parliament would not meet for another six months. In the interval the members went home to attend to their own affairs. D'Arcy, as usual, was involved in a number of interests. He now had a business address with Thomas Walsh, advocate, on Little St. James Street, Montreal. There he was presumably training for the practice of law. But it is hard to imagine him appearing regularly at his office as he accepted numerous lecture engagements which kept him travelling constantly. He was deep in negotiations for setting up the *Canadian Freeman*; he was also deep in writing a history of Ireland, a literary effort which would have absorbed all the energies of a less versatile man.

Galt and his two companions went on their mission to England in the fall of 1858 and waited upon Sir Edward Bulwer-Lytton, the Colonial Secretary, who received them with a polite lack of enthusiasm. The attention of the British government was taken up by affairs in the East. A not particularly successful war with Russia had just been concluded. There had been a mutiny of native troops in India and growing difficulties with China. The plan for a federation of the British North American colonies was sound and admirable in theory, but the time was not considered opportune. The British government had hoped that these colonies, having won all the rights of self-government after being very troublesome about it, would look after their own affairs.

Also this confederation plan was rather too obviously tied up with railways. Railway building in the British Isles had been profitable, but colonial railways were a different matter. They had to cover immense distances to serve a few people. The Grand Trunk Railway was the longest in the world, a dubious distinction when it rolled up debts faster than mileage. There was the military argument which the delegates used in asking for railway grants, but in many quarters doubt was growing as to whether these colonies were worth defending. All the world was Britain's market. What did it matter whether the British American colonies remained part of the empire or were absorbed into the United States?

Of course nothing as blunt as this was said to the Canadian delegates. Generations of practice in government and diplomacy had given the English ruling class an inbred faculty for masterly evasion. Courtesy and ceremony awaited the Canadians in every quarter where they sought to be heard. The perfection of English hospitality was spread before them like a carpet. They spent a week-end with Sir Edward in the country. They were presented at Court. Cartier, as Prime Minister of Canada, was a guest at Windsor Castle, where Queen Victoria, still young and happy in her marriage, performed her royal duties with tireless energy.

The purpose of their mission was stifled in bland sympathy beneath which, when they pressed too hard, the

174

baffled colonials ran into sharp objections. A terrible people, these English aristocrats, their politeness could be more deadly than ferocity! The delegates from Canada, shrewd men all three of them, soon realized that they had drifted beyond their depth on the gentle swells of English policy and that their mission was out of control. Before they left, Galt was exerting every effort to prevent the Colonial Office from specifically condemning confederation. Since it would undoubtedly be discussed among the British American colonies there would be dangerous complications if the Imperial government expressed disapproval beforehand. The Canadian delegates returned home having seemingly accomplished nothing.

One result did follow from the visit. While Cartier was the Queen's guest he invited Her Majesty and the Prince Consort to visit Canada. The Queen, startled a little out of the customary diplomatic reticence, replied that the idea of such a long journey was very disconcerting. Victoria, the ruler of a seafaring people, admitted that even the shortest sea voyage distressed her. However, she added with an official smile, the invitation would not be refused. One of the children should go in her place.

So it came about that in the summer of 1860, all the formalities on both sides having been carried out, the Queen's eldest son, Edward, Prince of Wales, set out on a royal tour of the British American colonies. He was a well-brought up young man, handsome, amiable and only nineteen years old. His visit had very slight political importance, but its social significance was immense. Never before had a reigning monarch or his heir made a state visit to North America. Even the republican United States was impressed and sent an official invitation to the royal visitor which was graciously accepted. As for the British subjects, the most indifferent were aware that this was a great occasion, and the excessively loyal were in a state of exaltation bordering on frenzy.

The royal party sailed first to Newfoundland, the oldest

of all England's colonies, and from there to the Maritimes. After these visits it proceeded around Gaspé into the St. Lawrence with Quebec as its first Canadian port of call.

The Governor-General and Prime Minister George Cartier went by ship to greet the visitors as they sailed into the St. Lawrence. At Quebec everything was in readiness, the guard of honour trained to ballet-like precision, the receptions of dignitaries of the Roman Catholic Church and the Church of England arranged. The members of the government and the Parliament were all in town practising their bows. Those of the fair sex who had been fortunate enough to receive invitations to the ball were prostrate from sessions with their dressmakers. The evergreen arches were complete, the flags and bunting out. Then something like panic gripped the venerable city.

It was not, you understand, that the royal visitor, the heir of an alien ruling house, caused in the Quebecois any deep emotion. But the young Prince represented the British Crown to which they gave formal allegiance and in receiving him certain forms, certain proprieties must be observed. How dreadful if Quebec, one of the oldest of the New World cities, accustomed to state and ceremony under two regimes, should fail on this unique occasion!

The newspaper reporters, as always sensitive spirits, reacted to the atmosphere and wrote in nervous irritation to their papers. The weather was bad, cold and inclined to rain, the hotels were overcrowded and the prices raised beyond all reason to $4.00 a day. The people were a stiff, reserved lot. No one paid any attention to the journalists but the politicians. This last obscure complaint, whatever its cause, seems to have been eliminated early in the royal tour, because on later occasions the press box was so overflowing with ladies in crinolines that the reporters were all but squeezed out.

The dreaded moment arrived—the royal party accompanied by the Governor-General and the Prime Minister landed at the Lower Town where the mayor and council awaited them. They drove through the crowded streets to the Upper Town, winding around the great rock crowned by the citadel. All the ceremonies were carried out creditably. The royal visitor met the ecclesiastical dignitaries. The members of Parliament were presented, bowed and retired. The ball was held and the Prince departed for Montreal. The worst was over, the ice broken.

The people of the St. Lawrence valley, being of sociable temperament, began to enjoy the visit. As the royal flotilla steamed up the river, the church bells rang out in each village as it passed and festively decorated small craft came out to accompany it on a stretch of the journey. On board the *Hero*, Cartier was in his element. He was a born entertainer, with a fund of amusing stories and comic French songs which he sang with great vivacity in his high rather shrill voice. The Prince was captivated. The tunes were catchy and the French words not difficult. Soon His Royal Highness and the gentlemen of his suite were joining in the choruses with full-throated gusto.

Stage fright was not likely to trouble Montreal. The island city had played host to many people. Missionaries and Indian delegates, fur traders and governor-generals, armies of occupation both English and American, plague-striken immigrants, all kinds of people, common, noble or royal—its worldly experience was equal to any occasion.

For the royal visit the city was *en fête*. The reporters, in good humour now that they had something to write about, marshalled their vocabularies to describe the decorations, the devices illuminated by gas jets, the "allegorical and emblemical transparencies and mottoes", the mechanical designs and locomotive wheels decorating Victoria Bridge, the first bridge to connect the island with the mainland, which the Prince officially opened.

In the evening there were fireworks and dancing in the streets. The Prince—who after all was young—and some of his suite attempted to join incognito in the fun, but they were soon recognized and surrounded by a good-natured, laughing crowd. There were banquets and more receptions and of course a ball. The Prince, in fine form, danced indefatigably till four in the morning, but not more nimbly than Prime Minister George Cartier. He astonished even those who knew him with his buoyancy and may even have aroused some envy among his less gifted political colleagues as he displayed his terpsichorean talents in the ballroom.

The reporters inspected the train prepared for the Prince. Railways were still something of a novelty and the fittings of these coaches, as described in painstaking detail by an Ottawa journalist, would have been a novelty in any period. The salon coach with white walls and gilded mouldings and cornices, very rich and chaste, was furnished with sofas and armchairs in heavy curled maple. The royal armchair was elaborately (and possibly uncomfortably) carved with the Prince of Wales's crest surmounted by rose, shamrock and thistle intertwined with maple leaves. Maple leaves and beavers adorned the sofas, and the upholstery and curtains were all in royal blue. The exterior was equally handsome, painted dark crimson with gilding. The handrails were silver plated and all the iron work was bronzed.

Even so, this luxurious equipage was used only to transport the royal party over portages and into backwood places. Notwithstanding the fancy trimmings, trains were a sooty, jolting, cramped, unnerving means of travel compared to the ample accommodation and restful yet invigorating atmosphere of water travel. His Royal Highness travelled by steamboat on the St. Lawrence, the Ottawa, and the Great Lakes and the elegance of these vessels did not require description by the journalists as it was pleasantly familiar to everyone.

The royal party proceeded up the Ottawa in traditional fashion, portaging from Carillon to Grenville and taking ship again. Down river from Ottawa came their escort, one hundred and fifty canoes manned by twelve hundred lumbermen and Indians in blue and scarlet shirts or full Indian regalia. The canoes formed a great inverted V in front of the *Phoenix*, holding their positions with beautiful, practised uniformity while the crews kept pace to the rhythm of the traditional boat songs.

In this fashion the royal party moved upstream and towards evening came in sight of the city of Ottawa where a great crowd had waited since four in the afternoon with many glances at the sky, which threatened rain. Then after the manner of North American steamboats in a gala mood, the *Phoenix* put on more steam and charged towards the landing. With a whoop of delight the lumbermen bent to their paddles and the canoes shot forward with arrowy speed. Thirty kept up with her right to the wharf, while the rest crowded in behind, using all their dexterity to keep from dumping each other into the river. The artillery on the promontory, where the new Parliament Buildings were being erected, began firing a royal salute, the assembled school children sang the national anthem, the rain came down and the royal party courageously landed.

While the Prince was in Ottawa he laid the corner-stone for the new Parliament Buildings. The Ottawans made certain that this was the most important function of the tour. All the arrangements were on the most lavish scale possible. The Prince and his suite appeared in their most brilliant uniforms; spectators and participants wore their best clothes. Afterwards the Prince admired the lumbermen's arch—an amazing structure modelled upon the Marble Arch in London and erected from 200,000 feet of planking without the use of a nail. In turn he won the lumbermen's admiration by shooting down a timber chute on one of their rafts.

All in all it was a happy occasion for the lumbermen of the Ottawa valley. They had made their city the capital of the country. They had dedicated the foundation of the Parliament with more pomp and ceremony than had ever been seen in Canada. They had displayed their skill and prowess on the river. But even in the moment of their triumph the lumberjacks were being ushered off the historic scene. They were about to lose their identity with their city. The lumber trade would remain, but Ottawa would cease to be a lumber town. The city would grow dignified and sedate under the shadowing towers of its new

Parliament. The lumberjack in his gaudy shirt and spiked boots would give place to throngs of civil servants, well-bred and neat. The chansons would die away on the river as the sounds and murmur of debate grew louder on the Hill and the life of the lumberman would fade from the city's memory. The rowdy elections, the Irishmen getting drunk on Saturday night and fighting the Orangemen would be recalled only in some archivist's scandalous chronicle, written perhaps by a descendant of French lumbermen and repudiated indignantly by the descendants of the Irish.

At Ottawa Cartier said farewell to the royal party. According to a tacit understanding that kept the two provinces separate in spite of their formal union, John A. Macdonald was to accompany the tour in Upper Canada.

From this point matters did not go so smoothly as heretofore. In Upper Canada there were groups of people whose loyalty tended to run beyond the bounds of reason—in short, the Orangemen. The instructions covering receptions for the Prince of Wales forbade the display of party or sectarian emblems. The Orangemen took this prohibition to be directed especially against them, which in a measure was true, and to proceed from the machinations of the Catholics, which strictly speaking was not true. The instructions had been given by the British government very specifically to the Duke of Newcastle, who was in charge of the royal party. There were times in Ireland when the British government made use of the Orangemen's professional loyalty in ways that did not bear too close inspection; but it was no part of its policy to allow any shadow of these transactions to mar the graciousness of the royal visit, or to encourage demonstrations by a party whose particular and exclusive kind of patriotism had never produced anything but discord.

This the Orangemen did not understand. Accustomed to having their own way, they insisted in spite of the instructions in overlading the civic decorations with the

symbols of Orangeism. They met their match in the Duke
of Newcastle. When he discovered the prohibited symbols
in the decorations he re-routed the procession on the spot.
In one place, where the civic authorities admitted to Orange
displays, the Duke declared that the royal party would not
even land. At Kingston, possibly out of courtesy to John
A. Macdonald, the royal vessel waited for half an hour at
the wharf to give the Orangemen time to change their
minds. When nothing was done the royal party again
steamed away, leaving consternation in its wake. Deputa-
tions of Orangemen waited upon the Duke to protest.
Mayors came to offer apologies and beg the royal party to
return to their towns. The Duke stood firm.

John A. Macdonald, who had been solidly supported by
Orange votes, now found himself in the awkward position
of being regarded by the Orangemen as their champion.
Somewhere along the route he washed his hands of the
affair and went home, whether to sulk or to await more
favourable political weather is hard to say. The mind of
John A. is not easy to read.

The last attempt of the Orangemen was made at Toronto. Convinced that they could not get away with a blatant
display they tried to work in a few not too conspicuous
references to King William and the Battle of the Boyne—
just enough to put something over on the terrible Duke of
Newcastle. But his Grace took the precaution of pre-viewing
the route of the procession and his lynx eye spotted their
tricks. Down they must come!

That night the Toronto Orangemen burnt the Governor-
General, Sir Edmund Head, in effigy (he wasn't very popular
in any case) and likewise the Duke of Newcastle, a very
impolite act as the Duke was a guest in the country. There
is a story that they followed Newcastle down King Street
to his quarters with hootings and catcalls. On the steps he
turned and surveyed them wordlessly with aristocratic
hauteur. Their sporting instincts aroused at last, the Orangemen gave him a cheer which seemed to say, "All right, you
win." At least so runs the story.

In any case the firmness of the Duke and the growing annoyance of the majority of people who wanted to enjoy the royal visit put an end to Orange importunities. Through the western portion of the province the Prince progressed serenely under innocently green arches and through streets hung with banners of only the broadest patriotic significance, laying cornerstones, opening fall fairs (it was now September), holding receptions, dancing at balls. A long life of this sort of thing lay ahead of him, but this was his first royal tour and he performed all his duties with the spontaneity and resilience of youth.

Members of the Conservative party wrote to Macdonald that all was going well and urged him to rejoin the royal tour. His absence was causing comment. But John A. refused to emerge from his retirement.

The royal party came to Niagara, their last stop in Canada. Here the mighty cataract, once venerated by the Indians as the home of a god, had been jointly claimed by Canadians and Americans and regarded by them as a piece of international scenery with which to astonish strangers. Mr. Kohl, who took his sight-seeing seriously, had allotted a week to observing all the wonders of the falls. But the royal party were content, like most visitors, to spend one day marvelling at the sights. Then, the Canadian tour completed, they passed by ferry over to the United States. Nothing remained for the Canadians to do but to dismantle the arches, put the flags away, thank Providence that all had gone well, or at least had been no worse, and retain the mingled happy memories, envies and grudges which a royal visit must inevitably leave.

The royal party left the shores of North America in late autumn. The young Prince presumably benefited by the tour as an educational experience. Certainly the Duke of Newcastle had had exceptional opportunities for observing the Canadian scene. He returned to England with definite ideas on the British American provinces, one of which was the advisability of confederation. This was to prove of importance as the British government had changed and the Duke was now Colonial Secretary.

Chapter Twenty-Two

THE TRIALS AND SORROWS OF A PUBLIC MAN

O<small>NE WHO MIGHT</small> have had reason for resentment at the time of the royal visit was D'Arcy McGee. When the committee in charge had drawn up the programme for the Prince's banquet at Montreal it had considered asking McGee to propose the toast to the guest of honour. The committee thought that, without going beyond the bounds of good taste, it would add a piquant touch to the occasion to have the honours done by the eloquent Irishman who had been a rebel and was now a member of Parliament. But Cartier decided against any public speaking at the banquet. As for piquancy he felt capable of providing that himself. For that matter he too had been a rebel—in 1837—and in any event he did not choose to give the centre of the stage to the adventurer McGee. It was not a matter of supreme importance although the honour, as McGee was well aware, would have increased his prestige and reflected credit on his Irish supporters.

When Parliament met at Quebec with the same air of futility that had marked the session in Toronto, a rude remark of Cartier's directed against McGee gave him a chance to pay off his own little score. With elaborate mildness and one ear cocked for the ripples of laughter from the House, he described Cartier during the Prince's visit.

"He has told us himself of one of the functions he discharged during that historical period—his dancing—but he modestly suppressed all reference to the other constitutional duty he discharged, namely his singing. Yet we have it set down in sundry places in a history of the visit dedicated to the Commissioner of Crown Lands how the honourable gentleman transformed himself both on the St. Lawrence and on the Ottawa from a severe Prime Minister into an amusing Primo Buffo. At one place—I quote the page of history—Mr. Cartier is represented as volunteering a very earnest Canadian song of emphatic accent and tender purport. Oh, Mr. Speaker, if he would only have his speeches set to music and sing them from the Treasury Bench in the manner of an operatic hero, what a saving it would be to our ears, and who can tell but such siren arts might win over some of the stubborn Opposition."

"Baboon," muttered Cartier, but though he was a notoriously aggressive man, he thought twice about entering into a verbal duel with the Irishman. Mr. St. Denis had not come out very well from his encounter.

"According to legend," said McGee when that member undertook to heckle him, "St. Denis travelled to Paris without his head. He was not the last of his name to arrive in a capital city without the necessary capital to his spinal column."

Retorted Mr. St. Denis, "The honourable member crossed the Atlantic with his head but without his reputation."

"Since the honourable member accepts my hagiology," replied McGee, "he is welcome to any comments he likes on my exodus."

No one could keep up that sort of repartee for long and the time had not yet come for more heroic debate.

On the whole McGee was well pleased with the Prince's visit, especially as the Orangemen had disgraced themselves. For the past two years he had urged the Toronto Irish to give up the rowdy St. Patrick's Day parade and had succeeded to the surprise and even disgust of some bright green Hibernians. During the Prince's visit the Irish had the reward of their forbearance in witnessing the humiliation of their enemies. D'Arcy wrote delightedly to Moylan to keep the tone of the *Freeman* moderate and discourage unseemly exultation among the Irish Catholics. But the time was ripe, he thought, for suggesting a Commission to investigate the many charges of violence made against the Orangemen.

The *Freeman* at this time was co-operating with McGee in his efforts to organize the Irish Canadians to carry the weight in public affairs that their numbers warranted. There were those who accused him of trying to form a political party with himself at the head, or even of forming political cliques to corner local appointments. But McGee's letters to Moylan show that he was working for something much broader. He constantly urged that his name be kept out of organization plans. People must feel that these efforts came from themselves. Indirectly they must be instructed in their powers and responsibilities.

The *True Witness* of Montreal was now his relentless opponent. It supported the Conservative government which was pledged to make no change in the Act of Union. Because McGee believed constitutional change was needed it rejected him as having deserted "the high and holy cause for which he had been elected".

There were several proposals for changing the Act of Union, one of which, representation by population, would destroy the equality between Upper and Lower Canada, leaving Lower Canada in an inferior position. Another proposal was a federal union which would leave to each province its own government for local affairs and provide a central government which might be extended to include all the British American provinces. This was the plan McGee favoured.

But to the *True Witness* the matter was simply one of yes or no, black or white, the Act of Union or Rep. by Pop. Acting on this the *True Witness* induced several Lower Canadian bishops to denounce McGee's policy and took care to keep the episcopal thunders reverberating in its columns as long as possible. It produced a great uproar. Most of the newspapers rallied to McGee's side. Even those that did not like him disliked the clergy in politics even more.

The *Freeman* supported him vigorously and arranged

a public dinner in Toronto in his honour. A letter from Bishop Charbonnel of Toronto, read at the dinner, commended his worth and respectability, proving nothing but that in politics bishops do not always agree. In the hubbub McGee seemed the least upset of anyone. This was not the first time he had been in trouble with the clergy.

It is a paradox that this man who was fair-minded and moderate from his boyhood passed his whole life in a furore of controversy. It is true that those with whom he was associated did not take their politics calmly, but the paradox also lay deep in himself involving a contrast in temperament and intention. He pursued his moderate ends with headlong impetuosity and imparted to his sober purposes the challenge of a crusade.

The trouble stirred up by the *True Witness* disturbed the harmony he was trying to create among the Irish Canadians. He began his speech at the banquet in Toronto by declaring frankly that it was regrettable that such an occasion should be necessary. Several times he wrote to Moylan not to prolong the controversy in the *Freeman* as it would harm the paper; he was not afraid of the bishops, or what was closer to the truth, the *True Witness* talking like a bishop. "I can survive the storm. I never felt in better health or conscience, never in fuller control of my powers. I cannot long be kept out of my rank, but I am most anxious to carry you along to success."

In the summer of 1861 there was a general election which among other matters tested the effectiveness of McGee's attempts to organize and educate the Irish Catholics in the direction of the Reform party. The result was disappointing. There had been a time, under the leadership of Baldwin and LaFontaine, when the Reform party had been a natural ally for the Irish Catholics; but George Brown had changed its character. The Irish were not prepared to accept Brown just because Mr. McGee fancied he had come to an understanding with him through meeting him in Parliament. Brown had always been notoriously anti-Catholic. Had Mr. McGee ever read the back numbers of the *Globe*?

Certainly not, McGee admitted. He never read the back files of newspapers. He might have gone further and added that he gave even the current issues only casual reading. He had been a journalist too long not to know the limitations as well as the value of newspapers. He was aware that print gave a permanence to opinions and reactions that did not always rightly belong to them.

But James Moylan, editor of the *Canadian Freeman,* read the *Globe* carefully. Up to the summer of 1861 the *Freeman* printed all McGee's articles and letters and gave cautious editorial support to George Brown. It even conceded that the *Globe* was less offensive than formerly. Then in the summer of 1861 James Moylan decided that the tone of the *Globe* was deteriorating. Mr. Brown had broken the compact; the dog had returned to its vomit. In an editorial Moylan regretfully and respectfully informed McGee that the *Freeman* could no longer support the Reformers.

In the election which took place about this time the Reformers improved their position little if at all and George Brown personally was defeated. But the worst result for McGee was the defection of the *Freeman* which left him without a paper in which to express his opinions.

For a week or two relations between McGee and Moylan were of exquisite politeness. Each leaned backwards in attributing to the other the most honourable and conscientious motives. Both had come out too strongly for harmony not to feel some embarrassment about the position in which they found themselves. The very delicacy of the situation made it impossible to maintain. D'Arcy seems to have been the first to break the thin ice with one of his belittling remarks.

He referred with some bitterness to Moylan as the obscure country schoolteacher from Guelph, C. W., who thanks to his influence, had been made editor of the finest Catholic paper in Canada West.

Obscure country schoolteacher, indeed! retorted Moylan editorially. Mr. McGee chose to forget that he had also

been on the staff of the *New York Times* and a member of
the Chilean Legation in Washington. Besides, what was
wrong with having been a teacher?

From this point Moylan cast aside fine feeling and if he
did not descend to the lowest abuse he nevertheless made
McGee's past look rather murky. Strange, he said, that
there should be so many episodes in McGee's life never fully
explained. All those accusations by Mitchel and Meagher.
So many changes of opinion. Strange, strange, indeed!

D'Arcy was at a disadvantage as he had no paper.
Besides, his tactics in controversy were the surprise attack,
the sudden thrust rather than the long-drawn-out verbal
battle. This time as far as can be learned from the *Freeman*
he was acting on the defensive, endeavouring to start
another paper, warning people that the *Freeman* no longer
represented his political opinions; behaving, according to
the *Freeman*, in a dictatorial, objectionable fashion.

The height of the quarrel came after McGee's visit to
London, Canada West, in September. The opposition had
locked the Separate School where his political followers
had planned to hear McGee address a meeting. The supporters broke the lock and succeeded in starting the meeting, but when McGee realized the situation and that disorders lay ahead, he persuaded supporters and hecklers to
break up quietly and go home.

As it happened the key to the school was in the possession of the parish priest, which made the building techni-
cally church property. Taking this scrap of an incident
the *Freeman* worked up a fantastic issue. In breaking into
church property, it held that McGee had committed a grave
offence and incurred extreme ecclesiastical penalties even
extending to excommunication. Going deeper into this
alarming case the *Freeman* disclosed that no authority short
of the Pope himself could re-instate the offender. The point
roused considerable interest among the readers; several
wrote in discussing it learnedly with Latin quotations from
Canon Law. The feeling seemed to be that the unfortunate
Mr. McGee was indeed *excommunicatus ipso facto*. But it

does not appear that the culprit allowed the *Freeman's* assumption of ecclesiastical jurisdiction to affect his peace of mind in the slightest.

What did this quarrel amount to? In a few weeks it had died out. In a few months the *Freeman* was reporting favourably McGee's activities. The old cordiality and fulsome praise were never resumed, but henceforth the *Freeman* gave McGee reasonable, intelligent support which he very likely found just as satisfactory. The moral of this may be that it would be well for the student of history to follow McGee's example and avoid reading old newspapers. But as this seems to have been the only occasion on which anyone tried to excommunicate that much abused man, it is included in this narrative as a journalistic curiosity.

Chapter Twenty-Three
STORM TO THE SOUTH

T HE AMERICAN crisis at the turn of the year 1860-61 gave McGee an excellent subject for his lectures. It was timely and had also those broad historical implications that especially appealed to him. When the crisis grew worse and became the war between the North and South, interest in the subject was thereby heightened. To Canadians of that generation war was something remote in time and space. It was awe-inspiring to think of a conflict going on within travelling distance from their own doors. Young men seeking adventure crossed the border to join the Northern armies.

For a very short time the Canadians looked on the Northern cause as a crusade against slavery and heartily approved. But in the course of a few months they realized that the Civil War was a little too close to their own lives to retain this simple heroic character. A certain discontent had always marked the attitude of Canadians who strove to keep pace with the flaunting wealth and relentless progress of the Republic and who were gnawed by envy when they failed. Now it looked as though that dangerous experiment in democracy was breaking up. The United States of America, born in rebellion, was destined to die in civil strife. It was just as well.

For the moment the war was bringing prosperity to Canada as wars always did. Everything the Canadians had for export—cereals, horses, lumber—found a ready market in the States. Trade missions coming and going from both North and South became commonplace in Montreal. The Yankee traders had long been familiar to the city. They stayed at the hotels down by the quays and drove hard bargains in an atmosphere of cigar smoke and gin slings. But the Southerners were gentlemen and an addition to the social life of the city. Such beautiful manners, such charm, such horsemanship displayed on the mountain! At the beginning of the war when the South was prosperous they had plenty of money and were open-handed with it. Later when the war went badly for the Confederates their agents in Montreal took to desperate courses, stealing Republican vessels from the harbour, organizing a raid over the border to rob a New England bank. But even these deeds the Southerners carried out with grace and gallantry and although (since Canada was a neutral country) the Montrealers had most reluctantly to put them in jail and bring them to trial, they continued to sympathize with them as warmly as ever.

It was the week of the fall fair in London, C.W., or rather the Agricultural Exhibition as the Upper Canadians preferred to call it. All week visitors from the country came and went, jolting over dusty roads through the brilliant autumn landscape. They came to exhibit or look at the exhibits of others. The products of the district arranged in booths, bins and stalls were a homely rather than sensational spectacle; the basic agriculture of a pioneer community did not produce anything rare or exotic.

The range of smells was more impressive than the sights. There was the dry, clean storehouse smell of the grains; the sharp, rather nasty smell of the poultry; and the strong, heavy, satisfying stableyard smell of the cows and horses and the pigs cleaned up for the occasion. It impregnated the atmosphere richly and transferred itself to the clothes of the farmer as though in this one respect the beasts imposed their will upon the man. In contrast to all these the domestic section where the quilting and homespun and needlework were displayed, seemed, flavourlessly, to have no smell at all. But the improvised kitchens made up for this, where the ladies' societies prepared the mounds of food for the trestle tables and where in the great pots the beans, drenched with molasses and baked slowly for hours with chunks of salt pork, were reheated.

The heat of the autumn noonday drew out all these odours and added to them the smell of warm, sticky humanity and the fumes of whisky accumulated from many visits to the taverns. As the afternoon lengthened, races were run, contests held and prizes allotted. In the evening a good crowd gathered in a gaslit hall to hear Mr. Thomas D'Arcy McGee, member of Parliament and noted lecturer, speak on the American Civil War.

He spoke from a deep sense of the conflict as a decisive event in history. His attitude was all the more remarkable in that his years in the States had not left him with any special affection for the first country of his exile. Nevertheless he began and ended his speech with a rebuke to those who looked with satisfaction on what they regarded as the breakup of the American Republic. "I cannot conceive the perversity of nature, the hopeless scepticism in man's self-government, which could make anyone applaud such a national tragedy."

He differed sharply from the growing opinion throughout the British world that the Southern states had a right to secede if they chose. The states in joining the Union had once and for all surrendered their individual sovereignty and there was no provision in the Constitution giving them any right to resume it. Again, the Southern states misinterpreted the Constitution with regard to slavery, which the Founding Fathers had considered a "peculiar institution" to be restrained and tolerated with the intention that it would gradually die out. But "of late years, almost within my own recollection, a new doctrine has overrun the South, that slavery is national, not local—constitutional, not temporary." Because Lincoln had made the right of secession and not slavery the immediate issue did not mean that slavery was no longer the ultimate issue of the war. McGee asked his audience to consider the consequences to the world if the Southern states succeeded, as many expected they would, in breaking away from the Union.

"They intend to call it a Republic, but they do not attempt to deny that it is to be a pagan Republic, an oligarchy founded upon caste, the caste founded upon colour . . . Organize an American power on such a basis, give it a flag, a Senate, a military aristocracy, a literature, and a history and you condemn mankind on this continent to begin over again the great battle of first principles, which in the Christian parts of the earth were thought to have been settled and established some centuries ago. As long as the monstrous doctrines of the innate diversity of the black and the hereditary mastery of the white were confined to individuals or states or sections, they were comparatively harmless; but build a government on such a basis, accept 300,000 whites as the keepers and lords of life and death over 400,000 blacks, erect an entire social and political superstructure on that foundation and contemplate if you can, without horror, the problems and conflicts you are preparing for posterity."

He also begged his audience to consider the alarming consequences to Canada of two Republics to the south. "The different dogmas for which these combatants fight, the different systems they hold sacred must lead to an era of standing armies, of passports, of espionage, of fluctuating boundaries and border wars. Are we prepared to welcome a state of permanent and still increasing armaments for North America . . . ?"

Then committing himself with characteristic daring, he prophesied the outcome of the war. He foresaw a long, bitter struggle ending in victory for the North. In spite of the poor showing Union armies were making in the opening battles, he believed that the greater manpower, seapower and resources of the North would prevail over the dash and spirit of Southern cavalry.

The visitors to the London Agricultural Exhibition had listened to a discourse of acute historical penetration, they had heard a remarkably accurate forecast and the peroration which closed the speech was, for sustained eloquence, the supreme example of McGee's oratory.

"We do not, while the ship is driving on the rocks, her

signal gun pealing for aid above the din of the tempest—
we do not lurk along the shore, gloating over her danger,
in hope of enriching ourselves by the wreck. No, God for-
bid! Such is not the feeling of the people of Canada. On
the contrary, so far as their public opinion can be heard
throughout the British Empire and the United States, their
wish would be that the Republic, as it was twelve months
ago, might live to celebrate in concord, in 1876, the centenary of its independence. We prefer our own institutions
to theirs; but our preference is rational, not rancorous; we
may think, and we do think, it would have been well for
them to have retained more than they did retain of the long-
tried wisdom of their ancestors; we may think, and we do
think, that their overthrow of ancient precedents and venerable safeguards was too sweeping in 1776; but as between
continental peace and chronic civil war—as between natural
right and oligarchical oppression; as between the constitutional majority and the lawless minority; as between free
intercourse and armed frontiers; as between negro emancipation and a revival of the slave trade; as between the
golden rule and the cotton crop of 1861; as between the
revealed unity of the race and the heartless heresy of Afri-
can bestiality; as between North and South in this deplor-
able contest—I rest firmly in the belief that all who are
most liberal, most intelligent, and most magnanimous in
Canada and the Empire, are for continental peace, for
constitutional arbitrament, for universal, if gradual emancipation, for free intercourse, for justice, mercy, civilization,
and the North."

It is apparent from this lecture on the Civil War that
McGee was interested in extending political education to
all Canadians. He gave this lecture or variations of it in
many places, in Ottawa and the Eastern Townships of
Lower Canada. With the exception of the *Globe*, which
approved Lincoln's policies from the first, there were very
few sources from which Canadians could derive the broad,
thoughtful view of American issues which McGee gave
them. Before the year was out some of McGee's warnings

STORM TO THE SOUTH

came to pass. The detached spectators' view was no longer possible and Canadians found themselves menaced by the pressures of the Civil War.

In November of 1861 two Confederate agents, travelling on a British ship, the *Trent*, were removed by the captain of a Union warship. The British government was furious at this violation of the freedom of the seas. The Minister for Foreign Affairs, the truculent Lord Palmerston, told the British Parliament he'd be damned if he would stand for it. The notes he addressed to the American government were worded almost as bluntly. Lincoln and his advisers, already involved in a major war, preferred to avoid conflict with the British Empire, but popular feeling in the North was in favour of war.

For some months past influential papers, notably the *New York Herald*, had declared that, now that the country was organized in a military way, here was an excellent opportunity to acquire Canada. It must be conceded that these journals would have rejected the idea of conquest of an inoffensive neighbour, but they chose to believe that if the small British garrison was cleared out of the country, Canada would gladly join the Union. It was manifest destiny, declared the *New York Herald*, that all North America should be one United States.

Alarm spread from end to end of the British American colonies. The number of British troops, considerably reduced over a period of years, was far smaller than the American or even the Canadian public imagined. Only the British and Canadian governments were in a position to know the defencelessness of the country.

A Canadian travelling through the country that fall watched the volunteers mustering at London, C.W. The harvest was over and the farmers who had attended the Agricultural Exhibition came hurrying back to town armed with shotguns. An officer in the reserve militia, one of their neighbours, was attempting to drill them. He was on horseback and wore a kind of uniform which seemed to have been gathered from different regiments. The men apparently liked him and were greatly impressed by his martial attire. Their own appearance was completely un-military and their attempts to go through the rudimentary formations awkward beyond description. The visitor would have laughed aloud had they not been so earnest and the situation so grave. There were no weapons but the shot-guns, no ammunition, no uniforms except the officer's cos-tume, but spirits were high. Two small pieces of artillery arrived by train and these tokens of warlike preparation affected the whole town like a tonic.

In Montreal the tea-partying, band-playing garrison was put on a war basis. Recruiting for volunteer regiments went on all over the city. D'Arcy McGee and several of his friends were very active in Griffintown, the Irish quarter. The city volunteers drilled more briskly than the country people, but they lacked even the shotguns. In Quebec, the volunteers took like veterans to parade routines. They had a number of French songs which made excellent marching tunes and they delighted in marching past the House of Assembly when Parliament was in session and saluting the members with martial music. Everywhere the response was the same. Though arms were lacking, volunteers were plentiful. Morale was high. The people knew nothing of the realities of war.

The officers of these makeshift battalions were somewhat less confident than the men. As the picturesque officer of the London rally admitted, there was no hope of training the farmers as soldiers. But they were good shots and knew the country; they would be very effective as guerrillas. It was obvious that they would be very independent in the matter of discipline. Where they knew their officer and res-pected him they would give hearty co-operation. But early in the crisis, in their loud-voiced, argumentative and, it must be admitted, positively Yankee way, they made it clear that blundering old Tories in the reserve army would get short shrift from them, no matter what rank they might have acquired through patronage.

The Canadian government alone understood the extent

of the danger. The war would be fought on Canadian ground, even though Canada was not consulted in the negotiations between England and the United States and the war was not of its seeking. Eight thousand troops were on their way from England, but it was unlikely they would reach Canada before ice closed the St. Lawrence. In the United States the demand for the annexation of Canada was growing urgent. In England there was a considerable war party which wanted to support the South and save the source of the British cotton industry, and Lord Palmerston was a war party in himself. To use the language of a later age, more painfully familiar with such occasions, it was a deteriorating situation—it was a war of nerves.

Even John A. Macdonald, who believed that every problem solved itself if left to time, was affected. On his advice the Cabinet sent one of its members, the astute Alexander Galt, to make direct contact with the American government. This move annoyed the British ambassador in Washington who resented colonial interference in foreign affairs. But if the Canadian government chose to send an unofficial delegate to wait upon the American executive, there was nothing he could do about it. Mr. Galt was received very cordially by Mr. Seward, the American Secretary of State. He also had a long private interview with President Lincoln.

The remarkable character of this man made a strong impression on Galt. He found Lincoln unpretentious in manner, a typical backwoodsman, with a fund of amusing anecdotes which he worked in on every occasion. But Galt, in talking to him, also sensed the great strength and great weariness, as of a man oppressed by destiny, characteristics which became more apparent later in the war.

He told Galt that the American government did not want war with England or Canada and was using every honourable means to avoid it, and he cautioned him against paying too much attention to the ranting of the newspapers. The policies of the government were not dictated by newspapers.

Galt left his audience with Lincoln somewhat reassured, but not completely. He was an anxious, worrying kind of man. What he saw in Washington was both extraordinary and terrifying. In the midst of confusion, blunders and defeat the Union was forging the first modern war machine. Arms and equipment of all kinds were pouring into the city. Soldiers from all the states in the North detrained on their way to the front, which was uncomfortably near.

The Irish Regiment of New York was there nursing its wounds after the battle of Bull Run. Had D'Arcy McGee been with Galt he might have seen familiar faces; his brother James was in the army and Tom Meagher—Meagher of the Sword—had at last come into his own. He was Colonel of an Irish regiment which he had recruited by his own efforts and was to be seen about the capital between battles in a dashing Zouave uniform, a sight to make even jaded Washingtonians stare a little.

Galt had eyes only for the vast extent of the preparations. The very circumstances of adversity gave an air of relentlessness and implacability to these efforts. Galt shuddered to think of this armament or any portion of it being turned against his own country where he had left unarmed lads playing at soldiers, innocent as children. As a young man Galt had been one of those Canadians who had approved union with the United States and he had even signed the Annexation Manifesto of 1849. What he saw in Washington convinced him that the only union that would be offered Canada was that of conquest. He was disabused of his youthful notions. Even though he trusted Lincoln he doubted if the government of a democracy could ignore for long the screaming insistence of its influential newspapers. Mr. Seward implied that the American government would be glad if Canada would cease to be a temptation by putting itself in a state of defence.

There is good reason for believing that the affair of the *Trent* was finally settled by a mortally sick man in a regally furnished study in Windsor Castle. Prince Albert, the Consort of Queen Victoria, possessed his wife's confidence in the fullest sense. He saw all the state papers that passed through her hands including the intransigent letters of Lord Palmerston to the American Secretary of State. He seemed to appreciate more than the others involved the tragedy that threatened the English-speaking world if England and the Empire were drawn into the war between the States. Dismissing his doctors he took to his desk as a man might take to a last ditch. In the half light of the winter dawn he worked over the state papers, unravelling the web of war spun by Palmerston. Almost unnoticed in the excitement of the crisis the green-shaded lamp on his desk shone like Shakespeare's good deed in a naughty world. His moderation reaching out to the moderation of Lincoln prevailed. The American government consented to free (without apology) the two Confederates taken off the *Trent* and the war crisis passed.

In Canada, members of the government saw the moment of danger pass with feelings of profound relief, shared in varying degrees by the whole country with the possible exception of the younger recruits who regretted that the excitement had failed to lead to action. In December, Albert the Prince Consort died. Canadians joining the rest of the Empire in condolences to the Queen were not aware, so self-effacing had been the Prince's life, that their conventional expressions of mourning were made for one who had gambled his chance of recovery to save them from war.

In March of 1862 Parliament met at Quebec with a great deal of ceremony and fanfare to mark the arrival of Canada's new Governor-General, Lord Monck, who was presiding at the opening. The Cartier-Macdonald administration was still in power; an atmosphere of staleness amounting to stalemate soon blanketed the session.

In April the government brought in a Militia Bill which had been drawn up by a committee very conscious of the warning of the *Trent* affair. The bill provided for both volunteer and compulsory military service and a fivefold increase in military expenditure. John A. Macdonald supported the bill on its second reading with a dry speech. Some, at least, of his listeners felt that he did not have much confidence in it. There was no debate and a vote was called for immediately. Always a volatile assembly, subject to decided changes of mood, the House on this occasion was stiff with tension.

In the section where the voting began there was subdued argument and gesticulation among the members. They were a group of French Canadians from the back counties, representatives of conservative farmers who opposed tax increases, had an abhorrence of military service and knew from deeply ingrained tradition that the country of the St. Lawrence had never been involved in a war on its own account, but only as a pawn of the great powers. Although these representatives looked to Cartier as their leader, their responsibility was to their electors.

When the Clerk of the House asked for the "Yeas" none of them rose to cast a vote. Cartier's face clouded with anger. He and Macdonald drew slips of paper towards them and began keeping tally. The House grew very quiet as the voting continued. Staunch supporters of the government voted for the measure. Then the Clerk turned to the opposition. Some who usually opposed the government supported the bill in the interests of defence; others like McGee were too deeply committed to opposition policies to sacrifice an opportunity to defeat the administration. A little agitation continued over in the corner and at one point several of the original voters changed their minds and asked to have their votes recorded with the "Yeas". By this time those who had been keeping tally mentally quite lost count. Cartier and Macdonald concentrated on the score. There was no sound but the voices giving and recording the votes. When the voting was over there was dead silence. The Clerk made up the tally and handed it to the Speaker who announced the results. The Militia Bill had been defeated by seventeen votes.

The government had been defeated too,—for the first time in eight years—clearly and decisively on a major issue.

But instead of the burst of jubilation on the part of the opposition, the high spirits, the back-slapping and hand-shaking that should have greeted the event, the House continued to sit silent. The question seemed to press heavily on all of them: Had they played the game of politics once too often? Had they gambled with their existence as a people?

Cartier rose and, controlling the anger in his voice, moved an adjournment.

The government which replaced the Cartier-Macdonald administration brought in a new militia bill as one of its first acts. This bill provided for smaller expenditure than the first one, voluntary enlistment and the establishment of the Royal Military College for the training of officers for the permanent force, a useful provision overlooked in the first bill. The second bill Parliament passed without difficulty.

The news of the rejection of the first bill made a bad impression in England. Newspapers and even members of the British government spoke of the Canadians as a poor-spirited people, lost to shame and honour, who were unwilling to defend themselves. The Canadians were very annoyed by this criticism. It was their own business what bills they chose to pass or reject in their own Parliament. On the other hand they were painfully aware that in the matter of defence they were not independent.

Let the Canadians not think, warned one section of British opinion, that the Empire would defend them if they refused to help themselves.

To this threat D'Arcy McGee, who was a member of the new government, retorted that it was nonsense to talk of the Empire defending Canada. Canada *was* the Empire, just as much as any other part.

The quarrel died down in time, but not before stirring up a good deal of hard feeling.

Chapter Twenty-Four
BROWN THE TERRIBLE

In 1861 the English shareholders in the Grand Trunk sent Edward W. Watkin to Canada to report and make recommendations regarding that very troublesome railway. It was already of great length, over one thousand miles, extending from Lake Huron in Canada West to Rivière du Loup east of Quebec. The Canadian government was frequently in trouble with the electors for making extra and unauthorized grants to the line which was always in debt. The home government was reluctant to spend the British taxpayers' money on an unprofitable venture and the governments of the Maritime provinces were insistent that no good would come of the railway till it was extended to Halifax.

After carefully studying the case Mr. Watkin came to a conclusion that positively startled him. With something like embarrassment he wrote to a friend that he saw only one way in which the Grand Trunk could be made profitable.

". . . . I may be looked upon as somewhat visionary for even suggesting it, but that way to my mind lies through the extension of railway communications to the Pacific. Try for one moment to realize China opened to British commerce; Japan also opened; the new gold fields in the territory on the extreme west, and California also within reach. Try to realize again, assuming physical obstacles overcome, a main through railway of which the first thousand miles belong to the Grand Trunk Company, from the shores of the Atlantic to those of the Pacific, made just within—as regards the north-western and unexplored district—the

202

wheat-growing latitude. The result to the Empire would be beyond calculation—it would be something in fact to distinguish the age itself; and the doing of it would make the fortunes of the Grand Trunk."

D'Arcy McGee had many opportunities to meet Edward Watkin and he naturally welcomed a man with ideas like these as a rare and congenial spirit. It was not by chance that when he published a book of his addresses on federal union in British North America he dedicated it to Edward Watkin. McGee wrote and lectured on the idea of a Canada reaching to the Pacific and presented the vision to politicians and people with lonely enthusiasm.

"I see in the not remote distance, one great nationality bound like the shield of Achilles by the blue rim of ocean—I see it quartered into many communities—each disposing of its internal affairs, but all bound together by free institutions, free intercourse and free commerce; I see within the round of that shield the peaks of the western mountains and the crests of the eastern waves—the winding Assiniboine, the fivefold lakes, the St. Lawrence, the Ottawa, the Saguenay, the St. John, the Basin of Minas—by all these flowing waters, in all the valleys they fertilize, in all the cities they visit in their courses, I see a generation of industrious, contented, moral men, free in name and in fact—men capable of maintaining in peace and in war a constitution worthy of such a country."

The members cheered him in the House when he made this speech, although they feared to face the ideas that inspired it.

The union of all the British North American provinces including even the Hudson's Bay Company's territory westward, had been a familiar project for years. There was scarcely a man in public life who had not spoken of it as a highly desirable aspiration. It was what the Americans called "Manifest Destiny". But whereas the Americans leaped towards their manifest destiny and pursued it across the continent—at this point some were willing to pursue it to the Arctic—the British North Americans shrank from their challenging fate. It had to pursue them. At this point in various ways their destiny was closing in on them although they still expected and hoped that the problem would fall to a later generation.

In John A. Macdonald's opinion the Civil War was proving the folly of all federal unions. He was in favour of a strict legislative union of British North America when it took place—an event which he believed would be in the distant future.

George Brown gave qualified approval to confederation, but did not think it would happen in his time. He wanted the union between the Canadas changed to allow for representation by population. As this meant asking Lower Canada to accept an inferior in place of an equal status, every responsible public man knew that the obstacles to achieving Rep. by Pop. were practically insurmountable.

Dorion saw one way out of the difficulty—a limited federation that would include only Upper and Lower Canada. He did not think a larger federation would be acceptable to his compatriots and in this he was not far wrong. The French Canadians reacted to confederation schemes as they did initially to most suggestions of change, by going in the house, bolting the door and pulling down the blinds. As this attitude is incompatible with civilized living they invariably had to open the door again, if only to permit bargaining to be carried on.

The Maritimers wanted a railway connection with Canada, but they were not nearly so eager for the political union. Some felt that if they could have representation in the Imperial Parliament in London, it would be preferable to sending members to a Parliament in the Canadian hinterland.

McGee carried on missionary work in the cause of confederation among the people of the Maritimes as well as among the Canadians. Every summer he visited the provinces by the Atlantic, met their public men and in his speeches and lectures presented to them his dream of a northern nation.

"We have more Saxons than Alfred had when he founded the English realm; we have more Celts than Brien had when he put his heel on the neck of Odin; we have more Normans than William had when he marshalled his invading host along the strand of Falaise. We have the laws of St. Edward and St. Louis, Magna Carta and the Roman Code; we speak the speeches of Shakespeare and Bossuet; we copy the constitution which Burke and Somers and Sidney and Sir Thomas More lived and died to secure and save. Out of these august elements, in the name of the future generations who shall inherit all the vast regions we now call ours, I invoke the fortunate genius of a united British America, to solemnize law with the moral sanctions of religion and to crown the fair pillar of our freedom with its only appropriate capital, lawful authority, so that hand in hand we and our descendants may advance steadily to the accomplishment of a common destiny."

His words stirred the slow imaginations of his listeners and warmed their enthusiasm. It was not quick to take fire, but once alight it could be expected to burn with a steady flame.

The railroaders like Alexander Galt were the most forward of all in urging confederation as an immediate policy. But their motives were suspected of being not entirely disinterested. An over-all government would be more generous with grants than several small ones. A united country extending from Halifax to Lake Superior and possibly expanding westward would mean more traffic for the starving Grand Trunk.

Along with its own financial difficulties the Grand Trunk suffered from the bad reputation railways in general had acquired in Canada. The first Canadian railways were built in the tradition of coaching lines for comparatively short distances and sometimes with a rival company building in hot competition. Municipalities as well as private individuals invested money and lost heavily when the railways failed because operating expenses proved far more costly than had been expected. Railways came to be looked upon as a reckless and ruinous form of speculation.

The government was constantly under pressure from the Grand Trunk for more loans and grants while the opposition and its newspaper the *Globe* loudly cried: "Corruption!" They declared that the Conservatives were controlled by the railroaders who robbed the public treasury to assure themselves huge profits.

More considered historical opinion is that comfortable profits were made from the Grand Trunk by Canadian promoters and contractors, very little by the English financiers, and that most of the funds went into the cost of construction and upkeep. It must be conceded that if the railway was an evil it was a necessary one, for although it exercised an unwholesome influence in politics, it had made itself indispensable to the country.

The government that succeeded Cartier and Macdonald found that it too had to consider the railways. In 1862 its delegates met in convention with the Maritime provinces to discuss an intercolonial railway from Quebec to the sea. This caused Dorion, who was a member of the government, to resign as he believed that the railways should follow trade and population and not precede them.

Critics of the government accused it of breaking its promises of economy. But as McGee sensibly pointed out, economy was a poor, negative policy for a new country. The function of government was not retrenchment but development. He was always a good friend of the railways, although, unlike many men in public life he had no financial connection with them and unlike certain later historians did not regard railway building as romantic. Railways were useful, serving as a backbone for a country of scattered communities. He talked about railways as he talked about economics, with facts and figures. These subjects did not appeal to his imagination, nor inspire the splendidly sustained eloquence of his perorations.

The Reform government in which McGee held the office of President of the Council marked a new point in his career.

His efforts to win the support of the Irish Catholics for the Reformers seemed to be justified by events. The "corrupt" Conservatives had been defeated. A Reform government was in power, but without the objectionable George Brown who was not even in Parliament. The *Canadian Freeman* began to report more favourably of McGee. And his speech on the Separate School Bill went a long way to restoring its confidence.

Here was a matter of public policy involving three factors—the Church, which retained certain rights of education under the constitution; the Superintendent of Education, Dr. Egerton Ryerson, who wished to see the common school system extended to the whole population, but appreciated the need of compromise; and the *Globe,* which supported the common schools and wanted no compromise whatsoever. A problem pertaining only to Upper Canada, but even within its narrow setting a controversy of historic and philosophic significance. As such it appealed to D'Arcy McGee.

For the first time in history, education, in the sense of literacy, was possible for everyone. McGee was unhesitatingly in favour of it. His work for the night schools in New York made him one of the pioneers of adult education. But when it came to the instruction of children he was prepared to support to the limit the claims of the Church as a source of education.

According to his argument three agencies were concerned in the education of the child: the parents, the pastor and the State. It was obvious that he considered the first two much more important than the last. The idea of State education was modern; it came from Prussia and was non-Christian in its tendencies. Where the dogmas of religion were lacking the dogmas of the State might be put in their place. "No one can show me any enduring national character that ever was moulded without a strong infusion of dogmatic religion of some sort. Some have spoken of the demand for Separate Schools in Upper Canada as a priests' question. Nothing could be farther from the fact.

I assert of my own knowledge in the name of tens of thousands of parents whose petitions are on your table that this is a fathers' and mothers' bill . . ."

Certainly he spoke for himself as a parent, for on other occasions he had shown that his own theory of education was one of culture and tradition rooted in religion.

"If on the one hand it was in my power to give to my own children all the secular knowledge that Alexander von Humbolt carried to the grave—or give them on the other hand the Christian catechism and some of those old songs of our ancestors that infuse heroism, fortitude and affection into the heart—if I had to choose between them, I would not hesitate a moment to choose the old songs and the little sixpenny catechism."

This was a legitimate philosophy of education, but at a time when the trend was setting strongly towards State-controlled, secular education it was not likely to have a large following.

On the whole McGee's first experience as a Cabinet Minister was disappointing. His influence was far less than his position had led him to expect. It is true the Separate School Bill had been passed, but his carefully worked-out plans to assist immigrants, whose welfare he had said would always be his first concern, were discouraged by the other members of the Cabinet. The French Canadians did not favour immigration, as it upset the balance they held in the population of the country.

The Reform government did not have a dependable following in the House. Very soon after taking office, it learned that the humiliating condition upon which it held power was to shift and adapt in order to retain a vote here or a couple of votes there among the less attached members. The Reform Ministers were now in a position to appreciate the adroitness with which John A. had manipulated a shaky majority over a long period, and with which, in spite of alleged corruption, he had succeeded in passing useful legislation.

The Reformers were not furnished with a leader of comparable talents. The Reform premier, John Sandfield Macdonald was likely to be confused with the Conservative leader in name only. He was from the Highland Scottish settlement of Glengarry in Canada West, where he enjoyed the reputation of a skilful fiddler, very good-natured about providing a tune at weddings and festivities. This pleasant and neighbourly talent had no place in the House of Assembly. Under the strain of office J. S. Macdonald's health suffered; he grew nervous and irritable.

The attitude of the *Globe* did nothing to smooth his path. George Brown was not in Parliament, but in the editorial columns of his paper he commented with displeasure on the course of the administration. It had dropped Rep. by Pop; it had lent its support to the Separate School Act; it had dallied with that sure source of corruption, the Grand Trunk. In the spring of 1864 George Brown successfully contested a by-election, and with some trepidation the House, especially the Cabinet, learned that he would soon be among them. New members looked awe-struck on the towering austere-faced Mr. Brown dressed sombrely in black. Veteran members remembered what it had been like before when Brown was in the House. In his own words he had returned to Parliament as the avenger of liberalism.

He lost no time in putting the fear of George Brown and the *Globe* into J. S. Macdonald.

"Now, if at the time when the honourable member was chosen to be the head of the administration last year he had come to me and had asked me to join his government, I would have asked him at once whether he was prepared to go for representation by population. I know what his answer would have been. 'Oh, that is all nonsense, the government must be carried on.' I would then have said: 'I prefer you to the others and will support you against them, but on the first favourable opportunity I will kill you too.' If the Premier should ask what will I do when I have killed him off, I will answer, 'Kill others. I have killed more than one ministry in my day.'"

It is indicative of the depressed state into which Parlia-

ment had sunk that no one rose to protest this unseemly
language. It had the intended effect of cowing J. S. Macdonald who acted to save his administration. A period of
intrigue followed during which three members were
dropped from the Cabinet to make place for three of Mr.
Brown's colleagues, Oliver Mowat from Upper Canada,
Luther Holton from Montreal and Antoine Dorion who had
previously been a member of the Cabinet but had resigned
over the railway policy. One of the Ministers dropped was
the Honourable Thos. D'Arcy McGee.

J. S. Macdonald showed a great lack of tact in the way
he got rid of his Ministers. Negotiations for changing the
Cabinet personnel were carried on in a secret, if not under-
hand, manner. No adequate explanations were given to the
ousted Ministers. No effort made to retain their good will.
J. S. Macdonald, unsure of himself and careful, had found
McGee's forceful and exuberant temperament difficult to
cope with. He was rather too free in expressing his relief in
being rid of the Irishman.

The *Globe,* which was still critical in spite of the Premier's attempts to mollify it, expressed regret that McGee
had not been kept in the Cabinet. Even the editor of the
Globe, deficient as he was in many of a politician's qualifications, felt concern about J. S. Macdonald's folly in throw-
ing so much talent and fiery resentment on the political bargain counter.

If the Premier and the Reformers did not want D'Arcy
McGee there were others very willing to take him into their
ranks. Cartier, although he did not like McGee personally,
was interested in the Montreal Irish vote which, as he was
only too well aware, McGee controlled. And John A. Macdonald was always on the lookout for another man.

McGee, who had acted as an Independent until he became a Cabinet Minister, returned to Parliament as a private
member in the autumn of 1863. He resumed his role of Independent member, but it was noticed that now he acted
with the Conservatives rather than with the Reformers. John

A. took McGee off with him on a by-election tour in which they accomplished the defeat of one of John S.'s candidates in what must have been to McGee a very consoling fashion.

John A. Macdonald had always shown a friendly attitude towards McGee even in the face of McGee's attacks on the corruption of the Macdonald administration. There were very few men whom John A. could not win over if he chose and he knew how to bide his time. There was no personal animosity between these two men, nothing to prevent them, after an evening session, from exchanging casual remarks or sharing a joke over their glasses in the refreshment room of the House of Assembly.

When John A. grew old and famous and his words were taken down as pontifical utterances it was noted that he sometimes said that he had never had his youth. When others recalled the escapades of their younger days, his memory, looking back over the years spent in George MacKenzie's crowded little law office, found no spritely episode to add to the conversation. He could recall the Rebellion of 1837 when armed with a gun he had started out with some others in the general direction of Toronto. He was paired off with a veteran of the Napoleonic Wars who knew how to march. The young law student striving to keep up with him was soon drooping from fatigue. That had not been much of an adventure.

And yet he had a capacity for enjoyment that craved fulfilment. He brought to the social and convivial side of politics the zest of a man who in middle life was satisfying a boy's hunger for fun. D'Arcy McGee, ten years Macdonald's junior, made a congenial associate. Whatever afflictions McGee had suffered, suppression of enthusiasm had never been among them and his youthful high spirits had been only a little dimmed in the course of his wanderings.

Together and separately they toured the constituency of Leeds during the short November days, and harangued meetings and met with committees during the long November evenings. Incidentally their purpose was to elect the Conservative candidate but principally it was to defeat the

Reform candidate who was also the Attorney-General in J. S. Macdonald's Cabinet. In a loud and public way they shared in the life of the community. They met and talked with the lawyers and merchants in the towns and with the farmers, free at this season for politics. They ate formidable country suppers, beans and pies and pickles, venison in plenty, hot Johnny cake and maple syrup. They drank tea if their local supporters were temperance, harsh strong whisky if they were not. It was as good as a general election for the local people. A by-election seldom attracted two such speakers. The country people tucked their blankets around their knees, drove miles through the frosty evening and crowded into hot and stuffy little halls to hear the ex-Premier or Mr. McGee, the noted lecturer, who was said to be the best speaker in Canada. Other people paid money to hear him lecture but they could hear him for nothing by attending a Conservative meeting. It was the political game, if not at its highest, certainly at its merriest. Against the persuasion of speakers such as these J. S. Macdonald's Attorney-General did not have a chance.

As an incident in John A. Macdonald's career there was nothing unusual in his taking over the brilliant Irishman. George Brown had recently called him an old cat always on the watch for mice. In later life he was compared to a monster in a cave to which the footsteps of many beasts approached, but from which none was found returning. His ability to use and manage men was a cause of suspicion rather than of admiration in a society where frankness and independence were prized as the manly virtues. Macdonald's peculiar genius developed in spite of his environment. He had no vanity and was content to exercise his talents quietly. Although for years he had been the real leader of the Conservative party and for much of that time the real Prime Minister, he was often willing to let someone else pose as leader or hold the title.

In the company of men of abounding energy like Cartier, McGee or Brown he seemed to lack vitality. From time to time he said he would withdraw from public life and was dissuaded from the notion by his party. He sometimes wrote to his sister that he had been ill when his critics said he had been drinking—"hopelessly inebriated". A curious story is told by a friend of one of these occasions when John A. kept to his room and refused to see anyone. The friend succeeded in being admitted and found Macdonald sitting up in bed with his head wrapped in a towel, sipping what appeared to be sherry and reading a French novel. He seemed quite composed. It may be that he had his own way of taking the fashionable water cure with its relaxation and water-sipping—only in his case he preferred the waters strong. At this point something should be said of McGee's conduct. A good case might be made for him as an Independent who supported the party which came closest to his own programme and who, if he followed a zig-zag course, always followed it towards the same ends. But at this time the larger destiny of Canada was closing in on the parliamentarians relentlessly and political parties were ceasing to have much meaning.

George Brown was the first to acknowledge that the game had been played to a stalemate and that drastic changes would have to be made. He passed the fall session in a state of irritation at the hopeless impasse in public affairs and in Cromwellian mood wanted to sweep away parliamentary procedure like cobwebs. D'Arcy McGee undertook to rebuke him.

"The honourable member, accustomed to play the tribune out of doors, seems to forget that we are here sitting not as a public convention which shall decide its own internal arrangements by the will of the majority, but that we are sitting here in the ordinance of Parliament, for Parliament is not a convention of delegates, but is itself an ordinance and the highest ordinance known to the Constitution."

Then just at the end of the fall session Brown did an extraordinary thing, the full significance of which was only apparent afterwards. He asked for a committee to enquire and report on the suggestions for constitutional change (i.e., federal union) made by Galt and Cartier to the British government in 1859.

The Governor-General, Lord Monck, encouraged him in this course and there is some evidence, although it is not conclusive, that Brown also consulted with D'Arcy McGee about the motion. Certainly the wording and presentation, the idea of identifying the committee with Galt's and Cartier's earlier confederation plan, all suggest that Brown had had one or more advisers of greater tact and diplomacy than himself.

As it was already late in the session he made the motion, he explained, merely to have it on record. He would bring it up again in the spring. He kept his word and reintroduced the motion in March for debate and in May to put it to a vote.

By May J. S. Macdonald's government had resigned. Strictly speaking it was not defeated; it just gave up. The moral, which J. S. pointed out in the best speech of his anxiety-ridden career, was that government could not be carried on with an uncertain majority of two or three votes.

The Governor-General had some difficulty in finding anyone to form a new Cabinet. But in the end those serviceable perennials, George Cartier and John A. Macdonald were induced to take office. Among the members of this not very promising administration was the Conservative party's latest recruit, Thomas D'Arcy McGee.

These monotonous shifts in and out of office were of less importance than George Brown's efforts to form his committee. The brilliant idea of using the same words in the new proposal for confederation that Galt and Cartier had used in 1859 failed to entice either of these gentlemen. Cartier said that confederation was not a proper subject for a committee; it should be a matter of government policy. Galt said it was just a trick; Brown was after something else. They voted against the committee as did John A. Macdonald. But they must have been somewhat surprised when the motion was passed by a vote of fifty-nine to forty-eight, especially as all three were named among the twenty on the committee. The other names represented various parties and points of view and included D'Arcy McGee, Oliver Mowat, J. S. Macdonald and Antoine Dorion. George Brown was the chairman.

Twenty is a large number for a committee and in this case all knew each other as colleagues or opponents. The first meeting started off with a good deal of persiflage, until George Brown locked the door and put the key in his pocket.

"Gentlemen," he informed them, "now you must talk about this matter as you cannot leave this room without coming to me."

The committee met twice a week for a month. No minutes were kept, but Brown maintained discipline and the problem of confederation was discussed to such purpose that by the end of that time the members were ready to take a stand. A large majority were in favour of confederation either for Upper and Lower Canada or for all the British North American provinces. Of the four who voted "no" one was J. S. Macdonald, one was a Mr. Scoble who has no part in this narrative, one was Christopher Dunkin who made himself famous in a small way by knowing more reasons against confederation than everyone else put together. And finally, one was John A. Macdonald.

It is not quite clear why John A. voted against confederation at this point. But since the vote may be either against the person presenting the motion or against the motion itself, it may be that John A. was registering dislike for George Brown, his committee and his chairmanship. Also he still adhered to the idea of a legislative union. It was his last gesture of opposition toward confederation. A day or two later when the newly formed government was in difficulties following an adverse vote in the House, John A. realized that even he could no longer carry on an administration. He was ready at last to consider confederation as an immediate and practical policy.

Negotiations were opened with George Brown. The first meeting between the two men took place openly on the floor of the House before an afternoon session. It was

brief but conveyed with dramatic impact to those who saw
it that something unusual was about to happen. The antipathy between these two passed the bounds of ordinary
dislike. For years they had not spoken even to exchange
the merest civilities. Now there followed a series of informal meetings in Brown's hotel room in the course of
which Macdonald offered to form a coalition with Brown
to bring about a federal union.

Just for a moment Brown hedged and tried to hold out
for the idea he had sponsored for years. Why not a coalition
for Rep. by Pop.? But Macdonald and his colleagues firmly
quashed the idea. Lower Canada would never consent to
inferior representation under the present form of union.
No government could hope to pass that measure. They
would have nothing to do with it. Brown gave up the idea
and like Macdonald committed himself once and for all to
the scheme of confederation. Each consulted with his party
colleagues and found them in favour of the coalition.

When Macdonald, speaking as a member of the government, told Parliament that the coalition was imminent, the
members cheered. The excitement continued after the
session adjourned. A French Canadian rushed across the
floor and embraced George Brown; others gathered around
to congratulate him more sedately. In one sense they were
being trapped into confederation; in another it was offering
them an escape from a blind alley. But at least they had
the bracing satisfaction of making a decision, like people
getting married or going to war.

There was a general feeling that George Brown especially had shown great public spirit in overcoming his
animosity towards Macdonald and that this forbearance was
all on one side. John A. was considered the sort of person
who was willing to be friendly with anyone, but Brown was
a righteous man who did not like consorting with sinners.
No one was more conscious than Brown himself that he was
acting from the highest motives. He enjoyed being the hero
of the hour and was eager to continue in the leading role.

"For perhaps the first time in my political life I indulged in a regular chuckle of gratified pride at the thought of my presiding over such a discussion by such men," he wrote to his family after he had accepted a position in the coalition government. "I could not help recalling many furious scenes in which several of those around me had bitterly denounced me for proposing the consideration of the very subject they were then engaged in settling under my presidency."

Nonetheless he had struggled very hard to remain out of the Cabinet, fearing that he would be dominated by Macdonald, aware that his independence as editor of the *Globe* might be restricted if he were a member of the government. He was willing to have other Reformers join the Coalition, but he did not think "that parties who had so long and so strongly opposed each other, as he and some members of the administration had, should enter the same Cabinet."

Macdonald brushed aside this delicacy. He would not consider a coalition unless Brown was a member. Brown wavered for several days. He could not enter a Cabinet led by Macdonald. But John A. was used to *not* being Prime Minister and the highly esteemed Sir Etienne Taché was given the honour. On the number of Reformers in the Cabinet Macdonald was firm. Brown wanted five colleagues. Macdonald said two was all that was reasonable or practical. Brown accepted the arrangement finally and with Oliver Mowat and William McDougall joined the government. He spoke at some length in the House on the sacrifice he was making to help the cause of confederation and drew satisfaction from the good opinion in which he was held in many quarters. But he could not completely stifle his uneasiness. He was not certain whether he sat in the Cabinet as an equal associate or as a hostage for his own good behaviour and that of the *Globe*. The biggest beast in the forest had gone into the monster's cave.

Chapter Twenty-Five

NOONDAY OF SUCCESS

YOU CAN HARDLY imagine the interest I now take in this country and all that belongs to it," McGee wrote to James Sadlier in 1864. "But it does not and never can supply the field for mental labour and affectionate inspiration which Ireland would have been."

He had not had to forgo entirely the satisfaction of literary work on Irish subjects. In 1862 he published in the Dublin *Nation* a poem on the occasion of the death of John O'Donovan, the archaeologist whose studies had opened a new world to him when he had discovered them in the Library of the British Museum years ago. Rarely have scholarship and the victories of the pen been praised with greater spirit and vigour than in this long memorial poem. Letters congratulating him came from many quarters and one which especially pleased him from Samuel Ferguson, his friend of the Irish League days, who had increased greatly in stature as a poet himself during the intervening years.

Then in 1863 he published the *Popular History of Ireland* on which he had been working since coming to Canada. This history ended with O'Connell and the Catholic emancipation and so brought the story up to McGee's own time. The book was widely read and passed through several printings; a new edition appeared after his death. The book continued to live up to its title in a gratifying fashion until it fell behind in the course of time and was superseded by more recent publications.

McGee had made a full and lively story of what in less skilful hands easily became a chronicle of sodden tragedy.

He had lightened the sad record of political history by including Irish social life, Ireland's literature and scholarship and the achievements of her people who had fared forth as missionaries or exiles. When the literal-minded Gavan Duffy had undertaken the serious study of Irish history he had been scandalized by the amount of legend and fancy that adorned it. But D'Arcy McGee was not—after the science-conscious fashion of the nineteenth century—contemptuous of legends, believing that the folklore of a people gave a better idea of the national spirit than a chronology of its wars and rulers.

The Young Irelanders, in the brief period of Davis's leadership, when their literary fervour had been at its height, had planned and even begun a popular history, dividing the work among a number of them as a group project. Little was accomplished and the idea had dropped out of sight until McGee took it up again and with devoted energy produced the *Popular History of Ireland* himself. Achievements such as this led Duffy to compare McGee to Thomas Davis. In the year following the publication of the history the Royal Irish Academy recognized his work by making him a member.

As his letter to Sadlier indicates McGee was happy in Canada. The family was settled in Montreal. The two little girls went to the Sacred Heart Convent. They were Euphrasia, whom D'Arcy described as "studious, a good musician and a great letter writer", and Agnes the lively one, the last born. Mrs. Caffrey, D'Arcy's mother-in-law, made her home with them. Mary's grief on her death in 1866 was intense. She had appreciated her mother's help during family illnesses and other incidental domestic crises and she had especially depended on her companionship during D'Arcy's frequent absences. He was constantly from home, attending Parliament, travelling here and there in Canada or in the United States on lecture tours. D'Arcy's brother John also made his home with the McGees; he too was often away in Upper Canada where he was training in the field to be a public land surveyor.

219

Among the friends McGee made in Montreal the Sadliers were in a special sense family friends with the relationship extending to the wives, "our two Marys" as McGee sometimes called them. Usually, however, the stiff conventions of middle class Victorians were maintained and the two ladies were addressed and referred to as Mrs. McGee and Mrs. Sadlier.

While Mary Ann Sadlier wrote for the *True Witness* it had kinder things to say of McGee than it had later, and when the Sadliers moved from Montreal to New York in 1860 D'Arcy regarded their departure as a public and private loss. He reproached the *True Witness* with its behaviour towards "one who after contributing for years gratuitously to your columns was suffered to leave this city and province without a word of acknowledgment—merely because she was my friend".

Although separated, the two families carried on a correspondence and made plans to spend summer vacations together. When Mrs. Sadlier returned to Montreal for a visit, as a matter of course she stayed with the McGees. D'Arcy wrote a poem to celebrate the occasion as well as one or two others at different times in honour of the lady. They expressed edifying and abstract sentiments and were dedicated with a correct gesture of anonymity "To Mrs. S—".

Along with his other activities McGee kept up his connection with Thomas Walsh, the advocate on Little St. James Street. It was a vague partnership but entitled him by 1862 to call himself a lawyer and on one occasion he appeared as a counsel in the Court of Queen's Bench. This seemed to have been the only time he exercised his prerogative as an advocate, although he continued to use the office of Walsh and McGee as his business address.

The McGees found themselves at home in Montreal from the first but it was not until 1864 that D'Arcy became a property owner. That year his political supporters throughout the country, but especially in Montreal, presented him with a house on the corner of St. Catherine and Drummond

Streets, one of a row of new houses called Montgomery Terrace, flat-fronted and dignified with plain stone arches over the windows. This gift served the double purpose of honouring McGee and meeting a practical political need. The electoral laws of the period required that a candidate for Parliament be a property owner. Gavan Duffy was given a house by his party to meet this property qualification when he contested his first election in Australia. In McGee's case property may have been registered in his name or some such arrangement made when he first entered political life. But the house made merely formal arrangements unnecessary. It was solid and actual and enhanced McGee's position as a substantial Montreal citizen.

After the coalition government had been formed, McGee suggested that something might be done to promote confederation before Parliament met in the fall. This could take the form of a summer excursion to the Maritime provinces to make the acquaintance of the people with whom they were planning to form a union. McGee's colleagues in the Cabinet were considering a visit later in the year and did not respond to the summer plan, but a number of private members were willing to make the trip. These were joined by journalists, railwaymen and merchants; in all they numbered nearly a hundred. The Grand Trunk did its share by providing their transportation.

Through intense summer heat the train carried the perspiring excursionists eastward under conditions that could not but convince them of the discomfort of railway travel whatever they might think of it as a way of getting across the country quickly. At Portland, Maine, due to some miscalculation the steamer they had chartered was not on hand and heavy rain added to their misery. At this point some of the travellers turned back; this may have been just as well as the steamer, when it finally arrived, did not have adequate accommodation even for those who remained. Some had to sleep on deck and McGee attempted to rally them by punning that if they did not have bed they still had board. The party continued in low spirits until the bracing salt air coupled with the cordial welcome of the Saint John Board of Trade revived them.

The newsmen and politicians of the Maritimes were accustomed to D'Arcy McGee's summer visits and most of them had attended railway conferences in Quebec or reciprocity conventions in Upper Canada, but this was the first time they had entertained the Canadians in force.

"Oh, if you fellows could only now and then dine and drink with us fellows, we would make a great partnership directly," Joseph Howe had said on a recent visit to Upper Canada. The veteran leader of the Nova Scotia Liberals was present to greet the excursionists when they visited Halifax and he had some pleasant things to say about confederation.

He had a long record in public life and had stood for the rights of the governed against the arrogance of governors and long-term office holders. The tribune of Nova Scotia, the people called him. Although he was close to seventy his energies were undiminished and popularity had tended to increase his ambition. He aspired to play a part in imperial politics and had undertaken a rather disastrous venture in attempting to recruit Irish Americans for the Crimean War. This had involved him in international difficulties and lost him the support of his fairly numerous Irish followers in Nova Scotia. This in turn had lost his party an election and the premiership had passed to the rising leader of the Conservative party, Dr. Charles Tupper, a match for the old tribune in energy and audacity.

Maritime hospitality produced a fine glow of good fellowship in the visitors and the hosts alike and the sociable purpose of the expedition was accomplished. On the way home the American ship on which the Canadians travelled was pursued by, or in danger of pursuit from, a Confederate warship, an occurrence which they found more stimulating than alarming. When they arrived home they could look back on a vacation made up of receptions and banquets, hardship, danger and patriotic achievement.

The report of good will brought back by the excursionists spurred the Canadian Cabinet ministers to visit Charlottetown in September, when a conference to discuss a union of the three Maritime provinces would be in session. This, to the members of the Canadian government, seemed a singularly opportune time to drop in on the Maritimes. Avoiding the rigorous railway journey, eight members of the Cabinet including Macdonald, Cartier, Brown, Galt and the tireless McGee, boarded a government vessel, the *Victoria*, at Quebec and travelled comfortably by way of the Gulf to Charlottetown. The hospitable Maritimers for a second time found themselves hosts to self-invited guests.

The conference was already in session and not making much progress. Prince Edward Island refused to consider a legislative union unless Charlottetown was made the capital. The objection to this was not so much that Prince Edward Island was the smallest of the three provinces, but that Charlottetown was cut off by ice from the mainland for part of the year. The less insular of the Maritime delegates felt that the Islanders might as well ask them to hold Parliament in a lighthouse. Popular opinion in Charlottetown seemed apathetic to the conference; there was a circus in town and it attracted far more interest. Without suggesting that the Maritime politicians had gone to the circus, it must be recorded that when the members of the Canadian government arrived a solitary official in a rowboat was the only person to meet the ship.

But the Canadians, only recently reconciled to the idea of confederation, were filled with the convert's missionary zeal. Upon being received into the conference they talked for two days and by the end of that time had gone a long way in convincing the Maritimers that the federation of all the British North American provinces was to be preferred to the union of the three little provinces by the sea.

Maritime hospitality also had caught up with the situation and the members attending the conference found themselves visiting about and being entertained at Halifax and Saint John. They continued to confer, but in a relaxed atmosphere of picnics, banquets, torchlight processions and excursions to the seashore. In this mental climate the idea of confederation blossomed like a hothouse plant. The danger was that it would prove an exotic bloom, the product of after-dinner oratory and a long line of toasts which might not survive the chill winds of a provincial election. But for the moment the delegates had no thought of difficulties. They were getting acquainted, a process which Joseph Howe had promised would open the way to a great partnership.

It was unfortunate that the old tribune was not at the conference. He had been invited by the Premier, Dr. Tupper, who knew that in spite of his recent political defeat he was still a power in Nova Scotia. But imperial favour had beamed on Howe in the form of a commissionership on the International Commission that regulated fishery rights in coastal waters. He declined the invitation to the conference on the grounds that his imperial duties required him to be at sea at that time. In his absence Tupper became the most outstanding of the delegates from the Maritimes.

He was a short sturdily built man with a square face which in old age would fall into heavy bulldog folds, but which at forty-three was rather handsome and could be described by those two popular terms, open and manly. As a young man he had been as quick in an argument with his fists as with his tongue, a vigorous quality that did not make him the less popular. He was called the fighting doctor and the young lion of Nova Scotia.

John A. Macdonald was very favourably impressed by Tupper whom he met for the first time in Charlottetown. Here was a man capable of filling a much larger role than the narrow scope of Nova Scotian politics allowed him. Macdonald himself was becoming aware that confederation offered him also a wider field of action.

"For twenty long years," he told the conference, "I have been dragging myself through the dreary waste of colonial politics. I thought there was no end, nothing worthy of ambition, but now I see something which is well worthy of all I have suffered in the cause of my little country."

Since the members of the conference were pretty generally of one mind on the question of confederation and since the Canadians had to admit that they had reached the limit of their capacity to accept any more hospitality, it was agreed that they should adjourn the conference and meet the following month in Quebec to draw up the plan in detail.

The steamer *Victoria* did service again and brought the Maritime delegates to Quebec in October. As they disembarked they had the air of a large, prosperous, family party since a number of them had brought their wives and daughters. They represented four colonies, Nova Scotia, New Brunswick, Prince Edward Island and Newfoundland. With the delegates from Canada they numbered in all thirty-three.

As in Charlottetown no reporters were admitted to their meetings and no statements issued to the press. Complete minutes of the proceedings were not kept. As a result the Quebec Conference has caused as much dissatisfaction among later historians as it did among the newspapers of the time.

The Fathers of Confederation hardly considered their hagglings in committee over procedure and finance worthy of a verbatim account either for the electors or posterity. They were not making a constitution in the grand manner. There was no philosophical preamble to be drawn up or pronouncement on the rights of the people. All that was taken for granted. Even though they were more truly the representatives of the people than many a legislator of more high-flown and revolutionary constitutions, they knew that confederation when it was accomplished would not be an act of the people or even their own act, but in an exact and legal sense an act of the British Parliament. The form of government would be the one which they already had—a Parliament of two houses, a Senate and an elected assembly, with the executive drawn from the assembly and responsible to it. But as this was to be a federal union with each province retaining its own Parliament and a federal Parliament over all, a division of powers and revenue had to be made. The delegates worked on the problem and by the end of three weeks had drawn up seventy-two resolutions covering most of the points. The powers of the conference did not extend beyond this. It was necessary for the delegates to have their respective Parliaments accept the resolutions, after which they could present them to the British Parliament to be made the basis of a new constitution.

While the conference was in session the ladies who had come with the Maritime delegates were entertained in proper Quebec fashion; they passed their time viewing historic sites and visiting convents. Lady Monck, the wife of the Governor-General, held an evening reception for them.

Once the seventy-two resolutions were drawn up the delegates were free to enjoy themselves in the spirit of work well done. Some of them again had the feeling experienced at the Charlottetown Conference that the really large issues in public affairs resolved themselves with less strain and worry than the nagging little ones.

The delegates from the Maritimes now received a return for their hospitality of the summer. The weather had been persistently unpleasant ever since their arrival. The visitors, one newspaper grieved, would think that Canada had nothing but rain. It was a pity because the country usually looked beautiful in October. Since nothing could be done about the weather every effort was made to take the visitors' mind off it. With their ladies in bonnets and crinolines, they were carried by special train to Montreal where a ball was given in their honour, followed by a luncheon the next day. They visited Ottawa, Toronto, Hamilton and St. Catharines, partaking of banquets which, if the menus speak truly, really deserved the name and make the public dinners of a later period look meagre.

The entire range of sophisticated dining was covered from soup through the fish and entrée to the boiled, roast and game courses, with salad,—sometimes in the form of lobster mayonnaise—and ending with pastries and dessert, which of course included nuts and fruit. Each dish had its appropriate sauce, which reads like a culinary poem, and no menu was complete without a list of wines and liqueurs that leave little to be desired. The imagination boggles at the thought of the diners accepting all the dishes offered, but even if they restrained themselves to half the menu they still would have eaten very substantially. It was not unusual for a banquet to last six hours, but of course besides the dining there were also the toasts and speeches.

The Victorian ladies were not expected to undertake these gustatory efforts, but there was no objection to their presence in the gallery where some of them came towards the end of the banquet to watch the gentlemen drink the toasts and to listen to the speeches.

The special train that brought the delegates from Quebec was provided again for the visit to Canada West. The lateness of the season and the prevailing bad weather gave the railway an advantage over its rival the steamboat. Mr. Brydges, the manager of the Grand Trunk, took great pains to leave no doubt in the minds of the confederation delegates as to the convenience of travel by rail.

They were popularly acclaimed in Ottawa and the towns of Canada West. In Quebec venerable Laval University had hailed them as the men who had moulded the destiny of their country. In Toronto staid Upper Canada College greeted them in the name of union, prosperity and strength. For the brief space of the tour they could confidently assume the role in which posterity would confirm them—the Fathers of Confederation. They made their progress through the country in a more lordly spirit than even the royal tour. That had been merely a symbol of power; they were the true nation-builders. Behind them were the seventy-two resolutions, a plan of union definite and detailed. Ahead lay the glowing possibilities of the future: a federation of self-governing colonies and the peaceful conquest of the West—the great plains, the mountains La Vérendrye had sought, and beyond them the harbours of the Pacific. A great nationality bound like the shield of Achilles by the blue rim of ocean—a dominion from sea to sea and from the river unto the ends of the earth.

McGee was no longer alone in his poetic vision of Confederation; it was now shared by a goodly company. His many visits had made him better known among the Maritimers than the other Canadians, so that he acted as liaison agent between the two groups at Charlottetown and at Quebec. His wit and good humour fitted him well for this task and when he rose to speak at the banquet in Montreal, according to the newspaper report "the waving of handkerchiefs almost made a canopy over the heads of the guests and it was not till after protracted cheering he could be heard".

Was Mary McGee present when the ladies waved their handkerchiefs and the men cheered? This surely would be one time when she would take part in her husband's public life. The only existing picture of Mrs. McGee, taken by a Quebec photographer, is a full-length portrait against a pseudo-classical background, showing Mary in a crinoline dress of a silhouette and amplitude that was the height of fashion in the early 1860's. It is obviously a best dress designed for great occasions. By drawing a little on the imagination we might even say it was chosen for the pre-Confederation entertainments of the autumn of 1864. Certainly Mary's name appears with her husband's in lists of guests present at some of the functions, and the last group of Maritime delegates and their ladies passing through Montreal on their way home from their jaunt through Upper Canada were entertained in McGee's new home at Montgomery Terrace.

Had Mary McGee been a mild and tepid personality destined to blend inconspicuously into the domestic background, we might accept the lack of information about her without curiosity. Self-effacing she must have been, but the few scraps of description we have of her bear out the impression given by her picture that she was not a colourless person.

Mrs. Sadlier said of her: "She was a woman of much force of character, who was fitted to shine in society by her brilliant conversation and fine wit. She was devoted to her husband, admired his talents and was altogether a true helpmate. He was equally devoted to her, respected her sterling qualities of head and heart and was often guided by her wonderful perception of character."

A conventional tribute, but its very conventionality makes the choice of compliment all the more striking. The very word "woman" had practically dropped out of the speech of the period. "Lady" and "one of the fair sex" were the euphemisms in use and in cases where neither could possibly apply "female" was the accepted word. Also whereas North American ladies of the period aspired earnestly to good taste and refinement they made no pretence to wit or sparkling conversation. And to top it all this self-effacing Victorian wife had "a wonderful perception of character". It is regrettable that there is so little record of the part she played in D'Arcy McGee's life.

Chapter Twenty-Six
POLITICS AS THE ART OF THE POSSIBLE

It would be difficult to exaggerate the caution with which the Fathers of Confederation approached their task. Timid they were not for they were prepared to face the undertaking even though all too aware of its difficulties. But as a group they made a virtue of the practical and avoided flights of imagination and rhetorical flourishes in their speeches. Even the eloquence of D'Arcy McGee stands out all the more brightly because of its rarity. He was too sincere a patriot and too cunning an artist to produce a Confederation speech at every banquet. On these occasions he usually helped the company over the last sagging half hour of hospitality, that threatened to become interminable, with the aid of his ready wit and easy fellowship.

"Improvement", "progress", "commercial prosperity through free trade", "strength through union", "communication by railway"—these were the larger themes of their addresses. They respected facts and figures and used them constantly. More than one voiced the hope that under Confederation, politics would enter a broader and nobler field and public life would be freer from bitter contentions over small issues. More than one admitted to a sense of urgency simply expressed by the Canadian Prime Minister Sir E. P. Taché: "Do not suffer this opportunity to pass. It is one that may never recur."

George Brown, a journalist rather than a politician, spoke up more boldly than the others and drew attention to the original nature of their work: "I don't believe any of us appreciate in its true importance the immensity of the work we are engaged in. But there is one thing peculiar about our position. There is no other instance of a colony peacefully remodelling its own constitution. Such changes have always been the work of the parent state and not of the colonists themselves. Canada is rightly setting the example of a new and better state of things."

D'Arcy McGee said it was a miracle. "Can we ever expect, if we reject the scheme, that the same or similar things will occur again to favour it? No, sir, it is too much to expect. Miracles would cease to be miracles if they were events of everyday occurrence. The very nature of wonders requires that they should be rare. And this is a miraculous and wonderful circumstance that men at the head of the governments in five separate provinces and men at the head of the parties opposing them, all agreed at the same time to sink party differences for the good of all, and did not shrink, at the risk of having their motives misunderstood, from associating together for the purpose of bringing about this result." (He was referring to the Quebec Conference.)

His colleagues loved him for utterances like this. Too prudent themselves to venture upon dramatic expression they responded enthusiastically when he spoke for them.

When the Canadian legislators assembled for the first time in the Parliament Buildings in Ottawa they had on the agenda the seventy-two Confederation resolutions, a subject worthy of discussion in their new and splendid surroundings. The debate was a formality. The coalition government formed by Macdonald and Brown had a strong following in the House and the motion to accept the seventy-two resolutions was certain to be passed by a large majority. But the speeches were directed not only to the legislature but to the country at large. The five members of the Cabinet—Macdonald, Brown, Cartier, Galt and McGee—who supported the motion were speaking for the record. Each dealt with a particular aspect of Confederation and brought to the subject all his powers of persuasion and oratory, knowing that he was very probably making the most important speech of his career. McGee spoke last and was generally and generously considered to have excelled in eloquence.

Antoine Dorion and Christopher Dunkin spoke against the motion. Dorion, who had supported the idea of Confederation for Upper and Lower Canada only, feared that the wider union would mean the end of French-Canadian nationality. It was only a scheme of the Grand Trunk, he said, to get itself out of its financial difficulties.

Christopher Dunkin spoke against the motion in a speech that went on for two afternoons and two evenings. He too was speaking for the record and made a painstaking analysis of every weakness in the seventy-two resolutions and every objection to Confederation that might ever arise. It is to be feared that the attention of his listeners flagged; the very completeness of his criticism defeated its purpose.

Bad news came from New Brunswick where the Confederation leaders had risked a general election and been soundly defeated. The seventy-two resolutions had proved too much for the electorate to digest. They had soon been reduced to one—the matter of subsidies to be paid to the provincial governments—and this one had been bandied about among the voters as the odious proposition that they were being sold to the Canadians for eighty cents a head. Prince Edward Island and Newfoundland also turned down Confederation.

The opposition in Nova Scotia had a formidable leader in Joseph Howe. He wrote editorials and toured the country denouncing Dr. Tupper and the "Botheration Scheme" as he had once denounced irresponsible governors. He had the satisfaction of finding his hold on the people of the province as strong as ever.

When the whole of Howe's career is considered it would seem that he did not intend to oppose Confederation permanently. He wanted to drive Tupper from office and reintroduce it on his own terms. As he said to a friend in his rough, frank way: "If you had a circus and had got together a good show and were ready to open up, how would you like it if that fellow Tupper came and stood by the door and collected the shillings?"

The popular opposition to Confederation in Nova Scotia was so great that Tupper dared not risk the defeat of the seventy-two resolutions by presenting them to Parliament. But Howe was wrong in thinking he could force his rival's resignation as Premier. Tupper determined to lie low and ride out the gale.

And now correspondence from leaders in all the provinces that sent delegates to Quebec begins to gather on a Cabinet Minister's desk in Ottawa. It might have come to George Brown or George Cartier—to Prime Minister Taché or to D'Arcy McGee who is favourably known to them all. But as it so happens it comes to the desk of John A. Macdonald, the man who has unobtrusively but surely directed the affairs of the united Canadas for eighteen years even though he has never been Prime Minister (except for eight months—December 1857-July 1858), the man whom exasperated opponents call the monster in a cave.

Circumstances have placed the problems of Confederation on his desk. He has not sought them; he never seeks out problems. But when he cannot avoid them he deals with them in his own way. Politics is the art of the possible and Macdonald is a superb politician. His canny replies go out to his correspondents—his shrewd comments on the situation.

Confederation will not be submitted to a general election in Canada. "I hear of no meetings against it and as yet there have been no petitions transmitted adverse to the policy. Under the circumstances the government have a right to assume that the scheme in principle meets with the approbation of the country. It would be obviously absurd to submit the complicated details of such a measure to the people."

Hopeful letters pass between Macdonald and Mr. Shea of Newfoundland, a colony still expected to join the union. A word of consolation goes to Colonel Gray of little Prince Edward Island which has rejected Confederation. There is condemnation for Mr. Tilley of New Brunswick. "The course of the New Brunswick government in dissolving their Parliament and appealing to the people was unstatesmanlike and unsuccessful as it deserved to be . . . The scheme was submitted without its being understood or appreciated and the inevitable consequences followed." He allows himself a moment of natural complacency when he refers to the situation in Canada. "You see that we carried the Address (Confederation) in both Houses by majorities of three to one." From Dr. Tupper in Nova Scotia come long letters giving in detail his difficulties and the temporizing tactics he is using to meet the situation. Mr. Howe is raising a storm of opposition, but Macdonald from his first meeting with Tupper knew he was a man to depend on and events are proving the worth of his judgment.

While the struggle between the old tribune and the young lion was going on in Nova Scotia the Canadian statesmen could only hope for the best, but the pressure of events had become so strong that they could not wait for the outcome. Government under the union of the two Canadas had broken down; they could not go back to that. The end of the Civil War had come, marked grimly by the assassination of Lincoln. Relations between the British American colonies and the Northern states had never been good since the *Trent* affair. The old easy intercourse of the pre-war days seemed to have gone forever and the British Americans now had a neighbour grown militarily powerful and unfriendly.

"Let Canadians never forget for one hour they have now to do with democracy armed and insolent," McGee warned. "With democracy in square and column, with a sword at its side and a bitter humiliation in its heart."

And finally there was the problem of the West. The age of the great trading companies was over. Just as government had passed from the East India Company so it would soon pass from the Hudson's Bay Company. The heritage of the fur trade empire belonged to the Canadians if they were ready for it. In the Northern states the editors of newspapers were writing constantly about Manifest Destiny.

The Canadians could not afford to wait any longer. If they did not accept their destiny there were others ready to seize it from them.

In the spring of 1865 a delegation from the Canadian government composed of Macdonald, Cartier, Brown and Galt, set out for England taking with them the seventy-two resolutions.

Chapter Twenty-Seven
THE WEXFORD SPEECH

O<small>N THE SEVENTEENTH</small> of March, 1864, the Hibernian Society of Montreal held a dinner at the Exchange Hotel. A number of prominent Irishmen of the city were present, several as guests of the Society. Towards the end of the banquet when the toasts were being drunk, "The Wearin' o' the Green" and other rebel songs were sung; also a special version of "Columbia, the Gem of the Ocean" which ran "Britannia, the curse of the ocean, the scourge of the brave and the free", and ended with a rousing "To hell with the red, white and blue!"

The Society's guests were somewhat embarrassed, not so much by the boisterous Irish nationalism—on St. Patrick's Day a certain amount of exuberance could be overlooked— but (at least so it seemed to one of the guests, a level-headed lawyer) because the demonstration was something more than a spontaneous outburst of holiday spirits. He felt there was something deliberate and organized about it, an attempt to draw him and other respectable members of the Irish community into the orbit of the Fenian Brotherhood, a revolutionary society that had grown amazingly in the United States.

D'Arcy McGee, Minister of Agriculture, had not been present at the St. Patrick's Day dinner, but when told of the episode he did not hesitate to inform Mr. Clarke, the lawyer, that the Hibernian Society was actually a branch of the Fenian Brotherhood and that he was right in thinking that the attempt to secure adherents and sympathizers who only partly understood its aims was deliberate. That was part of its tactics.

McGee's first encounter with the Fenians had been as far back as 1861 at the time of the *Trent* affair. A meeting called to recruit an Irish battalion in case of war had been repeatedly heckled by an organized minority. McGee learned afterwards that half a dozen agitators had come from the States for the purpose. Since then he had followed the development of the Brotherhood and its underground activities in Canada closely.

The Fenians began in Ireland after 1848 as a secret society to liberate the country from England—merely another of the secret societies that were always coming into existence among that oppressed and frustrated people. It was not established in America till 1857. There it had for its head John O'Mahoney, who had at one time been connected with Young Ireland. He was a man of good education and family who had delved into the Irish past and had translated Keating's *History of Ireland* from Gaelic into English. He also dabbled in spiritualism and may have fancied he had communed with the great spirits of the past even more intimately than through these studies. He wished to revive the fianna or militia of the ancient Gaels and he rejected every hope for Ireland except liberation by the sword. Unhappily, along with his many-sided abilities, he was mentally unstable and twice while in America he had to be committed to an asylum for the insane.

Under O'Mahoney's erratic leadership the Fenian Brotherhood flourished beyond reason. The Irish Americans had ready money and any appeal for the relief of Ireland moved them to heedless generosity. Money poured in and out of the Fenian treasury in unaudited profusion. During the Civil War the military ambitions of the Fenians were used to stimulate enlistment in the Union army. Recruiting officers promised that after the war was won the Irish would be armed, equipped and aided in their struggle against England. They would be allowed to take Canada as their base for operations. Idealists yearning to be Irish patriots, schemers, adventurers and wastrels were attracted to the Brotherhood. The movement was a crusade and a racket.

Only in America could this wild project have reached such grandiose proportions.

D'Arcy McGee feared it and hated it like sin.

He knew only too well the fascination that schemes and fantasies had for the Irish temperament and he knew how grievously Fenianism could prejudice the position of the Irish in Canada.

In the fall of 1864 an episode occurred which was given wide publicity in Canadian newspapers. The fifth of November, Guy Fawkes Day, an obscure historical date celebrated by the Orangemen, was usually observed in Toronto with some demonstration, such as burning the Pope or Daniel O'Connell in effigy. In 1864 these amusements were overshadowed by a counter demonstration by the Irish Catholics. They assembled to the number of four hundred in Queen's Park. They divided into four bands and each marched to a different point on the outskirts of the city where the men disbanded quietly and went home. There was no violence; it was the very lack of disorder, the evidence of organization and discipline that alarmed and amazed the public. Extravagant rumours spread through the country. The Fenians were organizing in Canada. They were planning to overthrow the government and Catholic churches were being used as arsenals.

For a year McGee had been exhorting the Irish to have nothing to do with Fenianism. He warned them in the plainest language that it was seditious and treasonable, condemned everywhere by the Church. Early in 1865, barely two months after the demonstration in Toronto, he pointed out its disastrous consequences.

"See what the result has been in some parts of Upper Canada. Any two or more nervous or mischievous magistrates . . . may subject a neighbourhood to all the rigours of martial law. Already indecent and unauthorized searches have been made for concealed arms in Catholic churches. Already, as in some of the towns of Bruce, the magistrates are arming one class of people against another."

He went on to warn the Canadian Irish again.

"At the risk of sharing the fate of all unasked advisors, I would say to the Catholics of Upper Canada, if there is any proof that this foreign disease has seized on any, the least among you, establish at once for you own sakes, for the country's sake, a *cordon sanitaire* around your people; establish a committee which will purge your ranks of this political leprosy; weed out and cast off those rotten members, who without a single governmental grievance to complain of in Canada would yet weaken and divide us in these days of danger and anxiety. Instead of sympathy for the punishment they are drawing upon themselves, there ought to be a general indignation at the perils such wretches would draw upon the whole community, socially, politically and religiously."

These anxieties were weighing on McGee's mind when he set out for Ireland in the spring of 1865, about the same time that the delegation from the Canadian Cabinet was going to England. McGee, as Minister of Agriculture was also travelling in an official role; his mission was to represent Canada at the International Exhibition being held in Dublin. There was a tacit understanding that he would later join the other members of the Cabinet in London.

In some respects the visit to Ireland was of a kind to distract McGee's mind from his worries. It was an occasion when a public man might properly lay aside his responsibilities for a moment and enjoy the prestige of his position. McGee was at the highest point of his success, he was the emigrant returning home with fame and honour.

By a happy coincidence Gavan Duffy was in Ireland at the same time, a personality who commanded even more attention than McGee. Many wanted to meet again a man long familiar to Dubliners, although they declared that now they could hardly recognize him with a beard and deeply tanned by the Australian sun. His short period of exile had been marked with notable success and he also was attending the Exhibition in an official capacity as Premier of the self-governing colony of Victoria.

A number of former Young Irelanders felt that this was an occasion for celebration. The fate of those who had returned from exile at the time of the amnesty had not been especially happy. John Dillon had described it in a letter to Duffy.

"You, I think, could not exist here without being a public man, and being that you would be miserable. In the midst of this hopeless gloom the news of your success comes to your old friends like a ray of light. When our enemies attribute our failures (individual and collective) to our want of capacity and energy, we have but one answer, and it is a conclusive one—we point to men of Irish birth or blood who are prosperous and distinguished everywhere but at home."

This mood was strong among the men of '48 when Duffy and McGee visited the Old Country. In a generous spirit of congratulation they prepared to honour these two who had vindicated Irish genius in the comparative freedom of the colonies. Public dinners were given for them. Duffy in his memoirs writes of the pleasure of looking down the table and seeing the faces of his old colleagues on the Dublin *Nation* and among them D'Arcy McGee, "one of my closest associates in trial and danger, who in whatever else he had changed, had at least remained steadfast in his kindness to me."

But the stir and noise of Fenianism did not allow McGee to yield entirely to the mood of reminiscence and reunion. In America the Civil War had ended and the Fenians in the Union army were clamouring to have the promises made to them fulfilled and to be allowed to turn their arms against England. The Fenians in Ireland were working themselves up to the explosion point. They really believed that the American Fenians were coming, backed by the might of the United States, to rescue them in blood and glory from their long vassalage to England. McGee was too acutely conscious of this situation to remain silent. When he visited his home in Wexford and was invited to lecture, he spoke out.

240

"I state here as an indisputable truth that there is no more national sympathy for Ireland, as Ireland, in the United States, than for Japan and far less than exists for Russia."

He told his audience hard and unpalatable truths about the position of the Irish in the United States. "The six northern or New England States . . . hate the Irish Catholic emigrant for his creed, despise him for his poverty and underrate him for his want of book learning."

He etched with delicate malice the ward politician who flourished in the big cities, a type he profoundly despised. "He is not seldom a dealer by wholesale or retail in spirituous liquors; sometimes a lawyer, sometimes an editor. He is always ready with his subscriptions to the Church, but seldom goes to church. He lies up on Sunday after the toils of the week, reading a sporting journal or a police gazette . . . He is particularly savage against England and grows quite pathetic, unprepared as he is, at the mere mention of the old land . . . A fair share of mother wit, a sufficient stock of spending money and a vast deal of brass complete the equipment of this very active, very important, much courted individual . . . A dealer in the manufacture and sale of his countrymen's votes."

During the Civil War a morbid hatred of England had been played up by the bounty brokers and recruiting sergeants. McGee feared that in spite of their gallantry and the blood they had shed, the Irish who had been in the front of the battle would be found in the rear of the national memory. It was in this atmosphere of false promises and exploitation that Fenianism flourished.

He contrasted conditions in the United States with those in Canada where the Irish had been absorbed into a less highly urbanized society.

"The newcomer it is true brings to us his social and religious discontents. The first two or three years he is dissatisfied and home-sick, but as with time he gathers gear, he settles comfortably into the system of society; becomes a small proprietor and a great stickler for law and order.

241

The old sores begin to skin over; his only grievance is that he has no grievance."

As on his previous visit to Ireland he was more inclined to warn against emigration than to encourage it.

"You seem to have a mania for emigration upon you in Ireland, and I certainly feel it no part of my duty to pander to that mania. On the contrary I would say to every man and woman who can live at home, stay at home! If the New World has its attractions it also has its penalties. If wages are much higher, life is far shorter; the average life of the Irish labouring man in the great town does not exceed ten years from the date of his arrival. A strange climate—out of the frost into the fire; strange food; and strange diseases sweep the back streets of the Irish surplus year by year. And it is to be feared that it is not bodies only that are lost but souls also."

It was a cruel speech. Even some of his friends thought he should not have made it. But McGee had spoken deliberately and with forethought. Knowing that what he said would not be confined to the audience in the Wexford Assembly Rooms, he took the precaution of giving a copy of the speech to the Dublin *Evening Mail* so that one truthful version at least would appear in print. Later, in an open letter to the Irish press he reiterated what he had said with additional facts and arguments.

Even his choice of place for the original speech was in a measure deliberate. He had been called a renegade before when he failed to sing sweetly of the Irish in exile. But a renegade would hardly choose his home town as a place from which to deny his principles. Where could he have more suitably discussed the hard realities learned in his twenty years' experience in America than in frank intimacy among the people with whom he had been brought up?

McGee's Wexford speech was quoted, misquoted and reviewed. The Dublin *Nation*, which had been taken over after Duffy's departure by a new editor, approved the tone of the speech with candour worthy of McGee himself. "The sickening effects of confectionary or stimulant oratory among us prompts the idea that a few draughts of bitters may be a salutary tonic influence in Irish politics." The *Nation* went on to say. "We express our entire concurrence with Mr. McGee in the opinion that the masses of our countrymen in the States are simply *used* in American politics and have notably been heartlessly and thanklessly used in the recent war."

The Irish American newspapers were shrill and abusive, an attitude hardly surprising if they believed their own distorted reports. Mendacious versions of the Wexford speech turned a harsh, but definite and verifiable account of the evils of immigration into a series of indiscriminate insults against the Irish Americans.

The *Canadian Freeman* at first merely printed the editorial from the *Nation,* then after the spate of angry journalism had lasted for some weeks, it came out with a moderate editorial in defence of McGee's argument. If the picture of the Irish in the States was not true, said the *Freeman,* let the objectors produce facts and not abuse to prove their point.

The strangest reaction of all came from McGee's companions of 1848. In the speech he had made two passing references to Young Ireland. The first was near the beginning. "I was one of the Young Ireland fugitives of 1848. I am not at all ashamed of Young Ireland. Why should I be? Politically we were a pack of fools, but we were honest in our folly and no man need blush at forty for the follies of one-and-twenty, unless indeed he still perseveres in them, having no longer the fair excuse to plead of youth and inexperience." And again in speaking of the Fenians he said: "Some of these seem to think that as I was a Young Irelander some twenty years ago I ought to show some lenity for them. Why, Young Ireland, as I am free to say, was politically a folly, but the men were honest and manly. Men like Thomas Davis and Duffy and others still living would have scorned to range themselves with these Punch and Judy Jacobins whose sole scheme of action seems to be to get their heads broken."

243

It is hard to understand why these not very severe remarks should have deeply offended certain one-time Young Irelanders, especially as they all sooner or later expressed the same opinion though not so trenchantly. But time and the action of Celtic imagination had produced wonderful effects out of the fiasco of 1848 as it passed into the memory of the race—another lost cause, forlorn and splendid. And the darling boys who had given themselves to it were already part of the legend. A pack of fools they may have been in the eyes of the world, but in the memory of Dark Rosaleen they were as young gods in the morning.

As the Dublin *Nation* aptly remarked: "It is not so much what Mr. McGee says, as what he does not say." Once again he had failed to sing sweetly of either the immigrants or the fugitives.

John Dillon, who had planned a select dinner party with Duffy and McGee as the guests of honour, crossed McGee's name off the list. Duffy declared that the Wexford speech was the one act of McGee's life for which he could never excuse him. He wrote to him privately to the effect that although McGee seemed to regard himself as a fool at twenty and a philosopher or statesman at forty, in Duffy's opinion he was much to be preferred as the fool.

Since McGee loved and admired Gavan Duffy above all his friends this criticism must have rankled in his mind more than the abuse of the Irish press. Months later at a banquet given for him in Montreal he defended his attitude passionately against the strictures of his friends.

"God knows the Ireland I loved in my youth is near and dear to my heart. She was a fair and radiant vision, full of the holy self-sacrifice of the olden times, but this Billingsgate beldame, reeling and dishevelled from the purlieus of New York with blasphemy on her lips and all uncleanliness in her breast, this shameless impostor I resist with scorn and detestation."

He only said heatedly and angrily what he had already said temperately in the Wexford speech and the letter to the Irish press.

The rift between D'Arcy and his companions of 1848 was not new. It had always existed, even when he worked on the Dublin *Nation,* an odd, ungainly, clever boy, lacking the others' advantages of education and social background —not university bred, not quite a gentleman. It is true that Duffy also lacked these advantages, having grown up like McGee in humble and restricted surroundings. But Duffy, whom McGee once called the "mild star", adapted himself gracefully to the literary world of Dublin and London. He was of blander temperament than McGee who never lost the saltiness of his plebeian origins.

Dillon went ahead with his dinner, but even with McGee eliminated the mood of the party was not right. It never reached a festive level. Duffy was obliged to rebuke one of the guests who ventured a witticism about Smith O'Brien refusing to dodge the police bullets in 1848. No one was in the humour for jokes at the expense of Young Ireland. Dillon whispered to Duffy when he came in that he had not dared ask McGee as he feared that some of the others would refuse to take his hand. The former Young Irelanders were in a peculiarly sensitive state of mind.

The next day Duffy, who had heard very little about Fenianism in Australia, had a long, probing conversation with Dillon. The account Dillon gave him of the movement in America tallied in all essentials with the statements of McGee's speech. Still Duffy did not draw the obvious conclusion. One cannot help wondering whether Duffy actually read the Wexford speech (he certainly thought he had), or whether he accepted what others said of it and allowed his usually fair judgment to be imposed on by their emotional reaction.

McGee did not allow the embarrassment caused by his speech to spoil his visit to Dublin. He was enjoying the prestige of his official position and the reputation that had followed from his *History of Ireland* and the poem on John O'Donovan. His conscience was clear. Few of the Young Irelanders had done as much as he to advance Irish letters and politics; none of those who had gone to America had

done as much to help the immigrants, or had earned a
better right to speak frankly about them. If John Dillon
was hurt and did not choose to invite him to his party that
was too bad. No doubt John would get over it. McGee
sent him a little note which when opened read:

John B.
Dillon, he
Cannot put up with D'Arcy McGee.

When D'Arcy joined the delegates in London during
the last week of May, they had been negotiating with the
British government for several weeks. John A. Macdonald
had let Cartier and Galt sail for England ahead of him and
had followed shortly with George Brown. They spent the
ocean crossing in each other's company without the camara-
derie that ship travel usually promotes. Brown was a strict
temperance man, while Macdonald was fond of a drink—
too fond, some said. They were a nuisance and a scandal
to each other. Brown continued to stiffen his will with the
thought that he was suffering for the public good and Macdonald would have been more than human if he had not
permitted himself the reflection that Brown was not the
only one whose comfort was being sacrificed to patriotism.

This irksome association was easier after they arrived
in England and could turn their energies to the business of
their mission. Galt and Cartier had some idea of what they
faced, having come on a similar mission in 1858. Since
then another government had come into office in England,
but negotiations remained as formerly on a social and
ceremonious level.

The Canadian delegates were presented at court, where
the heavy and pompous ritual was more magnificent than
ever, although the Queen, who after the death of her husband devoted herself with gentle stubbornness to her
widowhood, appeared everywhere in deep mourning. They
also attended dinners and receptions—at the Marchioness
of Salisbury's where they met the Tories and at the Countess

of Waldegrave's where they met the Whigs. Of course there were committee meetings, but it was advisable to meet socially all the people of importance. That was what mattered. That was the way things were done. The Canadians exhausted themselves in a round of formal entertainments in the fashionable world to which they were not accustomed. But it made wonderful news to write to their families.

Alexander Galt's letters, which have survived, are full of their presentation at court, the dresses of the royal princesses, the appearance of the Duchess of Wellington (rather over-painted, Galt thought) and the affability of the Prince of Wales who was quite a grown-up young man now and married. He had entertained them charmingly at his house and after the formalities of the dinner, the port wine and the drawing-room, he had carried them off to his own particular snuggery, where he plied them with cigars and liquors and enthralled them with his royal talent for recalling names and incidents of his Canadian tour with wonderful accuracy.

"We are decidedly in the 'haute monde' at present," Galt wrote to his wife. "But I confess I would rather mix with my own class . . . No amount of wealth would secure the attention we receive and these attentions are given not to us but to our offices and in compliment to our people . . . We are treated quite as if we were ambassadors and not as mere colonists, as we have always been called."

Galt, earnest and anxious, was in no danger of having his head turned. Their present entertainment reminded him of the visit of 1858, which had come to nothing. As the elaborate courtesies continued and the negotiations reached no decision his letters to Mrs. Galt grew more and more despondent.

"I have never been sanguine and am not so now, though public opinion is generally favourable . . . Our business proceeds slowly and I much fear is going to become very involved. It seems to me as if the statesmen of England have lost many of the high qualities which used to distinguish them; they seem timid and hesitating . . . You must say nothing about it to anyone but I have the conviction we shall effect nothing satisfactory to our people. It is very grievous to see half a continent slipping away from the grasp of England with scarcely an effort to hold it."

McGee, writing from London to Samuel Ferguson and Mrs. Ferguson to acknowledge their hospitality which he had enjoyed in Dublin, gives the same opinion as Galt.

"Really what brought these four gentlemen here (my respected colleagues) seemed in so fair a way of being overlooked that I began to feel very uneasy."

The negotiations, for good or ill, were nearly completed when McGee came to London. As he was not officially one of the delegation, he was not included in its invitations. But he arrived in time to join in a jovial and entirely unofficial celebration of the Derby. The Canadians took a day off from diplomacy. Accompanied by one or two newspapermen and the inevitable railwaymen, several of whom were always in discreet attendance, they went to the races. Provided with hampers containing a caterer's lunch and wines, the party drove in two carriages to Epsom Downs where they arrived at noon. There was some doubt among them as to how freely they should bet on the horses. They had to remember that they were public figures and that they had with them the editor of the Toronto *Globe* who could be expected to take a severe view of horse racing. In the end they put their bets into a pool and drew the names of the horses. At the last minute John A. Macdonald exchanged with Galt and won the money.

The race was only one feature of the gala day. There were the games, gypsies, shows, a circus and above all the crowds from all classes of society. The return to London was an extraordinary affair, a British Bacchanalia. The Canadians supplied themselves with peas, pea-shooters and other nonsense, buttoned their coats up to the chin and climbed into their carriages which inched along the Road among every form of transportation from the costermonger's donkey cart to the nobleman's four-in-hand. They ex-

248

changed salvos of peas with the crowd and at one halt treated an appreciative Cockney audience to parodies of Canadian election speeches. Everyone was in the highest spirits. Even George Brown, as Macdonald noticed with amazement, thawed out. "I had given him a bag of peas and a pea-shooter," Macdonald related years afterwards. "And the old fellow shot out quite a lot of peas." They arrived in London covered with flour, but, all things considered, in fairly good condition.

The results of the mission to England were better than had appeared at the time. Slow and ponderous as its workings were the Colonial Office, thanks to the Duke of Newcastle, was no longer indifferent or hostile to British American federation as it had been in 1858. The creaking machinery began to move. A delegation from the Maritimes in favour of the union of the three Atlantic provinces was told that the British government would not consider proposals that did not have as their aim the larger union. The Colonial Secretary instructed the Governors of Nova Scotia and New Brunswick to use the influence and prestige of their position to support the Confederation party in each province. The Governor of Nova Scotia who proved recalcitrant was transferred to Hong Kong and a better disposed gentleman appointed in his place.

By spring of 1866 certain incidents south of the border helped to convince the Maritimers that their safety lay in union. Dr. Charles Tupper who had not dared produce the motion for Confederation in Nova Scotia for fear it would be rejected even by his own party, noted that the strength of Howe's opposition had passed its peak and prepared to take advantage of more favourable times.

Chapter Twenty-Eight
THE FENIAN RAIDS

Sooner or later an immigrant group is faced with the problem of divided loyalties. The emotional pull of the old land is all the greater in as much as the new-comers feel that they are strangers and not wholly accepted in their adopted country. Fenianism, McGee believed, was a symptom of the failure of the United States to assimilate rapidly enough the enormous immigration of the famine years.

"This very Fenian organization in the United States, what does it really prove but that the Irish are still an alien population, camped but not settled in America, with foreign hopes and aspirations, unshared by the people among whom they live? If their new country was their true country would they find time and money to spare in the construction of imaginary Republics beyond the seas? If their leaders were real rulers at Washington would they be playing at governments? It is because the active spirits are conscious that being Irish they have no hopeful public career in the land of the Know Nothings and the rank and file feel that while their stomachs are filled their affections are starved in that hard and fast new society, that all this weak and wicked yearning after the impossible has developed in both classes. It is on the one part folly, on the other part crime, but it is human nature after all."

This explanation might serve for the Irish Americans, but for Irish Canadians the folly and crime of Fenianism was much more serious. An invasion of Canada had always been considered a possibility. In December, 1865, when the military leaders, released from their wartime duties, arbitrarily took over full control from O'Mahoney, the invasion of Canada became a settled policy. From the point of view of the military men this was practical, while an expedition to Ireland was almost impossibly difficult. After that date membership in the Fenian Brotherhood for an Irish Canadian became treason beyond excuse or extenuating circumstances.

Still the insidious work of the Fenians in Canada continued. Although O'Mahoney had taken the name from the heroic ages of Irish legend, he had organized the Fenians according to methods copied from European revolutionary societies of his own period. The whole vocabulary of subversive and underground organizations, familiar to the twentieth century, applies equally to these earlier forms, although not so generally used. The Fenian Brotherhood was composed of cells or circles, each of which was under an organizer who received instructions from the head centre in New York. In Canada, where the Brotherhood dare not organize openly, it adopted various names or simply infiltrated existing societies.

Its ways of collecting money were questionable but effective. Raffles were held for prizes which no one could remember anyone winning. Collections were taken up for the "relief of Ireland"—a somewhat indirect relief as the money went no farther than the head centre at New York. The Brotherhood gathered about it sympathizers or fellow-travellers, well-meaning individuals who, mindful of the Church's ban on secret societies, did not join the Fenians, but who could not withhold money and good will from any organization professing to help dear old Ireland.

The strength of the Fenians in Canada was never precisely known. Eighty of the society's seven hundred circles were supposed to be in Canada, principally in the cities. Extravagant reports of success were made by organizers claiming 60,000 members in Montreal alone and the cordial support of the Bishop of Toronto. Apparently they adhered to the paradox that the more incredible a lie, the more likely it is to be believed. In this way a good deal of false information was passed on to the leaders. The Fenian Brotherhood had not achieved that perfection of organization wherein spies are sent to check on agents. The Canadian Fenian Brotherhood was expected to assist in an invasion of Canada, when in fact no such body existed.

The membership of Fenians in Canada was very difficult to determine. Even D'Arcy McGee who boasted frequently and contemptuously that he bought Fenian "secrets" freely, admitted he did not know. But he did have the record of the amounts of money sent by the organizers in Canada to New York. Allowing for a certain number of donations from soft-hearted people who ought to have known better, McGee judged from the amounts sent that the number of genuine Fenians was not more than a few score in each of the principal cities. But the danger from these few was not negligible. In the event of an invasion the treasonable behaviour of a small group could bring enough discredit on the whole Irish Canadian population to embarrass it for generations. McGee was determined that this disaster would not happen if he could prevent it.

In every part of the country he visited he attacked Fenianism unsparingly. An element of fanaticism in his nature showed itself for the first time. He would admit of no compromise, no weak hesitant sympathy. Fenians were lepers and pariahs whom Irish Canadians must thrust out or be destroyed by them. He knew from experience how easily the young and hot-headed are led unwittingly into conspiracy, to find themselves no longer free agents but bound by their loyalties and fears. He warned and threatened these young men.

"Have nothing to do with Fenianism. I tell you I know many of the men who are associated with Fenianism and I say this, that if they do not separate themselves from that organization I will denounce them to the government. There is evidence enough to hang them. Come out from among them. The organization will bring you to ruin. There are some who think that they cannot be found out, that they are secure. I tell you I know them and will denounce them if they do not mend their ways."

The Brotherhood appreciated McGee as a formidable opponent. Pro-Fenian papers exhausted the resources of journalistic abuse in vilifying him. He received anonymous threatening letters and there was some loose talk of assassinating him. These threats were all in keeping with the rest of the humbug, McGee declared. But for a time it was considered advisable to give him police protection. "Tramp, tramp, tramp", the Fenian papers wrote gleefully after his name in reference to the plainclothesmen who were supposed to attend him. They called him again and again renegade, informer and Judas Iscariot.

Fenian abuse made great inroads into his popularity. He may not have realized when he determined to put his influence to this use that it would thereby be expended and diminished. It seemed that many wanted the excitement of playing, just a little, at conspiracy; they thought they could be Fenians up to a point without going beyond it. They fiercely resented this man, whom they never forgot they had raised to office, who now wanted them to see the issue in terms of black and white and insisted that they stand and be counted.

In 1866 for the first time McGee spent St. Patrick's Day in Montreal. For some years past he had been successful, with the support of the *Canadian Freeman,* in turning Irish celebrations into orderly channels, but in Montreal the St. Patrick's Day parade continued to be held. This city had a weakness for parades. The French delight in fanfare and display, the presence of the garrison and regimental bands set a standard of urbane behaviour very different from the orange and green rowdyism of Toronto. McGee not only attended this particular St. Patrick's Day celebration, but had some part in arranging it from behind the scenes.

During the winter of 1866 the activities of the Fenian Brotherhood in the United States took an alarming turn. Quantities of supplies and arms were purchased from the demobilizing Union army and sent north to the Canadian border, while the Fenian militia mustered with warlike intentions. The Canadian government was obliged to take measures against a possible invasion even though John A. Macdonald, as always, avoided meeting trouble until it forced its way through the door. The Canadians had counted on the American government restraining the Fenians, but Washington remained blind to what was going on. An election was coming up in the States and neither party wished to alienate the large Irish vote.

Rumours spread through the British American provinces that something would happen on the seventeenth of March and that it would probably be an invasion. In this state of public anxiety it seemed a good time to D'Arcy McGee and others of like mind to keep the Irish population of Montreal out of mischief on that date by occupying them with a respectable programme.

Accordingly they were marshalled out to High Mass on the morning of the seventeenth—all the Irish organizations, the Irish Benevolent Society, the Temperance Society, the Young Men's Society and not least the influential St. Patrick's Society that had secured McGee's election to Parliament. In McGee's opinion it had sadly deteriorated in the last year or two. The younger and more radical members used the Society's rooms before and after the regular meetings for making pro-Fenian speeches and singing rebelly songs and no one undertook to control them.

The Society's new president, Bernard Devlin, was not a man of whom McGee approved. In his late thirties, a lawyer especially successful in handling criminal cases, active in city affairs, a colonel of the Irish regiment, Devlin was ambitious to move on to a political career. His brother openly supported the Fenians, but Bernard Devlin's connection with the Brotherhood was more difficult to gauge. He was too experienced in law and practical affairs to entangle himself in hare-brained, treasonable enterprises, but he was prepared to use the Fenians to further his own plans. It must have seemed very strange to him that a man like McGee, dependent on votes for his position, should dare to follow an unpopular course, but since this was the case he intended to take advantage of it.

After Mass the procession formed and proceeded with banners unfurled through the streets of Montreal between admiring crowds, from Lagauchetière before St. Patrick's Church up Bleury to St. Catherine, east to St. Dennis and down to Notre Dame and the Place d'Armes in the old part of the city. It was after one o'clock when it reached St. Lawrence Hall where the Governor-General, Lord Monck, was to receive it.

The various dignitaries and officials had preceded the parade to wait upon His Excellency, among them the Hon. D'Arcy McGee and Lt.-Colonel Devlin who greeted each other with cool civility. The president of the St. Jean Baptiste Society was present more or less as a gesture of courtesy to the good St. Patrick as was also the president of the German Society, representing the latest newcomers to the city.

There they stood, the Irish of Montreal in their parade ranks, facing the Governor-General on his balcony, a pleasant Anglo-Irish nobleman, intelligently interested in Canadian affairs. He knew the situation and the purpose of McGee's request that he should be present. With courage and tact he addressed his audience.

"I do not consider this magnificent demonstration as one of personal respect to myself; I accept it as an evidence on your part of loyalty to our gracious sovereign and of attachment to the institutions of our land; and further as a protest on your part against the principles and designs of wicked men who would disgrace the name of Irishmen by their conduct, who have threatened to desecrate the day sacred to our National Patron Saint by a wanton attack on this peaceful, prosperous and happy community."

His Excellency's remarks were received with cheers.

"It was an occasion not unattended with anxiety," McGee said afterwards. "Had the Fenian faction mustered courage to give tongue all the intended good effects would have been lost."

As it was, two members of the St. Patrick's Society failed to remove their hats during the playing of "God Save the

Queen". To McGee's strained imagination they appeared to be in centre front, directly under the Governor's eye. He also believed he heard a distinct hissing mixed in with the cheers at the end. But these were only the slight flaws in performance that harass the soul of a director and pass unnoticed by the audience.

The Irish next visited the site of the new St. Patrick's Hall where they heard suitable addresses from all the dignitaries attending the parade. Then with nothing more dangerous on their minds, one imagines, than a longing for a good meal and an easy chair they dispersed to their homes. In the evening two thousand attended the Grand Concert in the City Hall where they were privileged to see in the reserved seats not only the Hon. D'Arcy McGee but most of the other honourable members of the Cabinet. These were presented at the end of the concert and duly cheered.

As a counter demonstration to Fenianism the St. Patrick's Day celebrations in Montreal were a success. Tension throughout the country relaxed. The government dropped its tentative military preparations—rather unwisely, as the plans for invasion in the United States continued as briskly as ever.

The Fenians struck in the beginning of June. They gathered their forces at three points along the border, near New Brunswick, between Vermont and Lower Canada, and on the Niagara River near Buffalo.

Before dawn on the first of June about 1,000 men crossed the Niagara at Fort Erie. They wore various and nondescript uniforms but were seasoned soldiers with competent officers. Their leader, Colonel John O'Neil, was a veteran of twenty-five who had achieved an honourable record and promotion in the Civil War. He must have been a man of magnetic personality. Most of our information about him comes from the inhabitants of the Niagara peninsula among whom he intruded himself as an invader. But even his enemies attest to his soldierly bearing and the discipline he maintained among his men. He is described as fairly tall, lean, and of sandy colouring. In manner he was courteous and quiet-voiced. There is no doubt that he had complete trust in the integrity of his superiors and believed he was fighting in an honourable cause.

The Fenians entered the sleeping village and, as one of their first acts, cut the telegraph wires. O'Neil and his officers proceeded directly to the house of the reeve, Dr. Kempson. When the household was roused the doctor's intrepid wife came to the door and attempted to send the callers away, but upon their insistence that the reeve present himself, the doctor came downstairs and placed himself at their disposal. They took him out into the street and ordered him to assemble the leading citizens. The awakened villagers were by this time hanging out of their doors or peering fearfully between the window curtains. Two men attempting to get away in a row-boat were forced to return by shots from the Fenian sentries. When the village corporation of three had gathered, O'Neil informed them that the Fenians had come to liberate them and that no one would be harmed if all behaved themselves. The business in hand was to provide breakfast for the troops. The village elders heard without satisfaction the news of their liberation. But they were essentially practical people and knew it was useless for unarmed men to argue politics with soldiers, so they issued instructions to the village to prepare breakfast.

The housewives and the kitchen staff of the local hotel set to work at their stoves and presently pails of tea and coffee and mounds of bread and fried ham were passed into the street and the nearby fields and orchards. O'Neil had provided sentries to keep the men out of the houses and gardens. After breakfast, drowsy from the food and warm sunshine, the Fenians, who had been up all night, stretched themselves out in the shade and slept.

At nine o'clock the villagers, having surmounted the first emergency, consulted anxiously among themselves. The breakfast had exhausted the ample but not unlimited supplies of a rural community. What would they do if ordered to provide dinner and then supper? This problem they were not required to solve, because at eleven o'clock O'Neil roused his men and, leaving a small force behind to hold the village, marched off along the river road presumably with Port Colborne and the Welland Canal as his goal.

Their next stop was at the prosperous Newbiggin farm near Frenchman's Creek. This property the Fenians took over and prepared for defence, to the distress of the family who foresaw their farm turned into a battlefield. Late in the day scouts brought news that Canadian forces were gathering at each end of the Welland Canal, Port Colborne and St. Catharines. If he knew where they were, O'Neil shrewdly concluded they probably knew where he was. So about midnight he withdrew his men, all but a few pickets, from the farm, so quickly and quietly that the Newbiggin family who had orders to remain indoors did not know about it till morning.

That day, June 2, the Fenians marched to Ridgeway Road along which O'Neil expected the enemy forces to attempt a conjunction which it was his purpose to prevent. Very early in the morning his patrols reported that Canadian troops were detraining at Ridgeway station and preparing to set out along the road.

The force advancing toward the Fenians was made up of about four hundred volunteer reserves from Toronto and Hamilton—young lads, most of them under twenty—led by a nervous colonel who also was facing an enemy for the first time. They wore new uniforms, the 13th of Hamilton in red and the Queen's Own of Toronto in green; each man had thirty-five rounds of ammunition. As they came up the road they had a strip of field and the Limestone Ridge on their right and farmland on their left stretching away to the woods. A pleasant garden-like country of orchards and fields of green wheat and rye crossed with zig-zag railings called snake fences. In the ditches and pastures buttercups and daisies stood in the tall grass. The whole countryside had the fresh unspoiled look of early June. The comfortable red brick farm-houses had been deserted on the approach of the Fenians by all but an occasional hardy soul who had stayed behind to look after the cattle. It was about 7.30 in the morning and the day promised to be hot.

An exchange of shots announced that the Canadians' advance guard had come upon the outlying Fenians. The volunteers began to deploy into the fields on either side of the road. From a farm-house on the slope of the Ridge where O'Neil had made his headquarters he watched the Canadians' movements.

"When they advanced in line of battle in their red uniforms they presented a beautiful appearance," he wrote afterwards. "It was one of the prettiest sights I ever witnessed. The line was well formed and their advance was brave."

They came across the fields and over the snake fences, steadily, firing as they came. Their bullets did little damage as the Fenians were under cover. On the other hand the Fenians' bullets flew high and did little to stop the advance. After about ten minutes those in the front lines, where ammunition was giving out, were replaced by fresh troops who carried on the advance. The Fenian outposts retired to the main line and both sides, now that the fighting was at close quarters, sought protected positions from which to fire. The Canadians succeeded in forcing back the Fenians' main line upon their reserves.

The tide of battle was not in favour of the invaders. O'Neil had had to deplete his forces by leaving pickets and patrols along his line of march from Fort Erie. He was not in a position to risk heavy losses and he was in danger of being caught by Canadian forces coming down the Ridge Road from the other direction. He therefore determined to retreat to Fort Erie. Preparations were made for this purpose, the supplies foraged from the countryside being reduced to a minimum so that the farm carts could be used for the wounded.

Then an extraordinary thing happened. Faintly but quite clearly the bugles of the Canadians could be heard sounding a retreat. The Fenians at first thought this was an attempt to lure them into a trap, but the firing died away and it was evident that the Canadians were withdrawing. Then the bugles sounded the warning for cavalry and the luckless volunteers formed squares to meet the expected charge. Massed in this fashion they made easy targets for the Fenians who were quick to press their advantage.

Such a disastrous reversal of tactics would have caused confusion even among veteran troops. It threw the green volunteers into a panic. In vain several officers tried to reform the ranks to protect the retreat; the lines were swept away by more men breaking through them in full flight. The Fenians chased them pell-mell down the Ridge Road, and the volunteers did not pause in their flight until somewhere past Ridgeway station a train picked them up and carried them back to Port Colborne. The casualties of the battle for the Canadians were nine dead. The forty-four wounded were cared for at the local inn.

The Fenians did not find their position greatly improved by this turn of events. They had now been at large without reinforcements for two days in the Niagara peninsula and their lines were dangerously extended. They had brought with them large quantities of arms and ammunition to equip the Canadian Fenians whom they expected to join them. But none of them had turned up. As O'Neil and his men began their withdrawal to Fort Erie these extra supplies were destroyed by dumping them into the creeks along the way.

They reached Fort Erie pursued, but not too closely, by Colonel Peacocke and the regular troops who had failed to join up with the unfortunate volunteers. The Canadians camped near Fort Erie that night, intending to give battle to the Fenians at daybreak. But O'Neil learned that he could expect no reinforcements as the American government had belatedly intervened and barred all movement of troops and arms along the border. That night boats stole quietly across the river and carried the Fenians back to the States. In the morning only a few stragglers and outlying pickets fell into the hands of the disappointed regulars.

The Canadians were deeply humiliated by the events of these two days. Only rarely in the course of many generations did they face the ordeal of fighting an enemy on their own soil. A foreign soldiery had wandered for two days about the western tip of Niagara peninsula, eating the hams and provisions, slaughtering the chickens, using the farmers' carts and horses, frightening peaceable folk till they took to the woods. And they had made fools of both the volunteers and the regulars sent against them. Why had the Canadian troops fumbled everything? What precisely had happened at Limestone Ridge?

The railway had played an important part in meeting the invasion, the local officials performing their duties with an enthusiasm and despatch which if equalled by the military might have made this little episode in Canadian history quite a different story. They shuttled trains back and forth to accommodate troops, they delivered telegrams in person, one even going so far as to take a hand car to Ridgeway station and expose himself to enemy bullets. They sent a train to pick up the defeated volunteers. And finally, a few days after the invasion, they ran sight-seeing excursions for the curious to the battlefield.

Among those who came from Hamilton was Alexander Somerville, a man of varied background who had seen active service in the British army; one of those exponents of public opinion who writes to the papers. From the very first hours of alarm ex-Sergeant Somerville had feared things would go badly. He had stood on the platform of the Hamilton depot watching the boys entrain in high spirits and singing songs, very smart in their new uniforms. The government—Somerville was a stern critic of the government—had seen to it that they were provided with the showier kinds of equipment. He confessed his tough sergeant's heart was moved to pity to see them set out without greatcoats or knapsacks, without mess tins or canteens for water.

What he learned at Ridgeway confirmed his worst fears. The poor lads had been sent into battle without breakfast, having spent the previous night cooped up in train cars.

They had not had enough ammunition. Colonel Booker's instructions had been to avoid contact with the enemy till he joined with Colonel Peacocke and the regulars. But neither Colonel had a map and each had taken the wrong road.

Somerville, assuming the role of a reporter, talked to officers and men as well as the farmers of the district and the inhabitants of Fort Erie. He even entered into correspondence with Colonel John O'Neil, who upon returning to the States was taken into mild custody. The result was a picture of confusion and ineptitude on the part of the Canadian command painful to consider. And subsequent formal military investigation did little to change the picture.

A regrettable exchange of criticism and recrimination sprang up between the cities of Toronto and Hamilton, always in a state of rivalry. Toronto claimed that the Queen's Own had not been properly supported by the 13th. Somerville deplored this attitude. The evidence all went to prove that the volunteers as a whole had behaved very well. Using their heads and such scanty training as they had received, they were actually winning the battle when the fantastic order to retreat was sounded. "The fight was a soldier's battle, not that of a general—the fight had been won," Somerville reported. Why then, was the order given to retreat? The more he sought the reason the more mysterious it became. Everyone, even Colonel Booker, denied having started the alarm about cavalry approaching. Nevertheless the bugler had sounded the warning for cavalry and he could have received his orders only from Colonel Booker. The only explanation Somerville arrived at was that the Colonel, in a state of nerves, had given the commands as he was accustomed to give them on the parade ground— advance on the enemy, retire, form a square, retire on the double.

It is true that the manner in which the Colonel conducted the battle of Limestone Ridge left little ground for congratulation, but he was particularly unfortunate in having his sole experience on active service recorded by the merciless pen of an old sergeant.

The Eastern Townships of Lower Canada were also harried by the Fenians during the first week in June. Volunteers and regular troops were sent from Montreal including the Irish Regiment. These developments forced Bernard Devlin to declare himself although up to the last moment he had tried to balance between both camps. He proposed to the Canadian government that it send him as an emissary to the Fenian head centre in New York to induce the leaders to call off the invasion. But he was coldly informed over the signature of George Cartier that the government had no intention of treating with marauders and filibusters. Lt.-Colonel Devlin then made his decision and marched to the front with his regiment, grumbling to friends that it was hard to be asked to fight his own countrymen.

"His own countrymen!" scoffed D'Arcy McGee. "An American city rabble!" Devlin in the end was spared the painful duty as the Fenians, faced with the presence of Canadian troops and the refusal of the American government to allow reinforcements over the border, withdrew, as they had done at Fort Erie. The leaders of the raid on the Eastern Townships were not of the calibre of John O'Neil and there had been considerable looting and damage to property.

But along the border of New Brunswick the Fenians played a decisive part in British North American history, although they never actually crossed the border. During the spring, bands of Fenians had stationed themselves within sight of the towns of St. Stephen and St. Andrew's whose inhabitants could watch them alternately drilling and drunk and disorderly. The sight in the course of time had a subtly demoralizing effect on the New Brunswickers. They were not reassured when a British warship came to the defence of St. Andrew's and the commander instructed the people: "If the Fenians get in here, clear away as fast as you can for we shall shell the city and burn it over the rascals' heads." People in the border places began sending their portable valuables to banks elsewhere. Perhaps they had been too hasty in rejecting Confederation the year before. If through union with the Canadas they might be spared the double menace of the Fenians and the Navy they were ready to reconsider their decision.

In this they were encouraged by the Governor of New Brunswick. Some said the Governor exceeded his instructions and was over-zealous in moving volunteer regiments to points where their votes would be most useful in swinging the province in favour of Confederation. These tactics plus the Americans' refusal to renew the Reciprocity Treaty and the very real and visual danger of the Fenians certainly proved effective. In the elections of 1866 New Brunswick reversed its decision and voted in favour of Confederation. As this was the key province of the Maritimes the Canadian government was now able to invite Maritime delegates from New Brunswick and Nova Scotia to join it on a final mission to England to complete the work of Confederation which they had begun together in 1864 at the Quebec Conference.

Chapter Twenty-Nine
THE NEW DOMINION

THE LAST SESSION of the Parliament of the united Canadas ended in high spirits and an impromptu celebration. The union that had been thrust on the Canadians after the rebellion of 1837 was a thing of the past. It had never been whole-heartedly accepted, never really successful. When Parliament met again Quebec and Ontario would have assumed their separate roles—each with its own government and both belonging to the larger federation of the Dominion of Canada. This time next year they would belong to a new and greater country with greater possibilities than they had ever dared consider before. Even the few in Parliament who still opposed Confederation, pointing out the clash of interests and the expense—the truly formidable expense—of the new form of government, could not escape the excitement of a prospect that made them all light-hearted.

"It was such a scene of jollification that I am nearly *hors de combat,*" McGee wrote to James Moylan of the *Canadian Freeman.* "I won't get caught that way again till we have another peaceful revolution." He wrote from Caledonia Springs where he was taking the water cure and recuperating from the fatigues of the session.

The Toronto *Globe* took a less lenient view of these closing festivities. George Brown was no longer a member of the Cabinet. His term of office in the coalition government had brought him no personal satisfaction. Although he had acted with the consent of the majority of his party, in his heart he belonged to those diehard Clear Grits who said he should never have joined with the Conservatives.

As his conviction grew that John A. Macdonald was the real head of the coalition he became more easily offended and his conscience troubled him. Were not all coalitions essentially immoral?

He resigned from the Cabinet in December, 1865, to the consternation of Macdonald and the other members who feared that he would cease to support Confederation. Cartier and Galt visited him in his hotel room in Ottawa and used every argument to induce him to change his mind but without success. It soon appeared, however, that Brown was not repudiating Confederation but only John A. Macdonald and the Conservatives. When this became clear there is no doubt that everyone felt better. Brown was happy in his old congenial role of editor, denouncing the follies and laxness of the government and the end of the session celebrations on which he wrote an editorial bluntly entitled "Drunkenness in High Places". Macdonald on his part found the strictures of the *Globe* not too great a price to pay to be rid of George Brown. Later he said of their relations:

"We had acted together, dined in public places together, played euchre in crossing the Atlantic and gone into society in England together and yet on the day after he resigned we resumed our old positions and ceased to speak."

Even without the *Globe*'s editorial the country was critical of the government during the summer of 1866. The poor showing made by the militia at Ridgeway stirred up a good deal of dissatisfaction. Blame was directed freely against a number of persons and departments and it was hardly likely that the do-nothing policies and half measures of the Macdonald government would escape censure.

John A.'s qualities as a statesman are not easy to assess. They seem to be a sum of negations. The art of government can be practised passively as well as actively; John A. was an exponent of the passive form. Nothing need be done till the last possible moment in the hope that nothing will have to be done at all because matters have a way of working themselves out if left alone. It is a dangerous technique, but its benefits are not to be despised. Young expanding societies especially have a capacity for thriving on this kind of non-government and certain men are remarkably successful at it. Their ability seems to be a form of intuition, although not all intuitively gifted men have it.

No contrast could be more striking than Macdonald's passivity and D'Arcy McGee's multiple activities. Macdonald ignored the specific duties of the Attorney-General's Department of which he was the formal head. But McGee, as Minister of Agriculture, although admittedly he knew next to nothing about the subject, explored the functions of his department in every detail. Fortunately his Deputy Minister, Dr. J. C. Taché, proved a congenial co-worker, sharing many of McGee's interests and ideas. Together they reorganized the department and planned many improvements in its sub-departments which included statistics and immigration. The groundwork for the first complete and accurate census of the country, published in 1871, was begun during McGee's term of office. His many plans for immigration and his Homestead Bill, he realized, would have to wait till after the completion of Confederation. Then he hoped to gain a hearing for them in Parliament.

If, during 1866, McGee expressed a wish for more action from the militia, which was part of Macdonald's department and strictly speaking not his business, he was moved by a strong interest in combating Fenianism which Macdonald did not seem to share. Both wished to minimize the importance of the Fenian Brotherhood but their motives and means were very different. McGee had been striving for months to keep excitable young Irish Canadians away from Fenian influences. Even one successful foray might undo his work. But Macdonald considered that in this instance responsibility for keeping peace along the border fell to the American government rather than the Canadian. For the sake of its own internal order and to maintain stable relations with England the American government would not dare allow the Fenians to get out of hand. Macdonald's assumption proved right. The invasion was frustrated far more by the interference of the American government than the action of the Canadian militia; but the Canadians paid for Macdonald's policy in extreme irritation and wounded pride.

Also in bringing the Fenian prisoners to trial Macdonald acted with great reluctance and only under necessity. McGee declared they deserved the extreme penalty of the law and would have made examples of them. But even after the trials were over Macdonald's policy was to put into action the machinery of the royal pardon in cases where no individual criminal act had been committed, and mitigate the sentence.

As a young lawyer he had acted for a madcap Polish nobleman, Von Shoultz, resident in the United States, who had associated himself with the rebels of 1837 under the illusion that he was rescuing the Canadians from a tyranny as rigorous as that which his own country endured under the Czar. Macdonald's efforts had not been successful and his client was hanged. Furthermore, he had been criticized by patriotic people for undertaking to defend an enemy of his country. But Macdonald had felt sorry for the man as a misguided individual who had got himself into grievous trouble. He had been greatly embarrassed when before the execution Von Shoultz had tried to give him a hundred dollars for his services.

An incident like this remains in a man's memory for life. Consciously or unconsciously it may have influenced Macdonald against exacting from the Fenian prisoners the penalty which more properly might have been visited on their superiors. Before long McGee reconsidered his opinion and agreed with Macdonald that morbid public excitement subsided more quickly under a policy of moderation than under one of severity.

One enterprise engaged John A. Macdonald's full attention. That was Confederation. Ever since the Quebec Conference in 1864 and the drawing up of the seventy-two resolutions his confidence had never wavered. He had appraised the situation, the time, the circumstances and recognized in them a suitable conjunction. "There may be obstructions, local prejudices may arise, disputes may occur, local jealousies may intervene, but it matters not—the wheel is now revolving and we are only the fly on the wheel—we cannot delay it—the union of the colonies of British America under the soverign is a fixed fact."

One accepted the inevitable and used it. And in the months between the Quebec Conference and the passage of the British North America Act he gathered the threads of the Confederation issue into his own hands and brought it to its conclusion. He undoubtedly enjoyed his work. He was something of a political genius and Confederation offered him an opportunity for statesmanship such as occurs rarely in even a long public career.

The more favourable attitude of New Brunswick towards Confederation following the Fenian raids and the refusal of Congress to renew the Reciprocity Treaty made it possible for the Canadian and Maritime delegates to meet again to make the final arrangements. London, England, was chosen as the place of meeting so that on the completion of their negotiations the act could be passed immediately by the British Parliament.

The high moment of enthusiasm had passed. That had come after the Quebec Conference when the Maritime delegates had made a tour of the Canadian cities, banqueting with the Canadian delegates and sharing with them a vision of the future. Now even before the Act was passed, manoeuvring for place began, the struggle of each province for representation and influence. These intrigues almost immediately affected the career of D'Arcy McGee.

In August McGee had written to Moylan that he had been asked with other Cabinet members to go to England. But when Macdonald, Cartier, Galt and three others set out in the fall, McGee was not among the number. The reason for omitting him is not perfectly clear. The committee, when the Maritime delegates joined it in London, consisted of sixteen members. They represented different interests and the task which fell to John A. of keeping them in agreement was exceedingly difficult. They were all independent, forceful men and he may have been well pleased to leave McGee behind because, even granting his good services, McGee was another of the same kind.

More specific reasons also have been suggested. McGee's criticism of military deficiencies during the Fenian troubles had annoyed Macdonald. James Moylan, who was sufficiently interested to try to find out the truth some years later, has left among his papers a letter from H. J. Morgan, a civil servant of long standing. He gives another reason, namely, that McGee was left out of the London delegation as the result of a conspiracy—that is the word he uses—between Macdonald and Galt, both of whom wished to give less in concessions to the Catholic separate schools than they knew McGee would consent to.

Whatever the reason for McGee's not sailing with the delegation in the first place, he was not left out entirely. As minister of Agriculture he was to attend the International Exhibition to be held in Paris in April, 1867. He sailed early in the new year and joined the delegates at the Westminster Palace Hotel in February. As on the occasion when he went with the Canadian delegates to the Derby, he arrived just in time for an unofficial celebration. John A. Macdonald, nine years a widower, was getting married. A letter describing the wedding refers to seventy guests and gives the names of the four bridesmaids as Tupper, McGee, Archibald and McDougall. If this somewhat facetious letter is to be taken literally, the bride had most unusual attendants, unless indeed it was Macdonald who was thus attended.

Even if the delegation completed its work without taking McGee very deeply into its counsel, he had both pleasant distractions and important assignments to keep him from noticing it. He found time to visit Samuel Ferguson in Dublin. He also went to Rome to lay before the Pope a petition from the clergy and laity of St. Patrick's parish, Montreal.

His visit to Rome was an experience different from any he had ever had. It had been his fate to pass most of his life in the New World, while his native disposition, as he once said, was "towards reverence of things old and veneration of the landmarks of the past". His short visit to Italy and the most venerable city of Western Christendom gave him keen and unforgettable pleasure.

In Paris honours awaited McGee and his French-speaking Deputy, Dr. Taché. Since this was their Confederation year special attention was paid to the Canadians as representing the youngest of the nations at the Exhibition. Paris, so soon to be humiliated in the Franco-Prussian War, was at one of her moments of triumph. Who among the delegates of many nations enjoying her hospitality would dispute her claim to be the most brilliant city in the world or imagine that the veiled future held for her anything but further triumphs? The Empress Eugenie and the ladies of the court moved through their parts in the state functions, ravishingly beautiful in their crinolines, veritable clouds of gauze, muslins and laces, the embodiment and glorification of the artistry of French dressmakers.

While he was in Paris illness marred McGee's pleasant journeyings. He had to take to his bed with ulceration of the leg, a malady that had afflicted him once or twice before. It seems from its symptoms to have been a disease of the circulatory system, later called Buerger's disease, which at that time had not been accurately diagnosed.

Also he learned that John A. Macdonald could not come to Paris, as he had planned, because he had to return to Canada and the urgent problems of forming the first Dominion of Canada government. The letter which advised McGee of this contained information which he found very disturbing. Its nature may be learned from his answer:

" . . . You observe in your last that my own political future is at stake. I feel the whole force of that remark, and will not lose a day in returning . . . Ever since we have acted together, I have recognized no other leader in Parliament or the country. And I only ask in return that you will protect my position in my absence till I am able to mount guard over it myself. I certainly have no desire to embarrass future arrangements, which will naturally be under your direction, but in a Confederation Government, founded upon principles which I have always zealously advocated I will, if in Parliament, give way neither to Galt nor to a third Frenchman nor any other man."

This letter Macdonald passed over to Cartier. McGee hardly understood his chief or the situation if he imagined Macdonald could save his position in the Cabinet. It was not that Macdonald was not capable of making a political appointment purely on grounds of friendship, but in this instance the problems were too complicated and far-reaching to leave scope for personal influence.

That McGee was aware that in the end he would have to protect his interests himself is shown by the promptness with which he cut short his Paris visit and as soon as he was well returned to Canada. On the day he arrived in Montreal it rained. The weather and the fact that the St. Patrick's Society—under its ambitious president, Bernard Devlin—no longer supported him, account for his welcome being less tumultuous than formerly. His personal friends and some two hundred loyal supporters were at the station and made a brave showing.

His arrival in Ottawa a few days later was almost up to the usual standard. As he landed from the steamer he was met by the mayor and a delegation of citizens. The mayor made a speech and one of the Ottawa clergy read a poem composed in McGee's honour. To these courtesies he made a fitting reply. Then he entered the city accompanied by "a large retinue of carriages and many hundreds on foot". The procession halted while the Hon. D'Arcy McGee stepped from his carriage to receive a deputation of children from St. Patrick's Orphanage, who presented him with a bouquet of flowers.

Parliament was not sitting but the members of the government and the Maritime delegates were meeting together to decide on the new Cabinet. Their mood was not cordial. In fact, they were at an impasse. Cartier had stated uncompromisingly that the French Canadians must have three members in the new Dominion Cabinet. Unless he could assure his people on that point it would be impossible for him to retain their support for Confederation.

Christopher Dunkin, when he had wearied the Legislative Assembly with his reckoning of every difficulty that would face the Fathers of Confederation, had laid particular stress on this complication in regard to Lower Canada, henceforth to be called Quebec. In this province representation had to be given to two religions, Catholic and Protestant, and three racial groups, French, English and Irish. In Dunkin's opinion this tangle of claims alone would be enough to wreck Confederation. It nearly wrecked the first Dominion government.

Since Quebec was entitled to only four members in the Cabinet and Cartier insisted that three should be French Canadians this meant leaving either the Irish or the English minority without representation. Either McGee or Galt must go. This was the situation when McGee arrived in Ottawa. John A. Macdonald was in one of his moods of masterly evasion. He could do nothing more, he declared, he would have to resign.

McGee did not propose to do anything either, and he did not offer to resign.

Galt wrote to his wife: "Things are turning out just as I told you I feared would be the case and I am so thoroughly disgusted that if it were not for the fear of deserting my friends in such a crisis I would shake off the dust of political life from my feet."

He was a business man rather than a politician. The political game fatigued and irritated him and, having secured the interests of the railways, he would gladly have withdrawn. Unfortunately this would not have helped McGee. Galt represented not only the Quebec English and the Protestants but also the very influential financial and commercial interests of Montreal. If he withdrew someone from that group would have to take his place. Because of his considerable parliamentary experience, he was induced to stay.

McGee's position was the weaker. The Irish were a dis-

tinct group solely in terms of nationality. As Catholics
their interests were similar to the French Canadians. Those
among them who might be classed as capitalists were served
as effectively by Galt as McGee. But the position he expected in the first Dominion Cabinet was in every respect
of great importance to him personally. His colleagues had
back of them the incomes of substantial businesses or law
firms; McGee's income from writing and lecturing was more
uncertain. Participation in public life was expensive and
he could not ignore the salary (about $4,000 a year) that
went with the Cabinet minister's position. Far more important was the achievement which this position in the
first Dominion government represented, the crowning
honour of his career that few would deny he had won fairly
by his long and brilliant advocacy of Confederation. John
A. had assured him he would be included in the new government. McGee had a letter from him to that effect. So he
continued to say nothing.

Dr. Charles Tupper of Nova Scotia solved the impasse.
He and McGee would both withdraw and their place could
be taken by Edward Kenny, an Irish Catholic from
Nova Scotia, a comparatively obscure member of Parliament. He could occupy a place in the Cabinet as one of the
four Maritime members and as a representative of the Irish
Catholics. And so the matter was settled in a very high-
minded way and with a fine gesture.

"The union of the provinces is going to end in a fiasco
unless we give way. We are the only two men who can
avert that calamity," Tupper told McGee. To quote again
from Tupper's memoirs: "I then proposed that he should
stand aside in favour of Sir Edward Kenny of Halifax as the
representative of the Irish Catholics and that I should likewise surrender my claim to a portfolio. McGee readily
agreed to my proposition." And this was the version that
passed into history. But it is also recorded that George
Cartier spent two mornings with McGee before this decision
was taken. It would seem that D'Arcy did not lightly give
up his honours and position.

It is not hard to credit the story of Cartier's morning calls. In moments of difficulty it was his role to persuade and cajole, to reason with and prevail upon the recalcitrant, while John A. maintained a detached attitude implying: "I have done all I can. I can do no more. I can only retire." —a suggestion that never failed to cause perturbation among the many people whose political fortunes he had linked to his own.

No record exists of the conversation between the two men during Cartier's visits. Although they were colleagues in the same government they had never been friends. It was a case of antipathy between men who were too much alike, for these two had much in common. Both were men of intense nervous energy. Each in his young days had suffered the sobering experience of finding himself forced beyond his depth into a rebellion which his intelligence told him was ridiculous. Both were ambitious, but capable of putting the good of their own people before personal interests. Cartier had succeeded better than most of his race in establishing himself as a corporation lawyer in the business world of Montreal. But he remained French Canadian to the last syllable of his wonderfully accented English speech. Concern for the position of his people rather than for his own career prompted him to take his firm stand on the number of French-speaking members in the Cabinet. He understood the tenacity of the French Canadians and their caution. He knew how quickly their consent to Confederation could turn to opposition if at this point anything happened to awaken their too easily aroused suspicion.

Did Cartier feel any sympathy for the man whose career had obviously passed its peak or was he in his heart pleased to usher the "adventurer" out? A few weeks later the Conservative French-language paper *La Minerve* wrote, flourishing the English phrase in quotations: C'est certain que M. McGee est "a dead duck". *La Minerve* spoke for Cartier and his followers.

At this time Cartier was at the pinnacle of his success. Crowds and torch light and all the paraphernalia of political demonstration attended his public appearances. His position was assured and the election of other French-Canadian supporters of Confederation was certain. Nevertheless, seen in the perspective of history, a thread of similarity runs through the careers of these two men.

Before long Cartier, too, would be rejected by the people he had represented and in a manner even more fickle than the behaviour of McGee's supporters. In a very few years he would leave public life, his great energy spent, broken in health and under not entirely deserved censure. Over the end of both these men lay a shadow.

The unrecorded arguments Cartier used proved effective. The logic of the situation favoured him. When he left at the end of the second interview, he had in his possession Macdonald's letter promising McGee the Cabinet appointment. Having given in, McGee decided to carry out his part in the graceful manner suggested by Dr. Tupper. Of Cartier he said publicly: "Nothing could be more upright and straightforward than Mr. Cartier's conduct throughout, and if at this moment I am not still his colleague it has resulted from no other action than my own voluntary decision." And of Tupper he said: "My friend Dr. Tupper and myself determined between us in a sort of committee of two that we would both decline seats at the Council."

July 1, 1867, marked the birthday of the Dominion of Canada. The new nation was welcomed with mixed feelings by its progenitors. The original Canadas, with certain doubts and reservations, were content. But the Nova Scotians were unreconciled and still listened to Joseph Howe who told them they had chosen not for better but for worse. Some of the Maritime newspapers announced the event in black-bordered columns. But calamity or not, the Dominion of Canada was a fact. The day had been proclaimed a public holiday and guns fired a salute from Parliament Hill in Ottawa. The country prepared for the first Dominion election.

August of 1867 was a season of great heat. The oldest inhabitant of Montreal could not remember anything like it. The island and the broad St. Lawrence plain lay under a pall of heat. In the streets eddies of warm air stirred the leaves of the tall elms and their shade offered no coolness. The city became like an oven under the sun. During the night the brick and cobblestone slowly gave out the stored heat so that the bright summer dawn found the city unrefreshed.

Nominations and preparations for the election went forward. It was known that the candidates for Montreal accepted Confederation so that it was no longer an issue. It would not have been surprising if, considering the weather, political meetings in stifling public halls or under hot gas flares out of doors had been poorly attended. But in Griffintown, where the Irish lived, election meetings were carried on in such disorder that it was impossible for speakers to make themselves heard. The occasions were street fights rather than political rallies. There was a long series of injuries and broken heads and one man was killed. While the Irish raged, the rest of the city stood aside almost indifferently. Why were the Irish fighting? Why exert oneself in the heat?

Bernard Devlin was contesting the election with the ex-Cabinet Minister the Hon. D'Arcy McGee. Fenianism embittered the contest, which actually was little more than a struggle between two men for position. It was even less than that, a struggle merely between two political factions. McGee took little part in the Montreal election. As well as running for the Dominion Parliament he was also a candidate for the Ontario provincial Parliament. He spent much of his time in the county of Prescott where he had been nominated.

In running for the Ontario legislature McGee does not seem to have been influenced by the fear of losing the election in Montreal. He appears to have been arrogantly confident that he could beat Devlin easily. There was no rule at that time against being a member of two legislatures and McGee, who had travelled and lectured constantly in Upper Canada, was well known there. After his heavy duties as

Cabinet minister the prospect of acting as a private member in two legislatures did not seem too much responsibility for a man of his experience. He told his nominators in Montreal that if, in the event of being elected in both legislatures, he found his double duties too much he would resign from the Ontario legislature in favour of the Dominion Parliament.

It was not in his nature to admit defeat or discouragement, but his omission from the Dominion Cabinet had diminished his prospects. Physically and financially he was at the end of his resources. After a few weeks he had to withdraw as candidate for Prescott because of lack of campaign funds.

In Montreal his friends looked after the election and met the expenses. It is possible that if McGee had given more time to Montreal the election campaign might have been carried out with greater decorum. He had often been remarkably successful in promoting good feeling and raising the level of political behaviour. But he preferred to give his personal attention to the new riding he was canvassing in Ontario. He had only partly recovered from the illness that had stricken him in Paris and his health that summer was very poor. He kept himself going on whisky, which sustained him for the time but did not delay the inevitable collapse.

Early in August when the trouble with his leg confined him to the house for a week he wrote a series of articles on Fenianism for the *Montreal Gazette* explaining, "I present this narrative of facts to my neighbours and fellow citizens to show them some of the dangers they have safely passed in the dark and the necessity of marking those gulfs and pitfalls with more lights and other precautions. Instead of overstating, I have understated my case."

This claim was borne out by the articles which were models of objectivity. In them he traced the growth of Fenian influences in Montreal and their infiltration into the St. Patrick's Society. The articles, in their detached, factual way were sensational because McGee named all the persons concerned and in them Bernard Devlin emerged as a would-be politician who was trying to use Fenianism for his own ends. McGee was not holding a post-mortem. The Fenian movement was as strong in the United States as it had ever been. The raids on the Canadian border were not over and Devlin was playing with fire.

The series "Fenianism in Montreal" was not without influence on the electors. The franchise at this time was not universal, although it extended to householders owning or renting property. With this electorate McGee's soberly-written statements carried more weight than the emotional mass appeal of his opponents. When the ballots were counted it was found that D'Arcy McGee had won the election. The majority was the smallest he had ever received, but nevertheless he had won. When the news was brought to his house he was too gravely ill to enjoy his triumph.

At the same time a mob of Barney Devlin's supporters stormed McGee's committee rooms expecting to find him there. From their threats and frenzied mood it was evident they had come with the intention of killing him.

Chapter Thirty
AFTER THE ELECTION

From END TO END of the St. Lawrence valley winter ruled with February rigour. On a grey afternoon D'Arcy McGee stood in a window of the house on St. Catherine Street, looking out on the snow-banked road where infrequent traffic jingled by musically, and hoping for the first fine day when he would be able to go out. The house was like a hospital at this time of the year with all the family suffering from colds and grippe. It had been his prison for many long weeks. In November he had felt well enough to be present at the opening of the Dominion Parliament, but his attempt to take up his public duties had been premature and before two weeks had passed his lame foot, as he called it, had him in bed again. This time he had to resign himself to a slow and tedious recovery.

Worries that had never greatly troubled him before nagged him now—his lack of a steady income, his debts, his health, his future. He had in prospect the position of Commissioner of Patents. This appointment would mean withdrawing from Parliament, a condition which after recent events he could accept almost with relief. The duties of the Commissioner were not onerous and the salary was between $3,000 and $3,500 a year. Sometimes McGee thought of this prospect with satisfaction, sometimes he quibbled about it. "I shall not feel that either a hampered or subordinate office is a sphere into which I ought to go," he wrote to Macdonald.

At other times he worried for fear the appointment might not be made. "If the Patent Commissioner doesn't come through I shall be obliged to devote myself to those infernal gods, the publishers, the only work I am now steadily fit for."

During his leisure he considered his past and found in it much to disapprove. He became stricter in his religious observances and resolved to go to the sacraments oftener. He gave up liquor once and for all and hereafter never drank even on social occasions. All this he mentions with candour and complete lack of self-consciousness in letters to his friends. A pleasant aspect of his reforms was that he made no attempt to force them on other people—a forbearance which must have come by the grace of God, because he was of missionary temperament and usually eager to convert others to his ideas.

Never did his characteristic ability to live intensely on different levels show up more clearly than during the period of his illness. He was only physically a sick-room prisoner, and only at intervals did he submit to the oppression of his worries. At other times his mind ranged freely and sought congenial climates. He read, sometimes for ten hours a day. He resumed his interest in literature and poetry. The most enticing feature of the Commissionership was the leisure and security it would give him. What might he not do with such a gift? What might he not accomplish even at this date? As a boy he had wanted to be a scholar and a poet. Even while busy with more ordinary affairs he had produced some poetry and history worthy to rank with the best—that is, until public life in Canada had absorbed his energies completely.

Had Samuel Ferguson chosen the better part? D'Arcy, who recently had been his guest, could compare his own hard, strenuous life, from which he had wrung time for the *Popular History of Ireland* and the tribute to John O'Donovan, with his friend's serener course and its fine flowering of poetry. Avoiding the controversies of public life, Ferguson had devoted himself to antiquarian studies and literature. He uncovered the vein of ancient myth and fairy lore into which the later poets of the Celtic renaissance delved deeply. The long, unruffled friendship between Ferguson and McGee grew out of their common interest in literature. Ferguson used his own literary prestige to obtain recognition for D'Arcy's work and it was not merely in the spirit of conventional compliment that he declared that in his generation D'Arcy was the greatest Irish poet of them all.

D'Arcy McGee wrote poetry as an untrained person of natural musical ability plays the piano and he was similarly impatient of the disciplines of art. But whereas the untrained musician plays by ear the tunes he has heard from others, not all McGee's poems were derivative. Many were created from his own heart and mind. He wrote poetry because it was as easy for him as writing prose, and more fun. He was always ready to dash off verses for a lady's album or to celebrate a birthday, to fill up a column in his paper or drive home an idea. Some have disposed of him politely as a second-rate poet; others, more discerning, have charged him with wasting his great gifts on a mass of inferior stuff.

But no matter how many poor verses a poet writes he is judged by his best and D'Arcy McGee's best is very good indeed. Not for him the haunted, dream-misted poetry and the love lyrics with a tear and a laugh in them that Ferguson wrote so well. The soaring, twisting, turning quality of McGee's most original verse is more like a sword tossed in the sunlight than a harp plucked when the lights are low. He looked to the old bards for his models and he was at his best when he took their themes, praising heroic action, honouring the noble dead and—for it must not be forgotten that the history of Ireland is tragic—lamenting the lost fight and the exile.

Death was often the burden of his song. "I have always been an old keener," he told a friend, "and half my lays are lamentations." But there was no shrinking or morbidity in his thoughts of death. His sense of eternity was strong and simple, untroubled by doubt. The most intimate ties bound him to eternity—his mother and sisters, his children, his only son. Death was a universal experience and a great occasion. It was a mystery to be celebrated, not a horror to be shunned. The quicksilver rhythm of his verse gave a challenging ring to the sombre theme.

> Give me again my harp of yew,
>   In consecrated soil 'twas grown—
> Shut out the day star from my view,
>   And leave me with the night alone!
> The children of this modern land
>   May deem our ancient custom vain
> But aye responsive to my hand
>   The harp must pour the funeral strain.

He had many to remember in his poems, friends he had made and lost to death since coming to Canada; and companions of the Young Ireland days. By 1868, Smith O'Brien was dead and John Dillon, stricken by cholera, and Richard D'Alton with whom McGee had worked on the *Nation* in the days when he and poor Devin Reilly disturbed the peace of Duffy's office with their wrangling.

Brigadier-General Thomas Francis Meagher, after surviving the battles of the Civil War, met a violent end in the summer of 1867. He had gone into the new western territories full of plans to make his fortune.

"I am resolved not to turn my back on the Rocky Mountains till I have the means to whip my carriage-and-four through New York Central Park and sail my yacht with the green flag at the mizzen peak within three miles of the Irish coast."

Then one night he fell from the unrailed deck of a steamer and was drowned in the Missouri River. The accident was hard to explain. He had enemies, and rumours of foul play were never completely laid. But no one was ever brought to trial for his death.

All these men were in the prime of life. The news of each death had the shock of the unexpected. They had belonged to the most passionate and hopeful period of D'Arcy's youth. He remembered them all, some with affection, some with bitterness. For the first he wrote his funeral songs; to the others he paid the tribute of silence.

Of course he did not spend all his convalescence on this lofty plane viewing death from the heights of poetry. In spite of calling them the "infernal gods" he was negotiating with the publishers against the day when he would retire from public life and have more time to give to a literary career.

The immigrants had never ceased to be in the forefront of his interests. He was one of them. As editor of the *American Celt*, he had referred to himself as the historian of the immigrants and had substantiated his claim with the Catholic History of North America. Nothing moved him to more impassioned protest than loose and disparaging talk about foreigners and immigrants.

"In a sense we are all foreigners to America; European civilization is foreign to it; the Christian religion is foreign to it. The term conveys no stigma to the well-informed mind. The man of reading or reflection knows that at one time or other it was true of all humanity—true of the first man as it may be of the last. The history of our race is a history of emigration . . . The cities of Enoch, Babylon, Nineveh, Tyre, Carthage, Rome—what are they? Landmarks and tidemarks of the endless emigration. In the days before history, in the mountain mists of tradition, we see the dim forms of pioneers and leaders, carrying their tribes from old homes to new homes, over mountains and across straits, and through the labyrinths of the primeval wilderness. And the tale did not end when Hercules set up pillars at the Straits of Gades and forbade his descendants to tempt the exterior ocean. In the dawn of classic light we see mankind with darkened and troubled brows gazing out to the forbidden West as they lean against those pillars. The fearless Phoenician came, and swept by without slacking sail or heeding Hercules; he went and came and went, disenchanting mankind of their fears. The Romans talked of having reached the earth's Ultima, and so Europe rested for ages, in full belief of the Roman geography. At last Columbus rose, that inspired sailor, who dedicating his ship and himself to the protection of the Blessed Virgin, launched fearlessly into the undiscovered sea and introduced the New World to the acquaintance of the Old. After Columbus we came . . ."

And in that "we" all were included, even the latest, most hapless arrivals in the New World.

As Minister of the Crown in Canada, McGee had hoped to bring in legislation pertaining to immigration. But as his political hopes faded he turned again to literary efforts. The idea of an epic to be called "The Emigrants" had fascinated him for a long time. Here was material for a saga of heroic proportions. But in the end his imagination quailed before this grandiose undertaking. Instead, spurred by the success of Mrs. Sadlier's books, he considered writing a novel on the emigrants and began evolving a plot and looking for a publisher to interest in his idea.

Besides these personal projects, in the fall of 1867, he took a large share in the work of a campaign for the relief of Nova Scotia fishermen who had taken a disastrously small catch that season and were facing a winter of destitution. It was most unfortunate that Nova Scotia should suffer economic disaster at the very beginning of Confederation, especially as the province had entered the union very reluctantly. Generosity on the part of the Canadians was clearly required. McGee, who was keenly aware of the attitude of the Nova Scotians, wrote appeals from his sick bed on their behalf.

Finally, he was contributing a weekly article on Irish politics to the *Montreal Gazette*. Had he been a cautious or even prudent man he would have left this subject alone. Irish politics had proved a fatal and thankless cause for all his generation. But having condemned the Fenian programme of help for Ireland he needs must offer something in its place.

He considered one by one the drastic reforms which were fundamental to good government in Ireland. The list of injustices was long and specific. They must be rectified, not only to settle the long quarrel between England and Ireland, but to prevent the evil from spreading. The

memory of their wrongs had been carried by Irish emigrants
to all parts of the English-speaking world and threatened to
disturb relations between England and the United States
and weaken the bonds between England and the self-
governing colonies.

McGee no longer advocated the repeal of the union
between England and Ireland, but argued that it could be
made to function only as a union between equal partners.
At that time no political party for repeal existed in Ireland
except the Fenians whose purpose was to establish a
republic by violence. In England, on the other hand, Gladstone, who had just become Prime Minister, had pledged
himself to right the injustice of Ireland's position by legislative reform. Between these two McGee, who even in the
fiery enthusiasm of youth had been opposed to a republic,
chose the policy of Gladstone in preference to Fenianism.

Had he in this instance deserted a principle and not
merely changed a policy? Duffy, who remained a Repealer
to the end of his long life, thought so. This and not the
Wexford speech was the real issue on which he never for-
gave McGee.

Gladstone in the end admitted that the only answer to
the Irish question was self-government. It is most unlikely
that McGee would have lagged behind Gladstone when
Parnell's movement for Irish Home Rule once more gave
repeal a solid political party. As it was, the accident of his
early death left McGee in the false position of appearing no
longer to believe in self-government for Ireland; of asking
for his native land less than he would have been willing to
accept for his adopted country.

Chapter Thirty-One
CAPTAIN MOONLIGHT

Early in March McGee was well enough to return to Ottawa for what he expected would be his last session in Parliament. He took his place on the government side of the House, but no longer occupied a seat in the front ranks with the Cabinet. As representative for the Irish Catholics he had been replaced by Edward Kenny from the Maritimes; the portfolio of Agriculture which he had held had been given to Jean Charles Chapais. But even among the back benchers he was a more dramatic figure than either of the men who had replaced him.

At the beginning of the session in November, when he had spoken on the speech from the throne, another member, Alexander Mackenzie, had followed with an attack on him. With great lack of originality he had dragged out the stale, cheap arguments used against McGee so often in the recent election, namely that the danger of Fenianism existed only in his mind and that he slandered Irish Canadians by talking about it. The attack was in rather poor taste in as much as Alexander Mackenzie had never previously shown any particular concern for Irish reputations.

The House pricked up its ears, remembering the scathing, pitiless retorts McGee had made on similar occasions. But this time, before he had a chance to speak, another member rose to defend him. Gustave Joly de Lotbinière spoke from the opposition benches and as one who had always been in political opposition to McGee, but he defended him now for his patriotic sacrifices.

Had McGee kept quiet, he said, the Fenian excitement might have ended very differently. He might have retained his personal popularity at the price of a national calamity, but McGee had sacrificed his power to the interests of his country and credit ought to be ungrudgingly accorded to him.

The words and form of speech mattered little. Mr. Joly de Lotbinière had expressed the sentiments of the House and every sentence was interrupted with desk-thumping approval. Never in the days of his greatest success had McGee's reputation stood higher in Parliament.

On St. Patrick's Day a banquet was given in Ottawa in D'Arcy McGee's honour. About a hundred guests were present—a distinguished gathering including the Bishop, the Prime Minister Sir John A. Macdonald, and the Hon. G. E. Cartier. Complimentary speeches were addressed to the guest of honour. John A. and Cartier affirmed their friendship and admiration for their colleague and their appreciation of his unselfish act in resigning from the Cabinet. They seemed to be trying to make amends for their strange indifference towards him during the election of the previous summer. Then he had been the forgotten man of the Conservative Party, bereft of campaign funds or even so much as a supporting speech from any of the party leaders, and written off as a "dead duck" by the principal French-Canadian Conservative paper.

One might speculate at some length on the mixed motives that prompted the attendance of Macdonald and Cartier at McGee's banquet—advantage to the party, twinges of personal remorse for recent neglect, frank recognition of the sporting or (to use the favourite adjective of the period) manly spirit in which McGee had taken the decline of his fortunes. It is sufficient to say that McGee, who had attended innumerable banquets of like kind given for himself or others, knew how to evaluate what was sham and what sincere in them.

This seventeenth of March he spoke on the Irish question, going further than he had done in accepting legislative reform rather than constitutional change as its solution. He implored the British government to "settle for our sakes and your own, for the sake of international peace, settle promptly and generously the social and ecclesiastical condition of Ireland on terms to satisfy the majority of the people to be governed. Everyone sees and feels that while England lifts her white cliffs above the waves she can never suffer a rival government, a hostile government on the other side of her. Whatever the aspirations for Irish autonomy, the union is an inexorable political necessity, as inexorable for England as for Ireland. But there is one miraculous agency which has yet to be fully and fairly tried out in Ireland. Brute force has failed, proselytism has failed, anglification has failed; try, if only as a novelty, try patiently and thoroughly, statesmen of Empire, the miraculous agency of equal and exact justice, for one or two generations."

Early in April he spent Sunday at the home of a friend, Alderman Goodwin. After the heavy noon dinner, as Sabbath afternoon drowsiness fell over the household McGee, taking example from the family, stretched out on the couch in the study. But his sleep was restless, broken by terrifying dreams. He rose and wandered about the quiet house until he met his hostess to whom he told his dream, thereby ridding his mind of it. He had dreamt that he ran along the bank of a river calling a warning to a boat drifting into dangerous currents, when lo! he found himself on the river being swept relentlessly towards the falls.

In a more composed and cheerful state of mind he returned to the study and at his host's desk he wrote an open letter to Lord Mayo, the Secretary of State for Ireland. The argument of the letter had been in his mind since certain comments of the Lord Secretary had come to his attention. It seemed that the government circles and newspapers in Great Britain thought very well of the Hon. D'Arcy McGee's reasonable attitude regarding the Irish question. That his demands for reform in Ireland should encourage the British government in a feeling of complacency was not at all his intention. With dignity and firmness he addressed the Lord Secretary.

He reiterated that the Irish in Canada were content

under British institutions and that he personally had combated Fenianism "*but* no lay advocacy and no ecclesiastical influence could have kept our countrymen here loyal and at peace if this country were governed as Ireland has been during the sixty-eight years of her legislative union with Great Britain. Everything our emigrants find in Canada is very unlike everything they left behind them in Ireland . . . We are loyal because our equal civil, social and religious rights are respected. Were it otherwise, we would be otherwise."

What was to become of this man? There was nothing unusual in Canadian politicians retiring from public life when in their prime. Indeed, it was unusual for anyone to remain long in politics which seemed to require a combination of ruggedness and pliancy that few possessed. Canadian public life demanded a great deal and gave little. Its triumphs and powers were short-lived; its friendships brittle. It is not necessary to review the imposing list of competent governors-general and public-spirited party leaders who ended their careers with broken health and embittered memories; a glance at the House of Commons during the session of 1868 gives all the examples needed.

The formidable George Brown had been defeated in the general election and had passed off the parliamentary scene. Alexander Galt, after all the fuss about retaining him in the Dominion Cabinet, had resigned after a few months. He remained in Parliament as a private member but withdrew from the Cabinet with the excuse that his business affairs required more attention than as a member of the government he had been able to give them. To his wife, the constant recipient of his political confidences, he wrote with more than usual pessimism: "The government, which is really no government at all, is doomed whatever else will follow it."

George Cartier remained in the Cabinet, but it was an open secret that he had intrigued a little and unsuccessfully with Galt to oust John A. Macdonald. Those who had met

Macdonald for the first time during the Confederation conferences—the leaders from the Maritimes and the British
statesmen in London—as a matter of course looked to him
as the leader. He became the guiding spirit of Confederation not because he was a man of great vision, but because
he was a practical man of long political experience. He also
had a far more subtle qualification—the ability to manage
men; and he used his talent adroitly because in its use too
he had long experience. With the passage of the British
North America Act he takes his place as the dominant figure
on the political stage of newly federated Canada. The long
apprenticeship is over. Ambiguity ceases. He is the Prime
Minister and will remain in office for some time.

But just at the beginning of the first session of the federal
Parliament there was pained surprise among some of his
colleagues. When royal honours were conferred on the
leaders of Confederation, Macdonald was given precedence
over Cartier although the curiously dual nature of Canadian
politics had always given them equal standing. This lapse
in tact on the part of the British government was as much
a matter of chagrin to Macdonald as to Cartier, and he
declared himself very well satisfied when the home government rectified its error by giving Cartier a slightly higher
honour than his own.

But time and diplomatic negotiation were needed to
adjust a matter of such delicacy and during the winter of
1868 the Prime Minister, Sir John A. Macdonald, in the
pride of his newly acquired honours, sat in the front ranks
on the government side of the House. Beside him sat
the Hon. George Etienne Cartier, without benefit of title,
having declined an inferior rank. Beneath the carefully
maintained front of cordiality a rift had come between
the two men that was never completely closed.

Notwithstanding the hidden dissensions and the open
antagonism of Joseph Howe, who had gone to England to
complain that Nova Scotia had been coerced into Confederation, the government of the new Dominion functioned
reasonably well and D'Arcy McGee, writing to Charles

Tupper, who had been sent to England to counteract Howe's purpose, was able to say without too much exaggeration: "Our friends in the Cabinet seem to be getting along very well together . . . The breakers ahead have gone down and all is plain sailing at present."

After everything has been said about the vanity and frustrations of political life, could a man like McGee, having known its tension and excitement for years, willingly resign his part in it? With the country entering upon a new era never did the shiny, half genuine, half tinsel rewards of politics gleam more temptingly.

"The human mind naturally adapts itself to the position it occupies," Tupper had said before Confederation. "The most gigantic intellect may be dwarfed by being 'cabin'd, cribb'd, confined.' It requires a great country and great circumstances to develop great men."

And Macdonald at the Charlottetown Conference had made remarks to the same effect. Certainly he pursued his own political career with greater zest after Confederation became his goal. At last the game was worth the effort.

Was there then no place on this new and wider stage for D'Arcy McGee? At this particular time in his career a good deal depended on the attitude of John A. Macdonald. And McGee with all his brilliancy and dependability where large issues were in question had not proved an exemplary party member. He remained incorrigibly an Independent and retained his right to voice his opinions with results that on several occasions had annoyed and disconcerted Macdonald and the party leaders.

D'Arcy's stand on Fenianism also left Macdonald a little baffled. It was very high-minded, of course, but a poor way to catch votes. Writing very frankly to James Moylan who had steadily supported McGee in the *Canadian Freeman* and who was considering running for Parliament, Macdonald had said: "In consequence of your bold and patriotic course in the Fenian matter you have alienated so many of the Catholic laity it would be impossible to elect you."

McGee's work in the cause of Confederation was done,

but there remained great issues to engage his exceptional talents. Although union had been secured by an act of Parliament, there remained the task of conciliating the various groups in the new nation, a task which McGee realized would require untiring patience and skill. On his return from Europe he had said to those who met him at the Montreal station:

"Many of the young men here today will live to see the proof of my words that all other politics that have been preached in British America will grow old and lose their lustre, but the conciliation of class and class . . . the policy of linking together all our people . . . the policy of linking order to order, of smoothing down the sharp and wounding edges of hostile prejudices—this policy will never grow old —never will lose its lustre."

The immediate problem of winning Nova Scotia to whole-hearted acceptance of Confederation confronted the government. On the evening of April 6, McGee spoke on this subject and in defence of Dr. Tupper who, absent in England, was being attacked by anti-Confederation Nova Scotians. Those who had often heard McGee realized that he was making—not one of his great speeches—but a notably shrewd and skilful one. Whatever disadvantages he was at in the slippery game of politics by reason of his impetuous temperament, he was far from naïve or inexperienced. He had his own particular methods. The House, as it listened to him, knew that in defending Tupper he was also defending himself.

"It has been charged against him that he has lost the confidence of his own people. Sir, I hope that in this House mere temporary or local popularity will never be made the test by which to measure the worth or efficiency of a public servant. He, Sir, who builds upon popularity builds upon shifting sand. It is . . . the leader of a forlorn hope who is ready to meet and stem the tide of temporary unpopularity —who shows us that he is ready not only to triumph with his principles, but even to suffer for his principles—who has proved himself, above all others, worthy of peculiar honour."

He passed on to the higher theme, the conciliation of Nova Scotia.

"We will compel them by our fairness and kindness. It has been said that the interests of Canada are diametrically opposed to the interests of Nova Scotia, but I ask which of the parties to the partnership has most interest in its successful conduct, or has most to fear from the failure which the misfortunes or losses of any of its members must occasion? Would it not be we who have embarked the largest share of the capital of Confederation? Our friends, Sir, need have no fear but that Confederation will ever be administered with serene and even justice. To its whole history, from its earliest inception to its final triumphant consummation, no stigma can be attached, no stain attributed. Its single aim from the beginning has been to consolidate the extent of British North America with the utmost regard to the independent power and privileges of each province and I, Sir, who have been and am still its warm and earnest advocate speak here not as the representative of any race, or of any province, but as thoroughly and emphatically a Canadian, ready and bound to recognize the claims of my Canadian fellow subjects from the farthest east to the farthest west, equally as those of my nearest neighbour or the friend who proposed me on the hustings."

Surely some at least of those who listened to McGee that night must have asked themselves if the new nation, not yet free from the narrow prejudices and jealousies of its component provinces, could afford to lose from public life the imagination, the broad sympathy and hard-won experience of its most brilliant orator.

It was after one o'clock when Parliament adjourned. It would not reassemble until after the Easter recess. The feeling that the holiday season had already begun was general and lent a special, genial quality to the last-minute conversations and casual good nights as groups of members made their way through the echoing, handsome vaulted corridors of the new Parliament Building.

None was more pleased than McGee at the prospect of the Easter recess. His strength was returning very slowly and he would benefit by a few days at home. He was to celebrate his forty-third birthday on Easter Monday. There was to be a party—not a large public affair, only a party with the family and a few close friends, a novelty for a man who had been surfeited with public banquets. His friends had arranged for his portrait to be painted and it was to be completed for the occasion.

Robert McFarlane, one of the younger members attending his first session in Parliament, helped McGee into his overcoat, exchanging good-natured banter with him, and handed him his hat and the cane which he carried since his illness. The two lit their cigars and left the building together.

Outside, the grounds sloped away from the Parliament Buildings toward the sleeping city, blanched with moonlight. The day had been springlike, not with any suggestion of growth or greenness—it was too early for that—but with a clear luminosity in the upper air that lingered on into the evening. After nightfall the air had become colder and sharper and ice formed over the puddles, but the sky still showed crystalline depths upon depths like the heart of a dark sapphire.

As McGee and his companion left the grounds a group of page-boys from the House passed them and called out: "Good night, Mr. McGee."

"Good morning," McGee called back. "Because it's morning now."

At the corner of Sparks and Metcalfe Streets Robert McFarlane left him.

"Good night," said McFarlane.

"God bless you," said McGee.

He walked a short distance along Sparks Street, which was divided between moonlight and dark shadows, to his lodgings at Mrs. Trotter's boarding-house. At the door of the house he took out his key and bent a little to insert it in the lock. At that instant a shot rang out, fired at such close range that the powder singed his hair as the bullet entered his temple. He dropped to his knees, convulsively tried to pull himself up and instead fell backwards, off the stoop and onto the sidewalk. There he lay without moving.

Among those making their way home at that hour was William Trotter, a thirteen-year-old House of Commons page. His mother kept the boarding-house where McGee and several other members of Parliament stayed and it was possibly due to their influence that young Trotter had received his appointment. Mrs. Trotter's guests had each his own key, but she did not consider her son old enough for this privilege. On the nights when he was on duty at the House of Commons she waited up to let him in.

Will Trotter came along Sparks Street shortly after McGee. He heard the single shot, but it was so quickly and utterly lost in the quiet of the night that he was scarcely aware of it. As he came opposite his house he noticed a dark shadow by the steps and the thought passed through his mind that it was a dog. His mother had opened the door and something in her attitude suggested great agitation. Suddenly Will's mind came into focus and he realized that what he saw lying in the street was a man.

He crossed the road and stood looking down at him. The man lay on his back, the left arm with a cane crooked on it, slightly extended. Blood was oozing from the mouth, a great deal of blood; it formed a little pool on the sidewalk, widening sluggishly. A new, light-coloured hat had been knocked a little over the eyes. It was Mr. McGee!

Without waiting to speak to his mother Will Trotter ran down the street to where the lights of the Ottawa *Times* office still burned. He stumbled as he ran, his feet breaking the thin ice in the ruts of the road. Rarely has sensational news been reported more promptly to its ultimate destination.

"Mr. McGee has been shot," he called out.

One of the printers came to the door. Then the staff poured out headlong, the printers in their aprons, the desk man in his vest and shirt-sleeves. They all ran down the street with Will to the house where several people had gathered. Will edged his way between them as close as possible to the prostrate man. Dr. Robitaille who lived at Mrs. Trotter's was bending over him. He lay exactly as Will had left him, but from the throat and motionless lips came a strange, rasping, choking sound. Dr. Robitaille straightened up and gravely told them that Mr. McGee was dead.

Other people gathered—a policeman, another doctor, several members of Parliament and the Prime Minister who had been told the shocking news. There was little enough to do. The second doctor made his examination, the policeman took down the names of witnesses—Will Trotter's because he had discovered the body and Mrs. Trotter's because, expecting her boy, she had opened the door in time to see the revolver flash and D'Arcy McGee fall. The printers went back to the press, to turn the type to form mourning borders and bring out the most sensational edition in the history of the paper.

At Mrs. Trotter's the people still stood about. Then Sir John A. Macdonald, with the help of others, lifted up the body of his colleague and carried it into the house.

Chapter Thirty-Two
REQUIESCAT

THEY gave him a grand funeral.

Officially the Canadian government assumed the responsibility, actually the city of Montreal took over the occasion and made it its own. Where else would a combination of conditions more suitable for a great public demonstration be found? The French, who knew how to be dramatic, with good taste; the military regiments, that knew better than any others in the country the procedure for formal occasions; the Irish, who loved a funeral better than a wedding.

On the terrible day of D'Arcy McGee's assassination, Parliament met in an emergency session. Shocked as the members were, their vocal chords had not been numbed and many moving tributes were paid to the murdered man. The Prime Minister spoke more to the point than the others, making certain practical suggestions about a pension for the widow and provision for the education of the children. D'Arcy McGee had died a poor man and John A. Macdonald knew from his own early experience how cruelly straitened means can oppress a family when added to a heavier affliction.

The news of the assassination spread in a few hours by telegraph and newspaper throughout Canada. The recently united provinces, under the impact of the tragedy, felt their unity for the first time in an emotional sense. The whole country went into mourning and even remote places planned memorial services.

The body of D'Arcy McGee was brought home to Montreal on Wednesday of Holy Week and the date of the interment was set for Easter Monday. The house on St. Catherine Street, where Mary had often been alone since her mother's death, was full of company now. All the family was home: the two children from their convent school; D'Arcy's brothers, John McGee and Colonel James McGee who had come from New York. And D'Arcy himself resting at last after all his labours. James and Mary Ann Sadlier came from New York, Mrs. Sadlier staying by Mary as there were no women of the family to be with her.

Montreal went forward with preparations for the most splendid funeral the city had ever witnessed. Every group and organization from the mayor and the council to the most recent fledgling society of the German immigrants was going to take part. Many had known him personally and most of them at some time or other had heard him speak. There was a robust, all-embracing quality about that funeral that recalls the epic burials of classic literature and the Norse sagas. Thousands paid their respects at the McGee home where the body lay in state. The reporters kept record of everything and though they may have failed to attain the Homeric standards they aspired to, they set down everything they saw in lingering, loving detail.

"The body lay in a metal coffin lined with satin and surrounded by a double veil of white crepe. At the head upon a pedestal stood a crucifix in gilded bronze from the arms of which depended wreaths of vine leaves, roses and other flowers. Upon a marble table at the foot stood three alabaster vases, enriched with allegorical figures. These were filled with white lilies and foliage. At one corner of the coffin was a vase of Parian marble, veined with black and filled with tulips, while around it were six massive waxen tapers ornamented with gold. Two others borne by statuettes burned on the mantel before a great mirror; beside them were two alabaster urns filled with flowers. The floor was covered with a white carpet ornamented with mosses and from the cornices of the ceiling fell heavy folds of black drapery strewn with silver tears and surrounded by folds of crepe fastened with silk ribbons."

The day of the funeral was cold and sunny, with a sharp wind. It had been declared a public holiday and from early morning crowds filled the streets along the route of the procession as well as every window, balcony and roof top. The soldiers of the Montreal regiments stood at attention along the way and the bands stationed at intervals played funeral music as the procession passed. Even more remarkable than the number of spectators was the variety of people taking part in the procession. The list of organizations and institutions represented is of forbidding length but how else than by naming them can an idea be given of the extent to which the country and above all the city of Montreal participated in D'Arcy McGee's funeral? For the procession was led by the city police and the fire brigade followed by the mayor and all the municipal government. Then came the members of the provincial governments and the members of the Dominion House of Commons, the Senators, the Cabinet, the foreign consuls and the Vice-regal party from Government House. The funeral car was drawn by six grey horses draped in black velvet, led by men with silver wands. It was followed by the immediate family and the pall-bearers of whom the Hon. George Cartier was one. Then followed the legal profession and the medical profession, the faculties of the English and French Universities; the law students, the medical students and the arts students. After them came a great number of national, benevolent and trade societies, among them the various Irish organizations, the St. Patrick's Society, the Irish Protestant Benevolent Society, St. Patrick's Benevolent Society, St. Patrick's Temperance Society.

It is impossible not to pause at this point to wonder how many who walked in the Irish ranks knew James Patrick Whelan who, before the month was out, lay in jail in Ottawa charged with the murder of D'Arcy McGee, and if any were privy to his crime. He was known to be a Fenian, but no proof was ever produced to show that he had acted under orders or as a Fenian agent in the matter of the assassination. His trial uncovered no accomplices. Although he went to his execution maintaining his innocence he was condemned on irrefutable evidence and, according to stories current at the time of his arrest, he had boasted of his deed.

But if Whelan acted in the assassination without direction from any organization or persons this only spreads the guilt more widely, and all those who had written scurrilously of McGee—the newspapers that had published lies about him, the political enemies who had whipped up mob feeling against him, all those who let loose forces of hatred that they could not control—were guilty of his death. The obscure fanatic who suffered the penalty had acted for all of them. This they did not choose to admit. The pro-Fenian papers were as emphatic as any in repudiating the foul murder of D'Arcy McGee, and all those who had held him in their enmity excused themselves with the formula that whereas they might have disagreed with Mr. McGee's political opinions they had always said he was a great orator.

The slow procession wound its way to Lagauchetière Street where the principal mourners and as many of the public as the building could accommodate entered St. Patrick's Church for the funeral Mass. The Rev. M. O'Farrell preached the sermon, mastering the difficult assignment of being eloquent in the praise of eloquence and of tempering praise of the dead with the proper degree of Christian humility. The panoply of public mourning, the soldiers at attention, the bands, the crepe hangings, the wreaths, hid the lonely fact of the soul gone solitary into eternity. The solemn meaning of the Requiem Mass was almost lost.

After the *Ite missa est*, the procession reformed and proceeded down town to Notre Dame Church where another sermon was preached in French and a magnificent *Libera* chanted. All Montreal claimed D'Arcy McGee this day. It was typical of the city's curious tangle of jealous duality and reasonable compromise that the Irish and French agreed to share his funeral but to claim him separately.

It was afternoon before the procession made its last stop at the Cemetery of Côte des Neiges, where the Catholics buried their dead without distinction of language, side by side, all national controversies composed in the last silence. There the people of Montreal laid the body of D'Arcy McGee.

Of all those who mourned him, only one, Mary McGee, was pierced to the heart. It would be misinterpreting the spirit of the day to deny that in a general public way McGee was sincerely mourned, or that the elaborate funeral expressed and eased that grief. But for those to whom his death was a personal loss the day must have been a long ordeal. Mary McGee's health never fully recovered from the shock and strain of that terrible Easter.

Oddly enough the last word on the funeral belongs to D'Arcy himself. Shortly before his assassination he had written a poem—a funeral song—commemorating the death of Lawrence Devaney, one of his Montreal friends. It is one of his best poems; John McGee preferred it to all the others. Read with the circumstances of D'Arcy McGee's death in mind the poem takes on special significance. Above the public show and fanfare of his funeral it rises high and clear with the *Dies Irae* and the *Libera*. D'Arcy McGee had unwittingly written his own requiem.

Verses from
Requiem Aeternam
(Written for Lawrence Devaney, died March 3, 1868)

With Villa Maria's faithful dead,
Among the just we made his bed.
The cross he loved to shield his head—
Miserere, Domine!

Deaf to the calls of love and care,
He bears no more his mortal share,
Nought can avail him now but prayer—
Miserere, Domine!

No more Saint Patrick's aisles prolong
The burden of his funeral song,
His noiseless night must now be long—
Miserere, Domine!

REQUIESCAT

Up from the depths we heard arise
A prayer of pity to the skies,
To him who dooms, or justifies—
    Miserere, Domine!

Down from the skies we heard descend
The promises the Psalmist penn'd
The benedictions without end—
    Miserere, Domine!

Mighty our Holy Church's will
To shield her parting souls from ill;
Jealous of Death, she guards them still—
    Miserere, Domine!

The dearest friend will turn away,
And leave the clay to keep the clay;
Ever and ever she will stay—
    Miserere, Domine!

His flaming heart is still for aye,
That held fast by thy clemency,
Oh! look on him with loving eye—
    Miserere, Domine!

His Faith was as the tested gold,
His Hope assured, not overbold,
His Charities past count, untold—
    Miserere, Domine!

Well may they grieve who laid him there,
Where shall they find his equal—where?
Nought can avail him now but prayer—
    Miserere, Domine!

Friend of my soul, farewell to thee!
Thy truth, thy trust, thy chivalry;
As thine, so may my last end 'be!
    Miserere, Domine!

EPILOGUE

Mary McGee gathered together all D'Arcy McGee's poems, those that had been published in various papers or in collections and many that had been written for special occasions but never printed, and gave them to Mrs. Sadlier. This material Mary Anne compiled and edited and it was published by James Sadlier in 1869, the only complete edition of D'Arcy's poetry. Besides the copious notes in the appendix, Mrs. Sadlier had written an introduction to the poems and a biographical sketch. The work, she said, was a labour of love. It remains for the careful reader a very valuable source of information about D'Arcy himself. Mary McGee survived her husband less than three years and with her death the McGee household was broken up. As a result few letters and personal relics were preserved. But among the three-hundred-odd poems published in Mrs. Sadlier's collection are many of a personal character that give sharp impressions of many little incidents and glimpses of moods and motives.

The other source of direct information is the memoirs of Sir Charles Gavan Duffy. He wrote of D'Arcy McGee and the other Young Irelanders as he knew them when he was the editor of the Dublin *Nation*. With a delicacy which later biographers would consider excessive, he scrupulously avoided any but the most general reference to their private lives. But, even within the narrow limits he allowed himself, the description he has left of D'Arcy is so apt and telling that for the student it colours all McGee's career.

D'Arcy would not have minded that. In some respects he remained to the end the boy who had worked on the Dublin *Nation*. To the last day of his life he wrote poems

304

about Ireland. He tried to write about Canada but with only moderate success. The roots of his poetry were not in Canadian soil. The allegiance of the patriot could be willed, but not the poet's inspiration. This was one aspect of the personal tragedy of the immigrant. He was aware of the division in his affections and did not fear to refer to it frankly. "I admit for my part, as an immigrant, of no divided allegiance to Canada and her interests; but it would be untrue and paltry to deny a divided affection between the old country and the new. Kept within just bounds, such an affection is reasonable, is right and creditable to those who cherish it."

In 1848, the year of revolutions, he said that to be remembered in Ireland was his only wish. To be forgotten would be death. What has become of the boy's not ignoble ambition for fame? What have the years done to his memory?

He has not been forgotten. Ireland does not forget her poets; his name and writings appear in anthologies of Irish literature. He has been remembered in other ways too, for his life was of the stuff that makes green memories. His statue is to be seen on Parliament Hill among the Fathers of Confederation. He stands in an oratorical attitude and at his feet sits the muse of poetry in the guise of a comely young woman. On the centenary of his birth in 1925 a banquet with many speeches was held in his memory. In the same year two scholarly biographies of which he was the subject were published. In Montreal, the city where McGee and his family found their only permanent home, a functional modern high school has been named after him. And so each generation pays him tribute. He has not been forgotten. But the links to his chain of memory are added, not in Ireland, but in the land of his adoption. Would the boy have been satisfied?

BIBLIOGRAPHY

General

BRADY, ALEXANDER   *Thomas D'Arcy McGee*. Toronto, Macmillan, 1925

DUFFY, (SIR) C. G.   *Young Ireland*. New York, Appleton, 1881
Four Years of Irish History. London, Cassell, 1883
My Life in Two Hemispheres. London, Unwin, 1898

McGEE, T. D.   *Poems*. New York, D. & J. Sadlier, 1869

POPE, (SIR) JOSEPH   *Memoirs of the Right Honourable Sir John A. Macdonald, G.C.B.* Toronto, O.U.P., 1930

SKELTON, ISABEL   *The Life of Thomas D'Arcy McGee*. Gardenvale, P. Q., Garden City Press, 1925
(This is the definitive biography on the subject.)

Part One

BARWICK, G. F.   *The Reading Room of the British Museum*. London, E. Benn, 1929

DICKENS, CHARLES   *American Notes*. London, Dent, 1907

DILLON, WILLIAM   *Life of John Mitchel*. London, Kegan Paul, 1888

MITCHEL, JOHN   *Jail Journal*. Dublin, M. H. Gill, 1913

MOTT, F. L.   *American Journalism*. New York, Macmillan, 1941

NICHOLS, T. L.   *Forty Years of American Life, 1821-1861*. New York, Stackpole, 1937

307

O'FAOLIN, SEAN   *King of the Beggars* (Daniel O'Connell). London, Nelson, 1938

O'ROURKE, JOHN   *The History of the Great Irish Famine of 1847.* Dublin, McGlashan & Gill, 1875.

Part Two

GUILLET, E. C.   *Early Life in Upper Canada.* Toronto, Ontario Publishing Co., 1933
The Great Migration. Toronto, Nelson, 1937

HATCHER, H. H.   *Lake Erie.* Indianapolis, Bobbs-Merrill, 1945

KOHL, J. G.   *Travels in Canada and Through the States of New York and Pennsylvania.* London, G. Mainwaring, 1861

McGEE, T. D.   *The Catholic History of North America.* Boston, Donahue, 1858

MAGUIRE, J. F.   *The Irish in America.* London, Longmans Green, 1868

Part Three

ATHERTON, W. H.   *History of Montreal.* Montreal, S. J. Clarke, 1914

BIGGAR, E. B.   *Sketch of Canadian Journalism.* (Pamphlet, 189-)

BOYD, JOHN   *Sir George Etienne Cartier, Bart.* Toronto, Macmillan, 1914

CAMERON, E. R.   *Memoirs of Ralph Van Sittart.* Toronto, Musson, 1902

CANADIAN PRESS ASSOCIATION   *A History of Canadian Journalism.* Toronto, Murray, 1908

COLLINS, J. E.   *Life and Times of the Right Honourable Sir John A. Macdonald.* Toronto, Rose, 1883

DAVIN, N. F.   *The Irishman in Canada.* London, Low-Marston, 1887

BIBLIOGRAPHY

DENT, J. C.　　　　　*The Last Forty Years, 1841-1881*. Toronto, Virtue, 1887

FERGUSON, (LADY) MARY *Sir Samuel Ferguson in the Ireland of His Day*. Edinburgh, Blackwood, 1896

FRASER, ALEXANDER　　*A History of Ontario*. Toronto, Canada History Co., 1907

GRAY, J. H.　　　　　*Confederation*. Toronto, Copp Clark, 1872

HOLMES, (SIR) RICHARD *Edward VII, His Life and Times*. London, Carmelite House, 1911

LEWIS, JOHN　　　　　*George Brown*. Toronto, Morang, 1906

LONGLEY, J. W.　　　　*Joseph Howe*. London, O.U.P., 1926
Sir Charles Tupper. Toronto, Morang, 1916

LOWER, A. R. M.　　　*Colony to Nation, A History of Canada*. Toronto, Longmans Green, 1946

MACDONALD, (SIR) JOHN A.　*Correspondence*. Toronto, O.U.P., 192-

McGEE, T. D.　　　　　*A Collection of Speeches and Addresses*. Toronto, Macmillan, 1937

MACKENZIE, ALEXANDER *The Life and Speeches of the Honourable George Brown*. Toronto, Globe Printing, 1882

MacPHERSON, J. P.　　*Life of the Right Honourable Sir John A. Macdonald*. St. John, N.B., Earle Publishing House, 1891

MORGAN, H. J.　　　　*Types of Canadian Women Past and Present*. Toronto, Wm. Briggs, 1903

SKELTON, O. D.　　　　*The Life and Times of Sir Alexander Tilloch Galt*. Toronto, O.U.P., 1920

SOMERVILLE, ALEXANDER *The Fenian Invasion*. Hamilton, Joseph Lyght, 1886

STRACHEY, G. L.　　　*Queen Victoria*. London, Chatto, 1924

TAYLOR, FENNINGS　　*Thomas D'Arcy McGee*. Montreal, Lovell, 1868

TROTTER, R. G.　　　　*Canadian Federation*. Toronto, Dent, 1924

TUPPER, (SIR) CHARLES *Political Reminiscences*. London, Constable, 1914

309

THE ARDENT EXILE

Documents

Canada, Public Archives, Ottawa   D'Arcy McGee, Letters
Moylan Papers
Murphy Papers
Coroner's Inquest on the death of the Honourable Thomas D'Arcy McGee

Newspapers

The *American Celt*   (Fraser Institute, Montreal)
The *Canadian Freeman*   (Reference Library, Toronto)
La Minerve   (Gagnon Collection, Civic Library, Montreal)
The *Montreal Gazette*   (The *Montreal Gazette* files)
The *Ottawa Times*   (Library of Parliament, Ottawa)

INDEX

A

Albert, the Prince Consort, 198-9, 246

American Celt, The, 102, 104; moved to Buffalo, 106; 110; Canadian subscribers, 111; 115, 118, 119, 121; letters on Canada in, 128; advice to immigrants, 133; description of, 140-1; staff, 141-2; immigrant policy, 142-4; McGee sells, 147

Annexation Manifesto, 87, 198

Arnold, Matthew, 22, 23

Australia, 57, 93, 136, 239, 245

B

Bagot, Sir Charles, 88

Baldwin, Robert, 84, 186

Ballad History of Ireland, 32, 41-42

Booker, Colonel, 262

Boston, 3-4, 102, 106, 115

British Museum (*see* Library of British Museum)

Brown, George, 87-8, 133; appearance, 159, 160; defends father, 165-6; prejudices, 166; 167, 168; in government, 169-70; 171; and Irish Catholics, 186-7; opinion of confederation, 204; opinion of Grand Trunk, 206; 209-10, 212; his committee, 213-5; coalition with Macdonald, 216-7; 223; later opinion of confederation, 230-1; 233, 235; to England, 246; 249; leaves coalition, 265-6; 290.

Buffalo, 106, 108-11, 113, 116, 121, 127, 142

Buffalo Convention, 142-3, 144

Bulwer-Lytton, Sir Edward, 173, 174

Bytown (*see* Ottawa)

C

Caffrey, Mrs. (Mary McGee's mother), 46, 148, 219, 299

Caffrey, Mary Theresa, *see* McGee, Mary

Callan, Dr., 59

Callan, Mrs., 68

Canadian Freeman, The, purpose, 164; 173, 185-6; McGee's quarrel with, 187-9; supports McGee again, 207; 243, 253, 265, 292

Carlyle, Thomas, 22, 35, 39, 51

Cartier, George Etienne, 159; appearance, 160; 161, 169; Premier, 170; 171; to England, 172; at Windsor Castle, 174-5; entertains Prince, 177-8; 180, 183-4, 200-1, 206, 210, 212; opinion of Brown's committee, 214; to Charlottetown, 223; 233, 246, 269; stand on first Dominion Cabinet, 272-3; persuades McGee, 274-6; at McGee's banquet, 288; rift between Macdonald and, 290-1; at McGee's funeral, 300

Catholic History of America, The, 113-5, 284

Charbonnel, Bishop of Toronto, 186

Charlottetown Conference, 223, 224-5, 226, 292

Citizen, The, 117-8, 119

Civil War, 137, 140; Canadian opinion on, 190-1; McGee on, 192-5; end of 234; Fenianism and, 237, 240, 241, 256, 283

Clontarf, cancelled meeting at, 10-11, 17

Confederation of British North American provinces, 171, 172; first proposal to British government, 173-5;

INDEX

tee, 215; forms coalition government, 215-7; to Charlottetown conference, 223-4; 231; his part in confederation, 233-4; 235; to England, 246; 248-9; as statesman, 266-7; Fenian policy, 267-8; confederation negotiations, 268-70, 271-3, 274, 275; 280; at McGee's banquet, 288; his dominant role after confederation, 291; 292; at scene of McGee's assassination, 297; 298

Macdonald, John Sandfield, 209, 210, 212, 214, 215

McDougall, William, 217, 270

McFarlane, Robert, 295

McGee, Agnes (daughter), 148, 219

McGee, Catherine Dorcas (McGee's mother), 6-7, 23, 47, 134, 282

McGee children, 148, 282

McGee, Euphrasia (daughter), 148, 219

McGee, James (brother), 47, 68, 95, 141, 148, 198, 299

McGee, James (father), 6-7, 47, 134

McGee, John (half-brother), 148, 219, 299, 302

McGee, Mary (wife), meets McGee, 32; 42; appearance, 45; marriage, 46-7; 64; visits McGee in hiding, 68, 70; 78, 90-91; joins McGee in America, 95-6; 99, 113; to Montreal, 148-51; family life in Montreal, 219-20; her character, 228-9; 299, 302; death, 304

McGee, Thomas D'Arcy, to Boston, 3-4; joins Boston *Pilot*, 5-6; family 6-7; career on *Pilot*, 7-8, 10-11; 12; meets Duffy, 15-8; reporter in Parliament, 20-2; British Museum, 22-4; discharged from Dublin *Freeman*, 24-5; joins Dublin *Nation*, 26-7; 29, 30; his interests, 32; 33, 34, 35; attitude toward O'Connell, 39-40; 41; break with Mitchel, 42-3; marriage and honeymoon, 45-7; associate editor, 48-9; 53-4; meets Ferguson, 56; 57, 58; acting editor, 59; in conspiracy, 61-3; to Scotland, 64; attempted insurrection, 65-7; in hiding, 67-8; escapes to America, 70; on emigrant ship, 76-

81; 82; manifesto to Canadians, 88-9; homesickness, 90-1; starts *New York Nation*, 91-2; radical views, 93; controversy with Bishop Hughes 93-5; correspondence with Duffy, 96-7; interest in night schools, 97; continued controversy with Bishop, 98-100; to Boston, 102; starts *American Celt*, 102; drops radical views, 103-5; to Buffalo, 106; 109, 110; first interest in Canada, 111-2; sympathy with immigrants, 112-5; 116; quarrel with Mitchel, 118-9; attacked by Reilly, 119-20; 121, 122; visit to Canada, 128-33; visit to Ireland, 134-5; conversations with Duffy, 135-7; appearance, 137; 138, 139; attitude towards United States, 140; 141; slum clearance plans, 142-3; their failure, 144; to Montreal, 147; 151, 154; runs for Parliament, 155; 157-8, 159, 160, 161; maiden speech in Parliament, 162-3; begins political education of Irish Canadians, 163-4; first session in Parliament, 165; opinion of Brown, 166; opinion of government, 167-8, 170-1; 173; and Cartier, 183-4; and *True Witness*, 185-6; trouble with *Canadian Freeman*, 187-9; 190; speech on Civil War, 192-4; 196, 198, 200-1; advocates confederation, 203-5; in Reform government, 206-7; on education, 207-8; joins with Macdonald, 210-3; 214, 215; literary work, 218-9; presented with house, 220-1; excursion to Maritimes, 221-2; to Charlottetown conference, 228, 229, 230; on Quebec Conference, 231, 233; on aftermath of Civil War, 234, 236, 237; warns Canadians against Fenianism, 238-9; to International Exhibition, Dublin, 239; 240; Wexford speech, 241-2; its effect, 242-6; with Canadian delegates in England, 246-9; on Fenianism, 250; 252; organizes counter-demonstration, 253-6; 263, 265; as Minister of Agriculture, 267; 268, 269-70; visit to Rome, 270-1; to

314

INDEX

International Exhibition, Paris, 271; illness, 271, 278, 279, 280; 272, 273; resignation from Cabinet, 274-6; first Dominion election, 277-9; as a poet, 281-3; speaks for the immigrant, 284-5; on the Irish question, 285-6; defended in Parliament, 287-8; 288; letter to Lord Mayo, 289-90; 291, 292; speech on Nova Scotia, 293-4; assassination, 295-7; funeral, 298-302; memorials, 305

Mackenzie, William Lyon, 160-1

McManus, Terence, 66, 69

Maginn, Bishop of Londonderry, 67, 70

Mangan, James Clarence, 31

Marx, Karl, 22, 59, 92, 154

Mathew, Father, 9, 32

Mayo, Lord, 289-90

Mazzini, Giuseppe, 15, 22

Meagher, Thomas Francis, appearance, 30; Sword Speech, 33-34; 37, 39; candidate for election, 49; 52, 53, 54, 57; in conspiracy, 61-3; 66; trial and sentence, 92-3; McGee's letter to, 103-5; arrival in New York, 116-7; Duffy's letter to, 119; 188; in Civil War, 198; death, 283

Metternich, Count, 13, 50

Minerve, La, 275

Mitchel, John, 30, 32, 34, revolutionary attitude, 39; radicalism, 42-3; starts the *United Irishman,* 48-9; 51-2, 55; trial and sentence, 57-8; 93, 94; starts the *Citizen,* 117-9; 120; evil genius of Young Ireland, 135-6; 188

"Mollie Maguires", 65, 67

Monck, Lady, 226

Monck, Lord, 199, 214, 255-6

Montreal, 83; burning of Parliament Building, 86-7; 122, 125; cholera epidemic, 128-9, 144, 147, 150, 151-4, 155, 156, 160, 161, 164, 166; royal visit to, 177-8; 183, 185; attitude towards Civil War, 190-1; 196, 210; McGees' home life in, 219-21, 226, 228; Fenianism in, 236-7; 244, 251; St. Patrick's Day

celebrations, 253-6; 263, 272, 273, 275; election in, 276-8; McGee's funeral, 298-302; 305

Montreal Gazette, 278

Moore, Thomas, 6, 16

Morgan, family name of McGee's mother, 7, 102

Morgan, H. J., 270

Mowat, Oliver, 159, 217

Moylan, James, G., editor of *Canadian Freeman,* 185; differs with McGee, 187-8; supports McGee, 207; 265, 292

N

Nation, The Dublin, its beginning, 12, 13-5; 16; O'Connell and, 17; 18; McGee writes for, 24; McGee joins staff, 25, 26-7; staff of, 30-2; 34; change in interest, 41-2; 43, 47; Mitchel leaves, 48-9; 51, 52, 54; McGee acting editor for, 59; 61, 64; files confiscated, 68; 91; Duffy revives, 96-7; 120, 135, 136, 218; opinion of Wexford speech, 242-3; 244; 245, 283, 304

New Era, The, 147, 164

New York Freeman, 94, 95, 98, 99

New York Herald, 195

New York Nation, 91-2, 96, 98, 99-100, 102, 106

Newfoundland, 75, 175-6, 225, 232, 233

Newspapers (*see also names of individual papers*), typical of period, 5-6; 82; weeklies and dailies, 91; 95; McGee's papers, 99-100; 105; McGee and Irish American papers, 139-40; 143, 163; McGee and Irish Canadian papers, 164; and royal visit, 176, 177; American papers and annexation of Canada, 195, 197-8, 234; 185, 201; not admitted to confederation conferences, 225, 228; attitude of Irish papers to Wexford speech, 242-3; Pro-Fenian papers threaten McGee, 253; 276, 298, 301

Niagara Falls, 182

Night Schools, 97-8, 142, 207

INDEX

T. H. Best Printing Co., Limited, Toronto

You will find enclosed a P.O. order for the subscription which you were so kind as to pay for me, in advance.

I beg you to thank, in the warmest terms, the Very Rev. President, the Rev. Dr. Reeves, Mr. Gilbert, and Mr. Hardinge, for me. McCarthy as an old personal friend I must write to myself. I enclose a Memorandum for Mr. Clibborn, which I beg you to give him, and to say that nothing but the pressure of official & Parliamentary duty — for we are here, in a state of crisis, at present — prevents me writing him,